INTO THE HEART OF

MEXICO

Into the Heart of México:

Expatriates Find Themselves Off the Beaten Path

by

John Scherber

San Miguel Allende Books
San Miguel de Allende,
Guanajuato, México

ACKNOWLEDGMENTS

Any book starts as an idea, and by its completion becomes a joint effort.

Thanks to my wife, Kristine, for editorial and critical help.

Cover Design by Lander Rodriguez
Cover painting: *Señora con Cubeta Naranja*, by Daniel Rueffert
Interior Book Design by Kristine Scherber
Web Page Design by Julio Mendez

ISBN:978-0-9832582-9-2

San Miguel Allende Books
San Miguel de Allende, GTO, México
www.sanmiguelallendebooks.com

Also by John Scherber

AUTHOR'S NOTE

The cover painting, *Señora con Cubeta Naranja*, (Woman with Orange Bucket) is one I first saw in the studio of Daniel Rueffert in Pozos, the town that is the focus of the first chapter of this book. The site of the painting I later discovered in San Luis de la Paz, the setting for the second chapter.

The picture was hanging on the wall next to the door and I was immediately struck by it. To me it expresses an aura of the indelible otherness that infuses indigenous México. While the native people of this country were trampled and disinherited by their conquerors, they were not subsequently banished from sight in the same way that they were in most of the United States. Any day of being out and about in México will bring you into contact with them. Their bloodlines run through the great majority of people here, and the culture owes a debt to them that can be seen everywhere in its richness and diversity.

The artist was most gracious to allow me to place it on my cover, and every time I see it I can almost imagine that he painted it with this book in mind.

If human nature ever does alter, it will be because individuals manage to look at themselves in a new way.

—E. M. Forster, *Aspects of the Novel*

TABLE OF CONTENTS

INTRODUCTION

Nearly everyone has been to Cancun. It can be found as a tiny dot on a few maps going back to the eighteenth century, yet when resort development began in the early 1970s only a handful of people lived there. Effectively, the city as it exists today has no past, so it's not a stretch to think that as enticing as they are in January, Cancun and some of the other recent beach developments don't represent the real México, which is layered with history.

That realization is what drove me to spend some time in México's hinterland after seven or eight delightful beach vacations. I was coming from Minnesota then, where in the winter the word *delightful* describes anything above freezing. What I found in the interior was infinitely more complex than on the beaches. Substantial expatriate communities flourish around Lake Chapala near Guadalajara, San Miguel de Allende, México City, and other towns and cities. I discovered a way of life less hurried, less expensive, and in many ways more colorful and rewarding than the life I was leading in the United States. I encountered values that are different in refreshing ways. It wasn't long before I found myself examining these expat enclaves more closely for the right one to adopt for myself.

For North Americans thinking about moving to another culture, another country, and immersing themselves in a different language, the support of a community of their own people seems vital. Their high school Spanish may serve adequately in a restaurant or on a plane, but what happens when the need arises to communicate with an electrician or a doctor who speaks no English? How well does their Spanish differentiate among plumbing parts or specify urgent auto repairs? Especially in terms of personal relations, Spanish is a language graced with levels of nuance that the average high school teacher never attempts to explain.

Ultimately I chose San Miguel de Allende as my home in México. It's a historic colonial town on a mountain plateau at 6,400 feet elevation. The broccoli capital of the Americas, it hosts an expat population of about 10,000 among the 75,000 people in the city itself.

Soon, the experiences of my American and Canadian neighbors inspired me to write a book about their lifestyle within this supportive community. I wanted to know what had caused them to leave their homeland and what they'd learned as they settled in. In the conversations that followed, their stories were far more diverse than I had anticipated, and I found no way beyond their simple collective presence in San Miguel to characterize them as a group. They had all come at their new home from different angles, different points on a compass that was not exclusively geographic. The resulting book was titled *San Miguel de Allende: A Place in the Heart,* and while it wasn't the book I set out to write, it was the book that awaited me when I dug more deeply into the project. Sometimes it goes like that when you listen carefully enough to hear the unexpected.

More gradually, as I settled in myself, I became aware of scattered groups of expats who had chosen different towns, places farther off the beaten path, where they were more on their own, or gathered into much smaller enclaves. They lived in cities where they weren't numerous enough to affect real estate prices, as others had in San Miguel, to influence what was available in the markets, or to stimulate the local people to learn some English.

The character of their lifestyle went well beyond doing without peanut butter and chocolate chips. In contrast to my own situation in San Miguel, where if I didn't know where to find kosher dill pickles someone would soon tell me, it led me to dig deeper into ways of living that were less dependent on the support of others from the same culture.

As I crisscrossed the country talking to people, I soon realized that this is a different kind of expat. This book is about their México and their way of life, away from large English-speaking settlements. Some of the people on these pages left the United States leaving little warmth in their wake. Others left with no intention whatever of becoming an expat. It's not about why or how you came, but about what you do when you arrive.

Like my other book, this volume is personal and anecdotal. Its purpose is to illustrate some examples of this way of life, but not to generalize about it. Whether it's the real México or not is a debate I leave to others, but I know it has its own detailed reality for those who live this lifestyle. And because they are necessarily more connected one on one among the local people, the experience is often accompanied by a more distinctive sense of place, one that they do not dominate through their numbers, and place is one of the principal characters driving this story.

Americans and Canadians do not readily think of themselves as emigrants. After all, we came from the tens of millions of Europeans and Asians and Africans that arrived on our shores as a destination, mostly willing and eager, except those who were marched ashore in chains, so it must be the proper place to be. If that's the case, where else is there to go, and why move on? It almost feels like going against the grain, since it often took a great deal of pain and effort for our forebears to get there. In many cases it put them in debt or servitude for years. This book is the story of some of their descendants who have packed up and headed for new destinations in México. Is it a reaction against their old way of life, or only the next link in a chain of migration that began generations before? In the pages that follow, these characters will speak about this for themselves.

This book is not a sequel to my earlier work on the expat experience in San Miguel. It is more a corollary, an accompanying piece that is meant to stand side-by-side with it and illustrate a range of alternative destinations.

Casting about for a place to begin, I settled on a unique town about an hour from San Miguel. When I was painting, I was always fascinated by the melancholy air of ghost towns. Usually their growth had been fueled by nearby mines, and when the ore ran out the life of the town ebbed away. This was nearly the case with our distant neighbor, a town, once a vibrant city, named Pozos, in the state of Guanajuato. It's an out-of-the-way place cradled in the mountains deep in the heart of México...

Chapter 1

POZOS: LIFE AMONG THE RUINS

D riving up the long, undulant slopes into Mineral de Pozos, mainly populated by grazing goats and meandering cattle, the visitor takes in the humpbacked mountains where silver was first discovered in the late sixteenth century. They are covered with green now in late September, the end of the rainy season. Near the hilltop first appears the cemetery, the *panteón*, before the town comes into view over the crest beyond. It seems a fitting introduction to a city that nearly died itself, falling from a population of about 75,000 in 1900 to only 200, fifty years later. It was not the plague, although it must have felt like it as house after house fell silent, as property became nearly worthless, as schools closed and civic life dried up. In the midst of this extended decline, the courthouse burned. For a variety of reasons—this and the revolution of 1910, the flooding of the silver mines, the depletion of productive ore—the glory days were over. The economic base of the city sank out of sight as if seeping back into the soil from which it originally came.

Driving into town, the first building that came into view looked fresh and recent in construction, although traditional in design, with a façade of irregular stone like that of the *panteón's* enclosing wall. Flanking it were the ruins and broken walls of many others. Open as if under an x-ray, these walls offer lessons in traditional construction techniques.

Beneath the stucco, long fallen away, layers of mud brick, dissolving year-by-year back into the soil, alternate with narrow courses of stone. The old roof beams are long gone, salvaged for firewood or distant construction as the town shrank. In some months, Pozos can take on a notable chill at night, standing as it does at 7,500 feet. In the complete absence of any new construction, at mid-century no further structural need could be found nearby for any beams that remained on abandoned properties, but the fireplace beckoned in a compelling way.

My visit began to feel like a survey of the wreckage of a bombed out city in Germany in 1946, where, although the streets were opened again, the rubble in many quarters hadn't yet been cleared. This condition continued the farther I went, but then, tiny stores (*tiendas*) began to appear, and soon a four-table restaurant. These were buildings with a different look; they had restored walls, and were covered to the weather. In another block I drove past a small plaza, the Jardín Juárez. It had living trees, and at its southern edge women poked at improvised grills, roasting ears of corn still in their husks. Sizzling *gorditas* popped and sputtered on flat griddles. Children chased each other, laughing. They were easily immune to the larger meaning of their surroundings, as children often are.

A few years ago I drove through a small town in the western part of Kansas. On many of the residential blocks one or more houses were boarded up. *For Sale* signs fronted a few of them, but most had given up. A realtor friend once told me that the presence of a single boarded up house on any block sinks the resale value of all the rest. What I was seeing in Pozos as I drove on was this picture reversed. Some blocks had only one or two buildings occupied at most. And this was on Calle Miguel Hidalgo, the main street.

Knowing what it is we're looking at is often a challenge in México. Peering through the invisible filter of our American or Canadian background distorts the people, places, and events we see. We often yield to an instinct to explain things in terms of what we already know, to try to make them fit our prior experience. After all, haven't we heard it said that so-and-so was only an observer, so how can it be a skill that matters much? Yet the fact is that being an honest and perceptive observer, which is always my task, requires more work than you might think. Whenever I travel in this very foreign country south of the border, I leave my gringo eyes at home—they are of little use here.

Seventy-five thousand people disappeared from this place over the course of fifty years. The math is not difficult. That's an average of 1,500 a year, or about four a day. Of course between the revolution of 1910 and the religious struggle (the Cristeros War) of the 1920s, the rate would have varied, although in which direction it's hard to say. Had Pozos been a peaceful refuge then or was it the front line of these conflicts as it already teetered on the edge of its own economic demise? Imagine that an average household might contain eight people—a good guess for México. The aging parents often lived with their mature children. If that was the case, then a house or apartment was abandoned on an average of once every two days—for fifty years.

In the United States we think of home ownership as the foundation of the middle class. It was the tragedy of Pozos that this financial underpinning, the most valuable asset most families ever acquire, became at first unsalable, and then unmaintainable, as jobs dried up, and finally *worthless* except for salvageable scrap at a time when construction materials were definitely not in demand. On street after street the story was the same. Ironically, these deserted homes also became mines of a different kind, where the more valuable removable features were scrapped out early on and hauled away. The plumbing fixtures, the doors and windows, the pipes and wiring would have most likely been carted out to the country, where agriculture was doing well, and reused in a building with a more predictable future, or placed with a scrap dealer where a family's despair was sold off for pocket money. The story of Pozos' decline is that of the end of dreams.

Farther down on Calle Miguel Hidalgo stands an old chapel, a foursquare stone ruin with no trace of stucco remaining. Maybe it was always rustic and informal in style, with the stone exposed. The two towered corners are severed above the second floor. A round arch frames the vacant entrance, with a gothic arch above. Within, a herd of goats now resides quite contentedly. I stuck my head in the door and waved to them as I moved on.

As midcentury loomed, with the economies of most North American countries in a postwar boom, Pozos increasingly resembled a process more than a place. Too far advanced to reverse, it was the ongoing dissolution of a society and even of its physical presence, then nearly at an end. Hardly more than an asterisk, by 1950, the town had almost forfeited its geography too, as it vanished from many maps of México.

By then, in a growing silence, only the 200 hardcore residents remained, and what an interesting group that must have been! Survivors all, as everything dried up around them. These were people with a committed sense of place, to the degree that they refused to be evicted from their chosen town by any mere reversal of fortune, even when that place proved less stable and persistent than they themselves were. I see the fundamental endurance of humanity reflected in that. Of course, they would have had outside means of support, since the economic life of the town was dead by then. But it took much more than an income or a pension to entice them to stay. They could have moved off to San Luis de la Paz, just a dozen kilometers to the north, but most did not. In Pozos, essential services would've almost all been gone by then, and only a minimal social life remained among people bound mainly by a shared sense of disaster and stubbornness in equal measures. If it really was the end, everyone who was willing to acknowledge that had already left. For the lack of a better word, I call that survival.

Water, sewer, electric power, and mail would all have ground to a halt as Pozos became too unimportant to bother with. Yet these 200 stayed on. Some, hopeful of a future as yet invisible, would have fenced in their neighbor's abandoned and ruined property with their own in anticipation of a better day. The decades passed; they lived on in this condition until they slowly died off and ascended to the waiting *panteón*, even as, slowly, tentatively, a few newcomers appeared to take their places. In these ruined corridors, the image of that decline was graphic and vivid.

I doubled back to the square, the Jardín Juárez, where at the north end stands a classic limestone building that houses a hopping bar enclosed by walls papered with sepia images of an older, vigorous Pozos, the once prosperous Pozos, before its near death and incipient resurrection. But do not look yet for its remains up at the *panteón*, it seems to say, especially on a Saturday night.

Pozos climbs both slopes of a narrow valley. The term *level* is more easily found in the dictionary than along its angular cobblestone streets. The small Jardín Juárez edges the main thoroughfare, but the pavement slopes away at both ends, so that a flight of stairs is needed to descend to the street on the opposite side. White walls capped with a red masonry crown frame this gathering place. An ornate wrought-iron band-stand in the center—still proud but rusting in patchy flakes here and there, a survivor of the good days—suggests there are still events to celebrate that require a closer look to under-stand. Why is anything happening again here worthy of no-tice, much less applause or enthusiasm? The answer isn't obvi-ous, but isn't that the case with most of México? While this country is as seductive as a sailor's dream, it never yields itself easily, especially to expats accustomed to the more predictable realities of Wichita or Wilmington, Toronto or Tacoma.

Descending from the plaza's corner, I discovered the art gallery I was looking for, one called Galería #6. Inside, a series of white-painted rooms opening to a garden were hung with photography and installation art. I was alone for a while until I was joined by one of the owners, a man named Nick Hamblen. He was expecting me.

Art often has to be sold, since the buyer can require reassurance that his taste on a particular piece is correct, and therefore gallery owners are generally a sociable lot. From a previous visit I knew Hamblen was receptive to sharing his thoughts about what had brought him to Pozos, and how it felt to be a businessman in a recovering ghost town in a foreign country a long way from home. That distance from home is not measured so much in miles, since I knew he came from Texas, but in its mental and cultural disconnect, which must have been far greater.

Nick is a man of average height and sturdy build. He was wearing a blue pullover shirt with jeans and a jaunty cap. He invited me into a long narrow garden behind the gallery. It was lined with chattery birdcages, including an enormous bell-shaped Victorian version, now as vacant as some other parts of Pozos, yet with the structure more intact. It might once have been the centerpiece of a country house conservatory in Essex, or in the horse country of Virginia. Their free-range gallery crow had been exiled there for a time after he'd lost his house privileges due to his growing incivility to clients. I could imagine that Nick likes to think he is at least as discriminating as the bird had become, but far better mannered. As the conversation began, I found no reason to disagree, and it was clear that Pozos was no dour place of exile for Nick Hamblen, but rather a kind of liberation. But into what, exactly? This was the question I had come to ask him.

"I love this setting," I said, with an inclusive gesture. "The peaceful, undistracting atmosphere, the supportive venue for art, but how did you ever come to settle in Pozos? How did you even find it?"

The story he told was that near the end of the 90s, a couple Nick knew was getting married in San Miguel de Allende. They loved Pozos and had already bought property there to build a house. Nick and his partner were guests at the ceremony. They had never visited that part of México before and were instantly charmed by it.

"Had you travelled much in México at that time?"

"Not really, a little bit around the beaches, like everybody else, but certainly we knew nothing about central México. We saw both San Miguel and Pozos at the same time, and spent a magical week in San Miguel. I fell in love with that town. We also met some people at the wedding who later became great friends."

A handsome young Méxican wearing a white jacket came out with coffee on a tray.

"How long did it take you to come back?" Nick's tale was not surprising to me, since I had heard stories like this before. They differed in detail, but they tended toward the same outcome, centered on a visit to México that turned into an unexpected hook that couldn't be removed, since it had taken hold in the mind more than just in the flesh.

"Well, that was in July, and I planned a trip back in September to see what it was like without the wedding."

"Sixty days later, then, to see if the magic was still there without the champagne and the dancing, the maria-chis," I said.

"Exactly." His expression grew vague and indistinct, as if seeing that again as it was then.

"Had you been in the gallery business in the States?"

"Not ever. That came a little bit later. After that September trip I saw that the area indeed had all the magic I thought it did. We started coming back at any opportunity we had for several years. We always visited Pozos every time we came to San Miguel, at least for a day trip."

"What was your background?"

"I was born and raised in Dallas and lived in that area all of my life. I still kept a home there until the time I moved to Pozos, although as a free lance art director I traveled all over the country and was seldom there. For the three years prior to moving to Pozos full time I came here any time I was not trav-eling for work to oversee and run the businesses we had begun here."

"You must've felt stretched out."

"I did, yet I thought that as I was already spending so much time here that the transition and adjustment when I moved here full time would be minimal, but I was wrong. Changing so drastically the daily patterns I'd followed for de-cades, suddenly not having a destination to fly off to loom-ing at any moment, and especially no more paychecks on the horizon, as well as just the general slower pace of life in Méxi-co took much more accommodation than I'd anticipated."

"Didn't you have a sense of giving up important parts of your life?"

"The main concern I had was the time away from family and friends, and that remains the most profound sacrifice today, even after four years here. Many are able to come and visit, albeit briefly, although many are not. I travel minimally back to the States due to the responsibility and demands of small business ownership here, so I still ache to see and be with loved ones."

"I've lived in México for years too," I said, "and I'm not sentimental about this place. As a writer, I can't afford to be, although there's nowhere else I'd rather live. So, when you talk about the magic, was it the visuals, the culture, the people? The food? The cheap sandals?"

"It was all of those things." Shaking his head, Nick stirred his coffee for a moment, staring out over the back wall. "It was certainly the visuals first; they were really fascinating. There's such an intact culture here, so close to where we lived, from Dallas. We couldn't believe what a different world it was. Then, definitely the people: not only the ones who lived here, but the ones who traveled to visit here, too. They tend to be people who are very interesting, and that hasn't changed over the years."

"What did you expect to be doing in Pozos? Didn't you have to work, to make a living?"

"Yes, I had always worked, and I'm still working now." He waved this aside with a small shake of his head, as if working at something he had never tried before was his preferred manner of retirement, what he'd always wanted to do in this land of *mañana*. "By the time we were ready to move here I knew we were going to be opening a gallery."

"Were you also a painter in Dallas?"

"No, I'm a photographer, but I've never pursued it much professionally. What happened was that my partner is a landscape designer. He was invited to come down and do a big garden for la Posada de las Minas, a hotel restoration project that at the time was just being planned. We were being hosted by a couple we knew with a home here, and they said that if we wanted to do that we could come and live there. We thought my partner would come down here for about six months and it turned into twelve years. He never went back. I traveled back and forth while I was still working in Dallas, and about four years ago I made the move myself full time. By then we had opened the bed and breakfast here, El Secreto de Pozos. The gallery was a space that soon became available. We thought it would be something interesting to do and we jumped on it, even with no experience."

I thought immediately of the risk involved in entering a business you don't know in a country not your own. Nervy was the word that came to mind. Still, Nick Hamblen has the look of someone who is comfortable in his own skin, although it may have taken him a while to get there. Isn't that the case with most of us? Yet many people never arrive on that path, although I've often speculated that México may be one of the best places to undertake the journey.

He went on to describe Galleria #6 as the sole art gallery in town. Initially it had been open only on weekends, and even then, there would be days when not a single person came through. Now they employ three people full time, and weekends are always busy. The bed and breakfast clientele is 90% Méxican, but the gallery draws expats and tourists, mainly from San Miguel. It shows about three-quarters painting and the rest of the shows are photography.

"Do you ever wish for more of an expat support group in Pozos? I've heard there are only about two dozen here full time, versus 10,000 Americans and Canadians in San Miguel. It's hardly a colony."

Nick responded with a wry look. "I'm of the philosophy that everything's happening as it should. There are plenty of expats in Pozos at any given time. The biggest draw for me in coming here was that it was a different world. I don't have any interest in making this place more like where I came from." Listening to this, I wondered whether I might be hearing the beginning of a theme.

"I love it like it is," he continued. "I'm a risk taker. It's a two edged sword because you want some growth here, of course, if you're running a business, but then you're reluctant to see it change because we loved it the day we got here. Change is inevitable, and we try to be responsible in helping Pozos to grow in the right direction, and not too quickly."

"And is that growth under control?" I hadn't seen any runaway activity driving in, but that was only a first impression. The cratered condition of the place had been my main observation.

"Lately it's been difficult to say. It chugged along so slowly for so long that it was a nonissue. In the last couple of years, with the Pueblo Mágico designation, there've been a lot of rumors about development."

The Pueblo Mágico Progam is an effort of the federal government to spotlight towns with especially rich resources in history, culture, and art.

"Certainly new construction of two different kinds is happening in town. One is the really beautiful historic preservation that's going on up and down the street. Then there are a lot of local Méxican people building homes up in the hills here. They're not historical at all. They're not doing anything illegal for the most part, and it's nice to see them coming back to Pozos."

"Is that a source of tension, different ideas about how the town ought to look in areas of new construction?"

"Issues have come up over the years, and there

are individuals who are pretty clear that they would prefer you weren't here, but as a community, we've been really accepted and befriended by the Méxican people. But there's a fear among some of them that their livelihood is going to be changed because of this growth, and to a degree that's understandable. To some extent the expats have the same sort of fears, with a little bit different edge to them. One of the good things about this potential growth is that it has brought us together more; it's forced a dialogue. You find you're in a meeting that's much more a mixture of locals and expats. That was something we struggled with in the past, getting them to come to our meetings. Now they're coming, and we're going to their meetings, because they have their own specific issues. By the nature of the process you get to know them better."

"Do you have Méxican friends in the first rank of your friends?"

"Absolutely. There are a couple of families in Pozos that from the minute we got here started treating us like sons. Our friendship with them has grown, and they have big extended families that we've gotten to know better. We share holidays and birthdays."

"Do you have a sense of where Pozos is going if you look ahead five or ten years?"

"It looks busier. The population seems like about 4,000 now, although there's been no census in a while. The biggest potential changes will come if one or two of these development projects happen. We're talking about many additional homes. They're not in the center of town, but they'll increase traffic. This is up by the mines, and it's difficult to say how much they would change the character of the town. You don't know who would buy these houses or lots, how often they would be here, or how important the culture is to them. Concerns about water are pretty big here too."

"You own the gallery and the adjacent bed and break-fast. Did you have title issues on the purchase?"

"There were no issues on these two parcels. One of the properties was owned by one of the old families in town. They all had clear titles. I also sell real estate, so I deal a lot with titles. You run into all kinds of situations. Very often everything is in hand, clean and clear, but other times there hasn't been a title in a hundred years. But there's a process to deal with that, and it is possible."

"Tell me more about what that's like, when you have a property that hasn't been occupied for generations. Is the ownership just anecdotal?"

"It can be. There is usually someone who claims to be the owner. There's not just a lot of land sitting around for the taking. It's a process of proving ownership, a series of steps. One thing we use is an ad placed in some of the local papers saying that this property is being put up for sale. It invites other claimants. There is also a conversation leading to an agreement with all the adjacent properties."

"If the low point of population occurred about 1950, a lot of the real estate would have been literally worth zero."

Nick nodded solemnly. "It was abandoned. Also, back in the 1920s, there was a fire, and city hall burned. All the records were destroyed. Now for twenty years people have been coming in from the outside and buying land. There are systems in place to accommodate that and it varies according to what the situation is with the title."

"I came out here essentially as a stranger today. I've been in this town a number of times before, but never for more than a few hours at a time, or overnight at most. What will I never see, coming in and out like this as a short-timer?" Hamblen began to nod again. "What immediately comes to mind is the word rhythm. It's taken me, although I'll work at it the rest of my life, a long time to slow down. It took me about three years, as I kept thinking I had slowed down, realizing there's so much more to do, and yet there is a *rhythm* here, that I now…"

"A rhythm specific to Pozos?"

"It's broader than that, but that's one reason I love México, and within that, central México, because I've now had the opportunity to travel out from here a lot. I can't say there's any part of México where I can't find redeeming qualities, but I'm always looking and asking, would I want to live here or there—it's a hobby. As of yet, I haven't found any set of circumstances that are as intact as those I have in Pozos. When I say rhythm, even walking the streets, which we do a lot, I love it that things are close together. If I want some milk, I have it in one minute from across the street. I don't have to use a car. Just by being on the street you build relationships. Some of them are only on the surface, like a smile, but what I love is that so many times at the same hour of the day I'll see the same people on the street, and because of what I know about them, I might have a sense of where they're going or what they're doing. That is something I never had before in my whole life."

Call it connection, I thought. Perhaps México furnishes a different variety or level of connection among people than many of us are accustomed to.

"That makes me think of something else, too," Nick continued. "Before I mentioned what an intact culture this is. There are indeed several *inner-city* grazing herds. One thing that I *love* now and will forever, is that on any given morning if I open my front door just about dawn there is a door across the Jardín Juárez that will fly open and out will come scores of sheep and goats on their way for a day of grazing in the campo. You can imagine the sights, sounds, and clamor. In an instant it's gone. So very often the tableau plays out as a misty dream in the dense fog of the early morning in Pozos, where we live here in the clouds. It is not unusual as well then, or in late afternoon, to encounter one of these herds making its way through a very *urban* intersection right here in the center of town where I must wait for whatever length of time it takes for them to pass to make my way through by car. Without exception I always say thank you for this visual feast that never seems to become less abstract to a lifelong city boy. There is much likelihood that this opportunity is a fleeting one that with the *progress* of Pueblo Mágico will disappear."

I pictured this for a moment. It reminded me of my thoughts about the 200 who had survived here without compromise. Maybe this had been one of their methods. "Do you get back to the States much?"

"I do not. I've been here for four years and I've been back once for four days."

Nick Hamblen went on to describe what he'd seen in changes to the U.S. as he rode the bus across the border—the urban sprawl, and the continual sameness of new developments. It was nothing unexpected, of course. But living in a town as quirky as Pozos would underline the relative uniformity of almost any other place.

"With all the the ruins, Pozos feels like it straddles the centuries. There's a real melancholy about this town. Am I wrong to see it in that way?"

"Not at all. I understand exactly what you mean. I keep using the word magical, but melancholy is a good word. I'd say it stops short of sadness; it's a feeling that lies over the town and the culture from way back. I've said that people walking down the street give me a smile—these same people are not already walking down the street smiling. Everyone is kind of straight-lipped somber, which often comes across like respect. People have this air of silence. By nature, they're quieter here than in other places, and by nature as well, that suits me too. Almost across the board, local people believe in ghosts. Pozos is always called el *pueblo fantasmo*. It's certainly less a ghost town now, being inhabited, than it was before. People here live with spirits and are very conscious of them. For example, in the property we have next door, you'll find that everyone in town says, oh yes, this one has ghosts, or that one had buried treasure. There's a shared knowledge that everyone has that's very melancholy."

"What might a typical property here sell for that's all in ruins?" I asked.

Nick gave me a practiced smile. No doubt he'd heard this question more than a few times. "Well, if it has ruins on it now it costs more. Property right here in the center, if it's vacant or it might have something insignificant, like a low wall, at this moment sells for around a thousand pesos per square meter. (About $8.00/sq. foot) That can easily double if there's any sort of ruin. They are tricky to build with. Of course, there are historical restrictions, and if you use existing walls you're going to have a lifestyle of water seeping up your brickwork and constant maintenance. That's just a fact of life. You have to do a lot of upkeep but you get to have these beautiful two-foot thick adobe walls. It's something I would always choose."

Later, as I walked up the hill toward la Posada de las Minas, I realized I had come away with no clear idea of whether Nick Hamblen had been plotting his escape from Dallas, or whether the exit simply appeared from nowhere when they came down for the wedding, and he seized the chance. I knew from discussing this phenomenon with a number of expats in San Miguel, that the decision to leave often takes a person by surprise—it can be as unexpected as it is startling, often taking over your mind on the day before you're due to leave. I turned to look back down toward the plaza. Beyond and across the valley I saw atop the far slope the caved-in ruins of two large churches less than a block apart. From the architectural style, they would have been no more than 100 or 150 years old, but when you don't maintain the roofs, you deliver them over to fate.

On Calle Manuel Doblado I turned and found the entrance to la Posada de las Minas. It borders a street that ultimately leads up to the old mines beyond the edge of town. I had eaten lunch there three or four times in the past and I thought of the building, with its stunning restoration, as not quite a monument, but at least a statement of what could be done for a collapsed mansion with enough determination, taste, and a significant pile of dollars. The current owners had knowingly bought a colossal ruin that still possessed three firm arches standing at the back of the foyer, dominating the rubble-filled courtyard below and defining the architecture.

Inside, I stood under a massive wrought-iron chandelier facing those three arches that now framed the sunken courtyard, filled with dining tables. The hotel marches down the hill with the street. At both sides of the foyer, four tiled steps lead up to the rooms. On the lower level, the restaurant occupies the center courtyard under a retractable roof and continues out to the back, where the architecture incorporates both ruined walls and new construction. The restored hotel seems to inhabit a different time from some of its neighbors.

The owners, David and Julie Winslow, met me at the office on the right side of the foyer. A tall, lanky individual, David wore a blue shirt with jeans and carried a Texas cowboy hat. Julie is also tall, with auburn hair and a quick smile. We stood under a ceramic tile wall panel showing the three tall smelter stacks of the Santa Brigida Mine.

We sat down in a long room facing the street on the other side of the foyer. As we went in, David remarked that this room was once, in earlier years, a *tienda*, a shop whose trade was hard to determine now. Was it groceries or clothing? Now it offers his own revealing photos of the town and countryside. Pozos possesses photo opportunities would bring any photographer to his knees.

"So," I began, "how did this happen in a town without many expats as a support group?"

They looked at each other as if to see who would start. David crossed his legs and clasped his hands over his knee.

"We had been traveling in México since the early 1980s. Our first driving trip in this area was to San Miguel, and we kept going back. We ended up buying a place there. Later, the ashes of a friend had been scattered in Pozos after he died, and that was when we first heard of Pozos."

"The first time we came here was October, 1999," Julie said. "That's probably the prettiest time of the year, because all the wild flowers are in bloom."

By that time they already had the small condo in San Miguel, but they weren't living there all the time.

"And to show you how much we liked Pozos, in September of 2000 we bought our first two pieces of property. We bought one parcel by the bullring. We haven't done anything with that, since there may be some title issues there. The second piece was the one we built our house on. We completed that in October 2001."

"What kind of title problems came with it?"

"Here there are two issues," said David. "One; is there a title, and two; is it *ejido* property? We bought the land down the street where our parking lot is from a guy and before we closed on it, he had to get his title. It took him two years."

The *ejido* system was part of the land reforms of the

1930s, when the haciendas were confiscated and broken into smaller units that were farmed communally. They were owned by the group or the village, and originally could not be divided further or sold.

"Do you feel secure in that regard on this hotel property?" I couldn't imagine that the title wasn't carved in stone after all the restoration they'd done. David was already nodding.

"We bought this property from the family of the ex-governor of the state of Guanajuato. We haven't had any problems with any of our properties except that first one, where the *ejido* was involved."

"And we've even bought a piece of land from the *ejido* directly," Julie said. "The government is now letting them sell property."

"We have a couple of friends who, after they bought some land, had someone else crop up and say, hey, this is my property. It's not just with gringos, some of the mine ruins are in dispute, too."

"What would you change about Pozos if you could?" I asked.

David laughed as if the topic were too large to address. "There are infrastructure issues I'd like to change. We've been hearing a lot lately about water. Once we went three months without any."

"But it wasn't because there *was* no water," said Julie. "One of the common things that happened was that the pump that brought the water into town would break. It would happen once a year."

"I loaned the local committee money on three separate occasions to fix the pump," said David. "Later the (nearby) city of San Luis de la Paz took over the system, but still, if there's a water shortage, Pozos will be the last place to get any. The hoped-for solution was that even before we got here a big dam was built eight or ten miles on the other side of San Luis. The state was supposed to do a treatment plant and a pipeline to bring the water into Pozos. Well, it's still not done. Electricity is another issue. It runs in spurts. Like this summer, it seemed that every Friday night, the electricity went out."

"When we first moved here it happened a lot when the weather was bad, like if it rained."

"There's a new power plant on Hwy 57," said David. "Bechtel built it about ten years ago. Here at the hotel we have a big tank of water on the roof, and we have a gas tank, so we can continue to cook, but when the water runs out and people are staying here…" He made a helpless shrug, one that closely approximated the one Méxicans always use. I've worked on learning it myself, because in some situations, there's no other response that fits quite as well. It suggests a level of indifference based on frustration.

"Another thing I'd like to change is the state that we're living in. We're in the state of Guanajuato. The capital is a two-hour drive from here. We're forty-five minutes from Querétaro (the capital of the state of Querétaro), and after what I've seen of what the state of Querétaro has done for some of their tourist sites like Bernal…(Another shrug.) But Pozos is different from Bernal. I think it has a lot more going for it, but the Querétaro state government went in there and did a good job in terms of creating a destination. They've also done those four or five missions that Junípero Serra built before he went up to California; they went in there and redid those very nicely. I'd like Pozos to secede from Guanajuato and become part of Querétaro."

"How about health care? Is there a doctor in town?"

"No, but we're ten minutes from the regional hospital (in San Luis de la Paz). It opened two or three years ago. For an emergency it's OK, but if you needed brain surgery you'd want to go somewhere else."

"If you had a heart attack you would go there?"

"If I thought I could make it I'd go to Querétaro. You can get there in a hurry and there are some very good hospitals there."

"It's the fastest growing city in México," said Julie.

"It's the next México City."

I was left wondering whether I'd want another México City that close. Was Pozos destined to become a bedroom community?

"What do people do for a living here?"

"There's a big industrial park, and a Flexi shoe plant in San Luis de la Paz. Taylor Farms is also on the way to San Luis. They supply all the lettuce to Subway, I guess." This region is generally referred to as the Bajío, and in addition to being the world capital of broccoli farming, it produces a dozen other vegetable crops. Strawberries are also a staple.

"Also," Julie added, "for the Méxicans and gringos who have moved here, the construction alone has given an alternative to a lot of the men who used to go to the States and send money back."

"We used local help on this hotel project except for the electrician and the plumber, and the carpentry work was done by a crew from San Miguel. There's a good construction labor force here. In fact, when the building boom was going on in San Miguel, there were probably forty or fifty guys going there to work from here. There are also some farmers around here who make a lot of money."

"With all this, I'm wondering where Pozos is heaed?"

"It's not just the gringos coming here and buying property," Julie said, "but you walk around the streets and there's a lot of new construction from the local Mexicans."

"I think many of them are from Querétaro and México City. Look at the location of the town. It's forty-five minutes from Querétaro, an hour and twenty minutes to San Luis Potosí, three hours to México City, two hours to León. There's a huge local population base here to support tourism. There are some real estate people now in town, we don't know if they're developers or just flippers from the capital, who have gotten in bed with the *ejido* here. They've floated three or four development plans. Supposedly they're going to do some projects up by the mines."

"We've been told they've bought huge parcels of *ejido* land, including the mines themselves."

"Well yes," David said, "there are all sorts of rumors that they bought all the *ejido* land, or they bought half of it, but the real story might be that they have a contract to purchase it. I don't think they've bought it yet. They're talking about some big deal up there. The first plan supposedly had two golf courses on it."

I tried not to look startled. This is in a town where the water often has to be trucked in because it vanishes for three months at a time? Still, I knew that golf is a major status symbol to upper class Méxicans. I tried without success to visualize fairways on the sloped areas near the mines, or missing a putt and having the ball roll back between your feet. You'd want to keep your heels together.

"They're still talking about the first phase as a twenty-six room hotel. They're already doing some work up there."

Pozos has a representative, a *delegada*, who represents them to the city government in San Luis de la Paz. To the Winslows, it's unclear what she does. After Pozos was named a Pueblo Mágico, it was decided to build a tourist center at the edge of town. It cost about two million dollars and presents a cold, institutional look. It could be anywhere, and it lacks parking, as if most tourists arrive on foot.

"Are there no design controls in Pozos?" I asked. I already knew that in San Miguel, although you can't cut a garage door into a house front in *centro*, zoning is still a foreign concept. There is no problem opening a combination slaughterhouse and barbecue restaurant next to a home for retired vegetarians. You can set up an ironmonger shop next to a music school. As elsewhere in México, individualism is always valued over community. Most team sports, aside from soccer, falter badly in a nation crowded with individual athletic stars.

David leaned forward over the coffee table. "That's the thing that bugs me the most here. The town proper was designated as a historic preservation area back in the nineties, I think. Anybody who does any kind of construction that can be seen, besides getting a permit from the *municipio*, first they have to get one through INAH, which is like the federal historical police. Their office that we have to coordinate with in this state is in Guanajuato. If you go back and look at every foreigner who has constructed something here in town, or even outside of the historical zone, they've had trouble with them. We had trouble when we built our own house. When we submitted plans to them we never heard anything, so our architect said, 'let's just start.'

"Of course they came in afterward and said that our second floor had to be eight meters back from the main street. Their reason was that it blocked the view of the church. I accepted that. We redid our plans and changed where we were going to have our bedroom."

"And then there are signs on buildings," said David, gaining momentum. "I had bought the property down on the corner. We had opened the hotel and I wanted to put a sign on it. Well, we had it designed, and it was painted on both walls going around the corner, and INAH came back to me and said, there are rules, you have to get a permit; you can't have one on both streets. You have to get rid of one, and change the size. I went through the whole process, paid for the permit, and you go around town now and there are some small stores where Coca Cola has painted the entire façade. The latest issue is with the president of the San Luis *municipio*. She opened a hotel and restaurant on the upper plaza. She put these horrible signs up there, huge, and I complained and nothing happened."

"It's not just us; others have been fighting the local government for twenty years."

Julie and David are both battered, but undefeated. They had lost their illusions, but not their determination. I speculated that if we had this conversation two years down the road, it would not be much different.

"Is it fair to say local government is not exactly supportive of business, and it's also wildly irregular in its enforcement policies?"

David's mouth took on a twist I hadn't seen earlier. "I don't know whether there's a subsurface prejudice against foreigners. I suspect there is. I think we're the biggest employer in town. We employ thirty people. I went down to protest that one house where they're putting the second story right on the street. I went and got a set of the plans and they weren't building what was drawn. The girl from INAH told me it was none of my business."

We sat there for a while waiting for the temperature in the room to drop back to normal levels.

"Has living here affected your view of the U.S.?" I didn't have to ask whether it had affected their view of México.

"My perspective," said David, "is more about the

Americans I see coming down here. They're often hard to please; much more demanding in general, I think, than Méxicans. They're much less forgiving when someone makes a mistake or if they have to wait too long for their food."

I could see Julie was itching to get into this.

"It's a whole different way of life here, where *mañana* doesn't mean tomorrow, it means whenever. The culture is totally different. If a businessman in the States makes an appointment with you, then you know that he's going to be there at that time. Here they may or may not even show up. There are different reasons in the Méxican mind, even that they don't want to meet with you or work with you, but they would never be rude enough to say that, so they just don't follow through. Even if it's a professional, they will do the same thing and not even call, and you will wait and wait. When you finally speak to them, you'll be given a good reason, "I had to take my mother to the doctor, or I forgot about this. But nobody calls, and you just have to learn to adapt to it. Being on time is not an issue. For people in the States, everything is to make money; time is money. You go to a restaurant to eat and those waiters want to get you in and get you out so they can get another table and make more money. Down here, you enjoy your meal, you're visiting with friends, there's no rush. When I go up to the States now I'm offended when they bring me my meal and put the check down on the table and say, 'We'll get that for you when you're ready.'

"I feel like saying, 'I'm not ready, you can take that check away.' David still wants to be on time for everything and I'm like, hey, what's the rush? They probably won't be there anyway. I love it down here because for my entire life I've been about thirty minutes late. I fit in really well here. I'm like Alfred E. Newman on Mad magazine, saying, 'What me worry?' You can't compare it to the U.S. It's like apples to oranges."

"So if we take the scale of that question down to this town, what is the actual flavor of Pozos on a day to day basis?"

"The people are lovely, very warm."

"The people in general are very nice," said David. "Most of them at first are shy but friendly. You go to the *tortillaria* in San Miguel to get tortillas by the kilo, but here they're hauling in their *masa* to get it ground so they can go back home and make their own."

"Do you feel a strong awareness of the past here? This whole town is a ruin. On most of the lots it's come down to piles of dissolving brick."

"We were much more aware of it when we first came. Now we're worried about the mines and what's going to happen up there."

"I don't feel they're as concerned about preservation as people from the U.S. are," said Julie. "I remember hearing a story about San Miguel when they started replacing cobblestones with pavers. It was the Americans that screamed the loudest. The Méxicans wanted to modernize it. People here don't want to preserve things. Maybe it's because back in those days they were more concerned about getting by on a day-to-day basis. They'd see an abandoned house not as a beautiful piece of architecture, but more like, let's see, maybe we can get the *vigas* (beams) out of there.

"Another thing that's happened since the gringos started buying property here is that it went from a quiet, laid back place where you could hike or ride your horses anyplace, to now, where everybody has run out and started fencing off pieces of property because they're trying to lay claim to everything they could to make a profit."

"Do you ever feel isolated without more of an expat community here?"

"No. That's never bothered me." Julie batted the

question off to the side.

"Not really," David shook his head. "I'd like to have a better relationship with our Méxican neighbors here. Some of the gringos are better at that than others."

"Your friends are chiefly gringos?"

"Mainly. A few Méxican friends."

"Any in the first tier?"

"Probably not."

"How has living in this town differed from your expectations?"

"When we came here," David said, "we never expected to be doing what we're doing. We had no intention of starting a business. We bought the two pieces of property, we built the house, and then this hotel property came up for sale, and we had seen it in passing. At the time we were coming down here from Texas once every two or three months. I don't know that the original owners had been involved with the mines, but it was a couple where her family had the money from owning some of the haciendas outside of town."

"So this was their town house," I suggested.

"We've heard conflicting stories," said Julie. "Anybody who lives here will tell you a conflicting story about anything. The story was that the *municipio* building burned."

This is a two-story foursquare building with a clock tower diagonally across the street. Occupying most of the block, it looks good now, like a lucky survivor. In Buffalo or Biloxi, we'd call it city hall.

"During the Cristero War this town was a hotbed of activity. The locals ambushed some federal troops and killed them. Others came back and sacked and burned the building across the street. The old *delegación*."

The Cristero War was an effort by the 'revolutionary' federal government to suppress the Catholic Church in the 1920s, in the belief that it had a baleful influence on the culture. The central part of México put up the stiffest resistance. The ranching states in the north, and the Mayan and Zapotec areas in the south and east, were less concerned, having retained more of their earlier religious heritage. They were OK with living without the Church.

"Is that an old school I see on the way up to the mines?"

"Those are the ruins of the Escuela Modelo, the Model School. Supposedly during his regime, (1877-1911), President Díaz took a big interest in Pozos and invested a lot of money in infrastructure. I think he was responsible for that school."

"It was the first coed school," said Julie. "And Pozos renamed itself Ciudad Porfirio Díaz in honor of all his good works."

"Then when they ran him off in the 1910 revolution they changed the name back. Another rumor is that they're going to renovate it and make it into an art school."

"What keeps you here, aside from the hotel?"

Julie leaned across the table toward me. "People are still buying property and building here and loving it. People who settle in Pozos want something they don't get in San Miguel. It takes a certain kind of person. I've had people say that if you don't like Pozos, it's because you just don't get it. It's not San Miguel."

"I don't think having seen San Miguel would help anyone to get this," I said.

"The mornings in terms of the natural surroundings are beautiful and the evenings very pretty too," added David. "From one day to the next the weather changes a lot and it alters the look of the town. The daily rhythms of this community are different than in a modern city. There are at least three or four goatherds. You go down to the next corner and a gal there has her herd of goats that she takes out somewhere in the morning and brings them back in the evening."

On the face of it, this may not sound that compelling, but in the context of what I'd been seeing, I could easily believe that it was.

"And we make our own tortillas downstairs in the kitchen every single morning. It's like any place new, you can reinvent yourself here. When you go to a place where nobody knows you and you start over, well... But the thing I like about Pozos is that the people who have moved here are from all over the U.S. They come from different backgrounds, but they all seem to gel, for the most part. Everyone gets along. They accept each other. Everyone seems to be happy as far as I can tell. The American dollar goes a lot farther down here. No high taxes, no high utility bills. No insurance. For all the things that sometimes make us angry, we really enjoy it."

This reminded me of something I've said about San Miguel often enough. The key to enjoying expat life in México is to manage your irritants. It's not a place that was made with expats in mind, but if you can move beyond that, you'll do just fine. Another thing I often hear expats say in San Miguel is, "If I wasn't retired, I wouldn't have time to live here."

Sometime later I said goodbye to David and Julie Winslow with the sense they had mostly achieved that, and the irritants that remained at least had a familiar look. I retrieved my car and drove up the long hill toward the mines, the core of the mineral wealth that had started everything, and despite their depletion, still occupied center stage in the current and future drama of Pozos in motion. Unique as this town is, the dominance of history is a feature most Méxican cities share. Urban renewal, like redevelopment, is a term most Méxicans would have to look up. The growth of cities is more organic.

At the edge of town, below the first tier of mining buildings, stands the Escuela Modelo, the Model School the Winslows had spoken of. Even with roof, windows and doors long gone, it's still a fine structure with a progressive attitude. Two tall stories high, it was clearly built for the ages with no fear of what they might bring. Today it looks emblematic of a muscular optimism long silent but with a tremor of reawakening.

Farther uphill, the great stone and concrete mine buildings graze like Cretaceous herbivores frozen in time. They have paused, listening as if trying without success to remember something important but just beyond reach. Memory has a way of fading like a watercolor hanging in direct sunlight. No one is left here who can recall the glory days. The mine buildings resemble witnesses, but they are mute. I had walked the empty landscape among these monsters in the past, careful to avoid the gaping holes that open to unimaginable depths. At noon, sometimes the light glances off the ancient black waters far below.

This field of ruined mines reminds me of ancient Egypt, where the housing, including the royal palaces, was built of mud brick, and over the ages has returned to the soil, leaving the great monumental stone structures of religion and burial still dominant, as they were when they were constructed. The surviving mine buildings in Pozos were dedicated to the extraction and processing of silver, a deity in its own right, no less then than now. They have survived that long period of danger that threatened when they were merely useless and unfashionable, so that now they stand a great chance of being saved mainly because of their good looks in old age, a prospect unavailable to humans.

The hopeful village of four thousand that today inhabits the shell of Pozos' prime, the ruptured sentimental pride of Porfirio Díaz, is also a growing denial of that fate.

Further on I paused at a great valley starting as a cleft below me in the hills. On both sides lay the continuous ruins of ore-processing haciendas, roofless and terraced upon the slopes.

Beyond, I came to a stop at the great Cinco Señores Mine. Here a quaint old man sitting at a table full of rusty trinkets and exotic mineral shards offered me access within the great fortress-like walls for a mere ten pesos.

It was like an ancient and empty city inside. Wandering through this blighted landscape of stone and concrete, I had the feeling of inhabiting someone else's ghostly dream. It would not be long before the kernel of life blooming in the central part of Pozos would spread up the hill to these battered walls, repopulating their silence.

How could this town at the same time be a place of liberation for Nick Hamblen, who may have been surprised that he needed it, or a site of unexpected renewal for the Winslows, who were nearly certain that they didn't? I had encountered this question before, in my conversations with people who had chosen San Miguel for their expat experience. It was more about the *person* in transit to these mariachi shores, and less the place. Or, looking back again at the quirky uniqueness of Pozos, was it?

CHAPTER 2

SAN LUIS de la PAZ: A PARTY OF FIVE

Only a dozen kilometers up the modern highway from Pozos lies San Luis de la Paz, a much different sort of town. The twenty or twenty-five expats in Pozos don't constitute a big support group, but none of the three I talked to was suffering from withdrawal. In San Luis the total number is five. I approached the town wondering whether they even knew each other, or worse, what if they did and they didn't get along? What kind of support would they provide for each other? Or, more to the point, how much support did any of them need?

I chose not to go by way of Pozos, but instead, from San Miguel I went north for a while up to Dolores Hidalgo. Here on the main plaza stands the church where Padre Miguel Hidalgo stood on the balcony and issued El Grito, the call, on September 16th of 1810. It was the rallying cry for the War of Independence. When I first settled in México and heard this story I was puzzled. Why was it such a big deal that he stood up there and yelled, among other things that no one accurately recorded, "Viva México!" After a while I realized that the country wasn't called México then; it was still New Spain. El Grito proclaimed the beginning of a new era with the freshly renamed country of México as its own master. Today the anniversary of this event marks Independence Day.

In the late morning sun the highway moved east toward San Luis de la Paz in a straight line, running through newly planted fields alternating with the stubble of harvested cornstalks. With irrigation here in the Bajío, farmers can grow two crops a year. I was on the way to meet Lamar Strickland and Ron Austin, who between them comprise about 40% of the expat population of San Luis.

Nothing much of any size appears between Dolores Hidalgo and San Luis de la Paz. The hamlet of El Bobo is a string of buildings fronting the highway whose back doors open on plowed fields. La Angelita is a smudge on the landscape one kilometer off the road. It is possible to arrive at the featureless edges of San Luis without ever slowing down.

Once past these newer layers, the town resembles most early Méxican cities in the sense that it began as another colonial settlement, one founded on the old silver road from the mines of Zacatecas in the north. In this respect its background was a bit like San Miguel, an early stopover point to rest, to feed and water the animals in a shady spot, and to hoist a shot or two of tequila into the setting sun before these early teamsters continued into México City, or the Gulf Coast to unload their pack animals onto the silver fleet bound for Spain. Some of it ended up in the shattered hulls of the great hurricane wrecks, like the *Atocha*.

Without the uniqueness that brings on a Pueblo Mágico or World Heritage Site designation, San Luis lacks both the classic expat-fueled glitziness of San Miguel and the crumbly chic of Pozos. As I headed into town I was wondering what species of magic it held for the tiny handful of expats who had come to earth there. I could visualize them as climbing ashore from a half-filled lifeboat of survivors from the gringo civilization of the twenty-first, or even an earlier century. To Pozos residents, San Luis probably looks like reality-down-the-road.

With a population of about 55,000, San Luis is a logical stop for people from Pozos looking for supermarket-style shopping, major banks, or a car repair. Here is the medical center and the maternity hospital. Its city government has a representative from Pozos who probably doesn't have much power. It is the place to pay utility bills and buy paint and hardware. It sounds like Peoria with sombreros, so how exotic could it be?

The answer is that it is exotic in the way that all of México is exotic, and this country can be as foreign and inscrutable as any place on earth. Don't be fooled by its proximity to the United States—they are the offspring of entirely different parents, nurtured in radically different circumstances, harboring a set of contrasting expectations. Rooted in the millennia-old indigenous culture, the collective mind of México is as remote as Tanzania and as difficult to approach.

Yet, in driving into the central part of this town I could see right away what it lacked—San Luis appears to cater in no way to expats or their needs. No messages in English are in view, and no franchise businesses have posted familiar signs. It does not seem to know about tourists or hamburgers. If it is off the beaten path, that path is the one trod by vacationing visitors. Someone had suggested to me that ecotourism was one exception to that, but in that case, the tourists were off roving the surrounding mountains, not this small city, which offers no boutique hotel or quaint bed and breakfast.

My GPS guided me through a maze of streets toward the most prominent landmark, a steep hill topped by a platform supporting a statue of Christ standing upon the orb of the earth. "Drive until you find Jesus," Ron Austin had told me when we were setting up this meeting. Amen.

The house that Ron and Lamar built is located on a new street that displays no name, one of several in a row in that condition. Of course, it really does have a name in the record office, but the city planners aren't in any rush to share it with visitors. It may be part of a widely held attitude in México that says this: If you don't already know the way, you've got no damn business trying to go there. Believing I had arrived approximately in the neighborhood, I stopped and spoke with an elderly indigenous man with two canes. Lifting one to point out the street in question destabilized his equilibrium for a moment and I reached out to support his elbow.

To even call it a street is something of an exaggeration; it is a space between two rows of houses as they climb the hill. City planners had played no role in this; it was if the lots were platted and then everyone went home for a siesta. The steep, rutted, and rocky passages between the houses and vacant lots await attention from earthmovers and pavers. Perhaps like me, the city road crew had been nearly unable to find it. I didn't attempt to drive past the front of the house, but instead came around to the back from a side road.

Their modern *casa* is the last and uppermost on that street. Across from the road I parked on begins the narrower course that climbs the Jesus hill, either to redemption or simply a better view. Aside from the privacy that being almost inaccessible brings, the best feature of the property is clearly the *mirador* (lookout) that expands from its rooftop.

Ron Austin met me at the door while a chocolate-colored dog wagged shyly behind him. Ron is a slender guy in his late fifties, average height, with a narrow face and clipped gray hair. His voice is a distillation of old Virginia beneath a newer Texas veneer.

It was a natural transition from my struggle in finding their house to ask him how they had found and selected the city of San Luis de la Paz to settle in. San Miguel, a World Heritage Site, and other Méxican towns that receive a lot of publicity in the travel press, are much more obvious choices. Clearly Ron and Lamar had something else in mind. Exploring that logic was the purpose of my visit.

"We had decided after visiting México a lot that we really liked it and wanted to live here," said Ron, gesturing to me to follow him upstairs. That seemed simple enough, I thought, the first step to becoming an expat.

The house interior fronts a main level garden on three sides, one that furnishes light to all the rooms, which are mostly faced with glass. From where I stood, I could see no windows that looked off the property, although the outside wall fronting the garden opens to a view of a neighbor's roof further down the slope. It is an intimate and inward-facing plan, where surfaces of steel and stone on the walls and the surrounding windows set a contemporary tone. The stone is called *sillar*; I had seen it before. It presents a rough buff-colored face, soft and abrasive to the touch, and full of darker inclusions. A twelve-year-old might be tempted to carve his initials into it. Although I've never lifted a block of it, this material appears to be light and almost airy for limestone. It probably has good insulating properties.

The upholstery is framed in primary colors, and much of the cabinetry is done in black lacquered wood. In the kitchen, an island unit like a small stainless steel aircraft carrier dominates the room, ready for business. It houses a stove and work counter, a deep sink, and a drawer-type dishwasher. On the opposite side, a breakfast bar runs the length of it.

Lamar joined us as we moved upstairs. He's a taller and more substantially framed man the same age as Ron, with shoulder-length white hair and the sound of the deep South in his voice. On the rooftop terrace we were met by Osa, a rescue dog. She and Hoppie, the brown dog that greeted us downstairs, detest each other and have to live on separate floors, a luxury in the dog world of México. As if in eager greeting, Osa squatted in her swimming pool and peed.

"We don't make decisions lightly," Ron continued, averting his eyes from this welcoming ritual, "so we traveled all over this country. We had friends that lived here in San Luis de la Paz and we'd been visiting them on and off since the early 90s. We never thought we wanted to live here, but we always ended up back here, so we decided to look into it. I think what made the difference was that it was a place where we could live almost anonymously."

I saw several ways to interpret this, and I made a note to bring it up later. I recalled one person's comment that you settled in México either because you were wanted, or you were not wanted.

From the top of the stairs, Ron turned toward the unwinding overlook as if to underline the obvious charm of the city. He went forward and leaned on the rail to point out several landmarks. Perched close to the top of the highest residential point in town, the house has long views covering three quarters of the horizon. Only the Jesus hill behind prevented a 360° vista. Lamar's white blond hair lifted in the breeze as we talked. Ron pointed out several notable churches, and the blue soccer stadium, built on the site of what had once been the Chichimeca prison. Descendants of the Spanish settlers were not mixed with the indigenous people in the incarcerated population. Social rank has always meant something here and it still does.

"When I look at places like San Miguel and Pozos," Ron continued, "it seems like when an expat community gets large enough it starts to impact the life of the town. I'm not saying that's a bad thing, because it can bring with it some benefits. But we wanted to settle in a place where being there didn't change it." My reaction was that this statement might provide a potential title for this chapter.

"That sounds like a kind of residential environmentalism, not much removed from camping, but with a good house," I said. "You don't want to leave any footprints, you bury the ashes from your campfire, and you cart your garbage away with you when you move on."

Ron nodded with a smile. "We wanted to enjoy it for what it was."

In all directions the low-rise city, in tones of pastel and white, spread outward toward the foothills.

Lamar moved up beside us. "We took a lot of driving trips over the course of the last ten years or so. Each time San Luis would be our first stop, then we'd branch out and do side trips from there. We got to know the town and we became comfortable here. It seemed like the right place. There was a good vibe, a good feeling. We also looked around at a variety of other places and made one trip down to the Yucatán during the heat of the summer just to see what that would be like. That was interesting, it was fun, but it was just way too hot. It was a nice place to visit, but we couldn't see living there full time. We always came back to San Luis in the end."

I considered the merits of this as a process of choosing a place to live. Certainly my own system had been no more scientific. Once we had found a place that could provide all the basic services, then it was more about the vibe, as Lamar would have it, the way it resonated as we walked through the historic streets, the way the local people looked back at us. "It almost sounds like this was the default choice, since that's where your trips always began. Maybe it seemed a little more like home for that reason. Home can be a jumping off place to explore other destinations, but it's the single place you always come back to."

"Although we almost bought a house in Progreso,

believe it or not," said Ron, with a shrug that said, "What were we thinking?"

Progreso is a beach town fifty kilometers north of Mérida at the top of the Yucatán Peninsula. Its economic base is built on fishing and container shipping, although it has attracted a population of expat retirees.

"We also went to Puerto Vallarta a couple of times," Lamar added, "on vacation trips. That was interesting, but it fell into the same category: a fun place to visit, but not where we wanted to live. We were both getting tired of working. México also seemed attractive because of the cost of living."

As he described how he continued to work on projects for Hewlett Packard after they moved to San Luis, I could see that between the two of them, Lamar was the numbers man. He has been fully retired for only about a year, and that may not last. Before that, he was able to alternate working for a couple weeks in the U.S., and then a couple more in San Luis online. After they moved here it became clear that a little more income would be welcome, but the commute must have left him feeling schizophrenic at times.

"I was a computer consultant working in the HP enterprise services group where we had contracts with state governments. We would redo their driver's license or vehicle registration systems, or motor vehicle applications. I was in the group that was taking on those jobs. Typically they were four or five year projects where I was a business analyst."

When Hewlett Packard began to go through some downsizing, Lamar seized the opportunity for a quiet exit with some benefits. Now he's thinking about taking on another project in New Mexico. "It isn't a big change in plans or strategy for me. I haven't gotten that ingrained in things in San Luis yet."

I turned to Ron. "And you were a social worker."

His eyebrows went up. How to summarize a career in two or three sentences? Labels couldn't express the experience of trying to help a thousand clients. "A medical social worker. Then, the last few years, I was a geriatric social worker. Before that I did HIV social work, and children's psychiatric social work."

"There's some edgy stuff in that." I was acutely aware of how inadequate a phrase this must be relative to his long experience. Many people, myself included, like to insulate themselves from some of these issues. Ron's job had placed him in the middle of it.

"Yes, there was." A brief summary of the experience. Ron's face was utterly sober.

"Do you miss that at all?"

"No."

Nothing more. There are times when simple, one-syllable words are all you need.

"OK, so you were clearly done with that when you were done. Does that make being down here feel like a rein-vention?" Perhaps it was an escape, I thought to myself.

"In some sense it is, because I've done some teaching in San Luis. Doing that was like a second career, although I'd also done a little of it in the U.S. with a few volunteer organizations. Here it was a paid job, so that was interesting. I enjoyed it, but I'm not sure it was a reinvention so much as a blossoming."

"Can you tell me more about what that was like?"

"Because I had been a volunteer teacher in the U.S., when I came down here, somehow, the word got around, and the director of the language center at the University of Leon asked me if I wanted to teach English at their center here in San Luis. I said I would try it, and I ended up teaching there for quite a while."

"You were teaching adults?"

"It was a mixed group because they tested the students on whatever level they were at. I had one kid who was twelve years old, and he was in the class with someone who was thirty-five. It was all based on their skill level, so it was a variety of ages."

"Moving down to México," I said, "a lot of people tend to shed their past. It's more about what you're doing now."

"To me it was more like a continuation, another chapter. It wasn't like we were running away from something. I wouldn't say reinvention. That doesn't seem like the right word."

"It was just a new adventure," said Lamar with a shrug. I was beginning to sense that for Lamar, changes of this kind were borne more lightly. He was able to go with it and commit to it, without being as reflective about the consequences as he watched it play out. Perhaps, after his career in a business top heavy with numbers, he welcomed the opportunity to observe a more subjective phenomenon without trying to quantify it at every point.

"Do you miss the support of a larger expat community in San Luis?"

"I don't."

"I don't either," said Ron, "and I guess you can't miss what you've never had. I don't ever find myself saying, gee, I wish there were more expats here that we could talk to. I'm not sure what the advantages of that are."

"We go to San Miguel once or twice a month, and we go to Pozos, where there's a pretty big expat community."

"Like that hoard of twenty-four of them?" I suggested. This was met with laughter.

"We go there once a week to eat." I took this to mean

that the restaurant scene was not the strongest point among the attractions of San Luis.

"We know the people there very well," Lamar added.

"They evidently have a dinner circuit, so there's always somebody going to someone else's house practically every night for dinner. We don't do that."

"We're not big socializers," Lamar said with no hint of understatement.

One part of the appeal of the area that emerged more slowly for them was its historic character. Their house is on the eastern side of San Luis, and we didn't have to drive far beyond it before we crossed an invisible line into la Misión, the reservation, as we would call it in the United States. It's continuous with the city because the indigenous people have been selling parcels of their land along the edges.

"We knew there was a Chichimeca reserve here," said Ron, "and we also knew the age of the city. It's more than 450 years old. But we didn't learn the details of the history until after we got here."

The Chichimeca are a collection of related indigenous groups that inhabit the north central part of México. Ron promised to show me a massive stone set in the sidewalk in the central part of town that marked the centuries-old boundary beyond which the Chichimeca were not allowed to pass when they came in to trade. Today they come and go freely, and the town supplies many jobs for members of their community. They do not mix much with the San Luis locals other than that. The *la Paz* (the Peace) in the town's name refers to a treaty that ended a long period of conflict centuries ago between the indigenous people and the later settlers.

As we bounced over these unpaved roads, the feeling of poverty was denser and more unyielding than anything I'd observed in the main part of San Luis. Because construction in all of México occurs in small stages as people assemble the money to buy the next truckload of bricks and mortar, the unfinished buildings often outnumber finished ones. Most still show their exposed red brick, since a covering of painted stucco is a sign of completion that is usually a long way off. Here and there we saw small groceries and workshops. The freshest and most optimistic-looking buildings were the schools. In the blazing sun we passed troops of children in uniforms that looked no different from those in other towns in México. The overall situation of the rest of the people reminded me of those reservations in the United States that were not supported by casino revenues. Life itself here is a sufficient gamble, and the payoffs are never large in a sense that Las Vegas would recognize.

As he drove, Ron Austin's social worker eyes must have been recording the same problems here as in the U.S.: drug and alcohol abuse, high suicide rates among the young, family breakdown. Yet, the Misión's loyalty to Catholic ritual, and especially, the feast days of the saints, is fierce; at least as strong and perhaps even stronger than in the more racially mixed Méxican population, where many people applaud the presence and ignore the message of the Church.

Half a kilometer on, we pulled onto a principal paved road and headed back into the main part of San Luis. Soon we were parked at the end of a long shady green space, the Alameda. Here the tall trees were painted white to shoulder height. Wide paved walks branched off into informal paths among the ground plantings, which looked like broadleafed philodendrons. A great calm prevailed. People read newspapers or chatted on Victorian cast iron benches against a counterpoint of bird commentary from above.

"If politics made it impossible for you to stay in México, where would you two go?" Even as I said this it was hard to imagine.

"I think we'd go somewhere in the southeast," replied Ron. "Lamar's family is in Mississippi, and mine is in Virginia. We might even go somewhere in between."

I didn't say so, but to me, the southeast meant somewhere in Chiapas or Tabasco, Belize or Honduras. "You don't think you'd venture deeper into Latin America? That's what I always think I'd do. Somewhere like Costa Rica, Panama, Argentina?"

"I don't think so."

"I haven't seriously thought about that," Lamar said. He dealt with what was on his plate and was little given to idle speculation.

"Have you two become part of the social fabric in San Luis?"

"Ron very much has, because he was here full time while I was still traveling. He was teaching and he got to know a lot of people. I think he's very much integrated into the town scene."

"I think we both have," agreed Ron. "We go to the weddings and the parties."

"How do people here look at you guys?"

Ron gave Lamar an amused glance. "I always say it must be like how Brittany Spears feels, because people always stare at us with a strange look, like they don't know what to expect. Even after six years here, people still do that. But for those who know us well, it's no different than anywhere else."

"I noticed that too." I said. "It's as if people in this town aren't used to tourists."

"It's not so unusual for all of them because a large percentage of the population has been to the U.S. to work," said Lamar. "There's that outflow mentality. You leave here to go to the States for extended periods. But to them it's unusual for people from the north to come to this part of México.

They find it hard to understand why people would make that choice, although I think many of them have gotten used to us. At first it was a little unusual."

"The other thing that's interesting," added Ron, "is how the local community reacts to us being a same-sex couple. People always seem interested in asking about it but also are often uncomfortable and kind of beat around the bush. Honestly, it is such a non-issue with us that we forget to even mention it unless we're asked. Although this is a very conservative town, in its formalities at least, we've experienced almost no negative reactions. Now and then young men may say something derogatory loud enough for us to hear, but in truth that happens less here than it did in the U.S., and the longer we are here the less it seems to be an issue even for that group. We just lead our own lives, and people seem to respect that. Even if we aren't exactly like them, it's all right if they decide that we are good friends and neighbors. Luckily for us, that usually seems to be the case."

I already knew that people in México tolerate a large degree of individuality among their neighbors and associates. Although this is not a society with widely diverse values, and people are encouraged by the Church to all face in the same direction, there is also an unexpected tolerance for individual differences because most people are reluctant to act as enforcers of a given orthodoxy among their neighbors. I often thought this came about as a reaction to the degree of intellectual and religious oppression imposed by the Conquest. Ron and Lamar may have stretched the normal limits of that tolerance, but they still easily fell within its outer borders. We passed the bowl of a huge fountain that launched a column of cool spray into the air.

I started thinking about how I see a lot of gay men in San Miguel and, as I travel, in many other places in México.

Did they find a special connection to this country? Ron hardly paused before he answered.

"Well, I think that is an interesting question. Of course there are the usual reasons that everyone has, such as climate, culture, costs, etc., but in thinking of what makes Mexico attractive to gay men in particular, I think it's a combination of factors. For what it's worth, Lamar and I have talked about it before and we came up with two trains of thought.

"One is that gay men quite often discover that 'live and let live' attitude in México. As long as you're not scandalizing the town, then people in general don't seem to have many concerns about what you do in your private life. As I think I mentioned previously, it seems to be more important what kind of person you are than anything else. Also there is the aging thing, especially salient if you are involved in the Méxican gay community. The general cultural model here seems to respect age as something that brings experience and wisdom, not just wrinkles. Maybe this is changing, but it still seems true particularly within the Méxican gay community that aging is not seen as a negative thing. This is such a big contrast with most gay communities in the U.S., where age discrimination can be a real issue and frankly, most gay expats that we have met are not young people. This acceptance (or at least non-concern) regarding sexuality and aging is a very attractive layer for gay men to add to the usual benefits of living in México. I in no way want to give the impression that México is free of discrimination or prejudice in these areas, but I think many people find it more liberating than other places, and expats often seem to be given more leeway in any case when it comes to 'different' behaviors of any kind, as opposed to what native Méxicans may experience."

I was beginning to think of this as *acceptance for different reasons*. México is not San Francisco, and there is certainly never an atmosphere of *anything goes*, yet the fundamental attitude here is to let your friends and neighbors live their own lives, no matter what conventions may be shattered in the process. Again, people have a reluctance here to be enforcers.

"This leads to a second thought," Ron continued. "While we too have wondered why there seem to be so many gay expats, we are not entirely sure that there really are that many more than in the population in general. What we can say is that the other gay men we have met here tend to be outgoing, dynamic people who were successful and very much out of the closet in the U.S. As a group they would most likely make their mark among any population, and only more so given the relative cultural freedoms in México as I described earlier. In other words, there may not be more gay men than anywhere else, but perhaps the combination of personal and cultural factors just adds up to a higher profile group and thus the appearance of larger numbers."

They were some of the taller trees in this forest, I thought.

As Ron spoke I was wondering whether coming this far south was a way of shedding the constraints of your prior environment. It was fine to be openly gay in San Francisco or Greenwich Village, but what about Biloxi or Bismarck? Wasn't the simple act of shedding your bonds to an earlier culture a release into a new kind of freedom? Part of the question may be only about visibility.

"That's our best take on the topic, but without any formal studies—sorry, that's the social worker in me—then who knows? It could be just as Susan Montana, former owner of the hotel Casa Montana in Pozos, once said when addressing this topic with me, 'It's just because gay men are always the first to discover the fabulous places.'"

Indeed. It may be only that. We could launch a conversation about whether or why gay men have better taste than some of us, but I don't like to overthink these things. We walked on a bit more, trailing thoughts lingering in all our heads. Ron took up the thread again.

"Lamar and I are also more visible than some other gringos in México, or even the ones from Pozos. If those people have errands to do they tend to send their staff to do it. We don't have a staff, so we go and do it ourselves and people see us." Earlier they had made a point that they do all their own cleaning, which is unusual for expats in México because household help is so affordable.

"We're very visible," added Lamar. "We go to all the cultural events. The Casa de Cultura is always putting on affairs throughout the year and we make a point to go to as many of those as we can."

"Mainly musical events?" I asked.

"Musical events and dancing, like ballet *folklorico*."

"At normal times during the day, how do you occupy your time?"

"I'm not sure," Ron said, "but we're always busy. Again, because we don't have a staff, we occupy our time doing the same things we did in the States. Taking care of the house, the yard and the garden. Going to the grocery store."

"Going to Costco. After I quit working at HP I decided to get healthier, so I started going to the gym in Pozos. I try to do that every day during the week. After that I come home and surf the Internet a little bit, and then do chores around the house."

"Even though it's the same kind of things we did before we came here, we're not so rushed about it now. We can take a whole day to work in the yard if we want to, but in the U.S., we'd have maybe no more than forty-five minutes before we'd have to rush off to do something else."

"If we go to San Miguel, that's a whole day trip. It's five or six o'clock before we get back home." San Miguel is a little more than an hour away.

"Or if we go to Querétaro to go shopping, then we always have lunch there." Querétaro is forty-five minutes off on an excellent highway.

"In the evenings you don't go out much in the absence of any of those special occasions?"

"Not a lot in the evening," Ron said. "We may go down to the center for coffee, because they have a few coffee shops now. Once in a while we'll visit a friend, but most of the time we like being at home."

We approached the bandstand, a lovely old Victorian-style creation with fluid ironwork and a shallow, conical cap. The base was a target for graffiti all around, which diminished the decorative effect, although in a way it did anchor it in twenty-first century reality.

"You don't ever miss all the attractions a town like San Miguel offers?"

Ron shook his head slowly. "That's not the kind of life I was looking for. My view of it is that people there tend to have a lot of money, and they would be just as comfortable living in South Beach as in San Miguel. And sometimes I've heard it referred to as the Hamptons South. But again, that's not animosity. If that's what people want, that's OK, but it's not what we were looking for."

I didn't say that I knew a number of people in San Miguel trying to get by on social security.

"I just don't have a strong opinion," added Lamar. "It seems like a lot of the people who move down to San Miguel are self-motivated and driven, it's like they have a mission. I think it's interesting some of the causes they take up. The issues seem a little different from what interests the local culture there, like the animal rescuers. There are always people talking about the differences in culture, yet they bring those values in and champion them, which may be a little different from the native priorities."

This echoed my own observations, but in the matter of animals, the difference between local attitudes and those of the expats is profound and cultural. I could spend an entire chapter on it, but it doesn't belong in this book.

"When you bring in a large expat community," added Ron, "that makes changes, and that's OK. But it does alter the community. San Miguel would be a very different place today without the expats there."

Yes, I thought, it would still be an agricultural community from 1960. While some of the locals would've thought that an improvement, most would suffer from it.

The great esplanade we were passing through had once been the orchard of the Jesuit establishment in San Luis. While their fruit trees were long gone, it was now a place that emanated peace and invited contemplation, just as it must have been then. I could easily imagine the black-robed priests reading their breviaries, strolling among the apples and limes and pecans. Almost anything will grow here.

The Alameda is an enormous asset for a small and unpretentious city, one with no tourism other than a few hikers headed into the hills, and for whom San Luis is mainly a colorless launching point. To me it felt like the town had gotten lucky, although I didn't know what transaction had brought it this park. It would certainly have changed hands when the Jesuits were expelled from México in 1767. Ron suggested it had been in private hands for about a century before its acquisition by the city in the 1860s. Now it was a place made for reflection, and walking through it in this leisurely fashion made me think again about my mission in coming here.

"Is there anything you think of as magical about San Luis?" I asked. Looking around us, I knew what I would've answered. We were leaving our footprints on the most enticing part of it, but Ron and Lamar were not there to leave any footprints.

A moment of silence passed before Ron brought up a broader view. "Two things pop into my head. One is the natural setting of it, the sunsets, the storms moving across the valley, the weather part of it, because the town is still small enough that it hasn't done away with nature. The other thing is that when you live here for a while you do feel a sense of history. Living across the hill from the Chichimeca reserve you hear the singing and the dancing. Then you go downtown and you see the ancient stone that marks the boundaries where the people from the Misión could never cross."

"I can see that. Part of my task in writing about San Luis de la Paz is going to be how to contrast this town with the extreme quirkiness of Pozos. I can only ask you this because you know Pozos as well. What would you come up with as a way of establishing that as a positive contrast? It goes way beyond saying that it's just not Pozos. No place is. So what is it in more affirmative terms? (more silence) This is what I face."

"It's hard to tell," said Lamar, slowly. "To me it has a totally different feel."

"I feel a sense of continuity in San Luis," Ron finally said. "It's 450 years old and it's always been a functioning city. It's never been a *failed* city, and Pozos is a place that died and now it's coming back. If Pozos is like Lazarus, then San Luis de la Paz is like Methuselah. It's been here forever and it *feels* like it. We will have to wait and see what Pozos is going to become, because I don't think it's ever going to be what it was again." Listening to this, I felt he was perfectly happy to watch this evolution, even as San Luis changed by no more than a centimeter every decade, like a process that was caused by gravity and the shift of tectonic plates, and had only the momentum of a monstrous statue embedded in the ground. It almost looked like the motion of Easter Island.

As we walked farther toward the old Jesuit abbey walls at the far end of the Alameda I couldn't think of a public space in the U.S. that had a similar feeling.

"Did you make a conscious effort to bring as little as possible of your U.S. life down here?"

"As far as material possessions, that's true," said Lamar, "but with technology, like the Internet, we had to have that going almost from day one. We spend a lot of time on the computer."

"You must have walked away from most of your possessions. I look at your current house and I see that you guys are not indifferent to your surroundings by any means. A great deal of care went into the design and ambience of that place. That suggests to me you left behind something that may have been equally as interesting in Dallas, but certainly quite different in style."

Ron smiled and paused at this point.

"We'd like to think that we left everything behind, but I have a Méxican friend here who says, 'You know, Ron, you gringos are like turtles. You can't help it, you carry your culture around like a shell, and wherever you go, that shell goes with you.' I think that's true."

"With a lot of the material stuff that we left behind," said Lamar, "it was because we wanted a fresh start as far as the house was concerned."

"We had a more traditional kind of house, marble floors with French provincial furniture. When we got here we said, let's go for clean and minimal."

"A fresh start? Does that imply a certain degree of

rejection of the past? On the one hand I'm hearing, OK, it's an adventure, which I can easily believe, but what else was it?"

Lamar was shaking is head. "It wasn't a fresh start in the sense that we were rejecting or running away from something. It was just a new chapter, an opportunity to do something different."

"Lamar had had his life in Dallas, and I'd also had my life in Dallas when we met. We had to meld those two. Coming here was a chance for us to have our life together, a house that we built together, the whole thing." I looked up to see his face glowing with this recollection.

"So it's not necessarily just one of a series of new starts."

Ron smiled at this. "We don't know. We won't know until it's over."

"It may be part of a series that stretches forward but not necessarily backward," I suggested.

"Right."

We left the Alameda as we came up to the old wall of the Jesuit enclave and headed toward the main plaza. The traffic wasn't dense, and the buildings were single story and unpretentious, housing businesses that served people's daily needs. The appearance was that of hundreds of other old towns in México.

"What would you change about San Luis?"

"I'm not sure I would change anything," said Lamar. I knew he would say this. Neither of them were missionaries for any cause.

"I would say the same, but if it changes by itself, that's OK."

"Neither of you is an advocate of change."

"Not without the need, and I'm not sure I see one."

"We feel very comfortable here," said Lamar. "There's

nothing that's out of kilter with it as far as we're concerned. Pozos is a different story. I'm fascinated by the changes that are going on there, and I'm looking forward to seeing how it evolves."

"We're also happy that we're not involved in that, and we can ignore it when we choose to."

"You're not in that state of flux," I said, "and you don't want it. You're in an ongoing 450-year-old continuity. México doesn't change much at some levels. Do you feel safe here?"

"Completely safe."

"It's safer than many places."

"What does it cost to live here?"

"Like anywhere in México," said Ron, "it can cost as much as you want it to, or as little."

"How about property taxes?"

"Right now we pay about $65 a year." He laughed, almost with chagrin. "It's ridiculously low. But if we were just going to move somewhere for the cost, it wouldn't necessarily have been here. Both where Lamar's family lives, and where my family lives, there's a low cost of living."

"And we spend a lot of time going over the budget," added Lamar, "because being retired, that's something you have to do to have some sense of your future security. Our budget is about $43,000 a year. That includes allowances for home and auto repairs, and unexpected medical expenses and insurance, saving money for travel—we try to hit all the major categories. We could get by with a lot less, but we do like to be comfortable."

"We have Méxican friends in San Luis who live on three or four hundred dollars a month. It's almost an embarrassment for us to say we need this much to be comfortable."

"We're very fortunate to be in that position," said

Lamar. "We could have a lot more resources, but we could also have a lot less. We're average middle Americans living in México." I could see that he ran the budget office.

"After six years what has living in Mexico taughtyou?"

"Patience," said Ron without missing a beat.

"The need for patience."

We rounded a corner and found that the street opened up into the plaza. It was filled with people without seeming crowded or hectic. Seeing no expats, I couldn't overlook the relaxed pace. San Miguel can often be rushed and full of people scanning their pocket maps and searching out the next photo op with their cell phones or I-pads, although its relaxed aspect is always present too. Playing out against the classic facades, one fronted by Moorish arches, here I still saw a balloon seller and vendors of street food and religious trinkets. Everything was aimed at the needs of local daily life. Many people did give us odd looks as we passed. They weren't at all hostile, only mildly surprised. We paused for a moment and sat on a bench. Patience was still on Ron's mind as he surveyed the activity.

"I have a lot more patience than when I came here. Also, one thing that's hard to get your head around is that seeing the world from a different viewpoint is neither good nor bad; it's only a different point of view. The biggest contrast to illustrate that is when we came here, we tried to get workers to do things to finish out our house the way we thought it should be done. No matter what we did, they still did it the way they thought it ought to be done. We'd offer them money, or we'd say, charge whatever you want to, to do it the way that we said. They got angry, because money was not a motivator for them, and that was a strange idea. Their way was the traditional way, or just the way they decided it should be done. End of discussion. They were the ones doing the building and we didn't have a right to tell them to do it differently. It took me a while, but I finally realized that it was just another way to look at the world, not good or bad, but just another way. One that was not ours."

I already knew that Méxican workers don't care to have people looking over their shoulders. This was an extreme example, but not surprising. They'd been hired to build a house, not to take orders.

"Now that you've lived with the choices they insisted on making, in the long run, were they correct?"

"No, not to us," Ron said emphatically. "I can see that they have a different way of looking at the world, but I haven't let go of mine."

Lamar was slowly shaking his head. "Those kinds of situations wouldn't upset me. They're just another step in life. I'm generally accused of being a Pollyanna, but I take things more in stride. That's the way it is here. One of the things I've learned is that you can do something out of the ordinary. Looking back, the major decision to pick up and get rid of a lot of things and make a move to another country, now that was a little scary."

"Looking back on it, it seems even scarier now," Ron said with an uncomfortable laugh.

"At the time it felt like the big adventure, but it still wasn't a show-stopper. But like Ron said, looking back we should've been a lot more scared of the decisions we were making. So the lesson is that you can make major decisions to change your life without falling apart."

I was watching the people coming and going. It was Thursday afternoon. Normal people were doing the things they did every day of their lives. This was not at all an exotic place in the way it functioned, and that was, after all, the charm of San Luis. It was the real thing, not dressed up or tilted this way or that to catch anyone's eye.

We got up and walked across the street to a group of churches. The main one, facing the plaza, was fronted by a massive gate, the only remnant of a wall that surrounded it when it was finished in 1908. A modern upstart among the ancient churches of México. It was dedicated to San Luis Rey, a king of France during the period of the Crusades who had left the campaign in Egypt in disfavor. He had found a way to make it up, somehow, at least in the eyes of the Church. Inside, the walls and ceiling exhibited an extravaganza of detailed stencil decoration.

My favorite part was a main-floor crypt in place of one of the side chapels. I stood inside among the tiers of burials, in the cool, still air. Some were fronted by marble slabs incised with gilt lettering, others with varnished wooden doors with locks, as if they could be opened and added to as needed. In the ceiling a small circular skylight offered a route to heaven. The most moving niche was at the bottom level, where a floral teddy bear sat on the floor, leaning against one of the niche doors, waiting.

Back outside in the sunlight we looked across at the plaza. It was two o'clock and the street vendors were serving lunch. Working people had been joined by their families.

"What do people do for a living here?"

"There's a Flexi shoe factory," said Ron, "and a Korean fabric mill that always has its own Korean manager. There aren't a lot of other factories here, but many of the people work in San Jose Iturbide. They run buses from here. It's about fifty kilometers away. Many people operate small businesses, stores or gift shops, welding places or bakeries."

"It's amazing to me how that works," Lamar said. "Everybody has a little shop or store and they're usually single-purpose; they only sell or do one thing. But they're all over. I guess there's enough business to keep them going."

"Then there's a tremendous amount of money that comes in from the U.S." That would be from people who had crossed the border to work. More migrant workers head north from Guanajuato than from any other state in México.

"There's also a lot of local farming."

We started moving back toward the car, passing a once elegant single-story ruin that was nearly a block long. Two shattered fountains waited behind iron gates. The tall windows were still mostly glazed and I could look through the house and out the matching arched openings across the rooms at the overgrown garden beyond. It was a stellar opportunity for restoration, one only in need of a person with the will and money. But nothing changes quickly in San Luis, and this project was still waiting for its moment. I suddenly had the sense that Ron wanted to sum things up.

"One thing that's interesting is that even though there are only five or six gringos in San Luis, you'd think maybe that once in a while we'd get together, but we never do. To me it's interesting that we don't have that much contact with each other. It's not that we consciously set out to avoid each other, but they live there and we live here. We each have our own communities."

"The common thing we have," Lamar added, "seems to be that we're all independent and we've made our own lives. We're all connected to the Méxican community, so there's no need for one expat to meet another expat to fill out something we're missing. It's not that we avoid each other, but there's not a strong need to have that contact."

"I want to ask somebody," said Ron, "what the advantage is of having an expat community. Not having one myself, I don't really know. I know that some people seek out communities with a large number of expats, and I wonder why, if only for my own curiosity. It was something that never crossed our minds."

After I thanked them and said goodbye to Lamar and Ron, I drove south into Pozos on the way back to San Miguel. A mere twelve kilometers separated one kind of world from another. One was mushrooming with change and development as it emerged from its near-death experience, and the other drifted forward in its own slow but steady walk through history. San Luis de la Paz had never known the kind of limelight that had lit up Pozos in its prime. It was easy to see Ron and Lamar as eco-expats, intent on savoring the tempo, learning the generations-old steps, but feeling no desire to alter the pace of the graceful music of time.

CHAPTER 3

AH, MORELIA

This midland city, the capital of the State of Michoacán, host to several colleges, and home to nearly a million people, is hardly off the beaten bath for Méxican travelers or for Europeans, but it is not an obvious destination to most Americans and Canadians. The expat community is comparatively recent and scattered, and I was not able get more than an approximate reading on how many might live there. Although one person I spoke to suggested that it might be in the area of 300 or so, no one else could confirm this. More commonly, the answer to this question began with the words, "Well, I do know a *few* others, but..." That was revealing in terms of the style in which this expat community hangs together, or does not.

Morelia is about a two and a half hour drive south of San Miguel. Like many other cities in México, it was established in the 1540s, when it initially took the name of Valladolid, after a city in Spain. After some awkward rivalry with neighboring Pátzcuaro, it became the state capital, and after the War of Independence in 1810-21, it was renamed for native son and revolutionary leader José Maria Morelos, whose birthplace and family residence still stand in the central part of town. Like most of the revolutionary leaders of México during any period, he came from a family of wealth and substance. The War of Independence was mainly a top down affair.

From the north I approached across the long, partially dry Lake Cuitzeo. In May, at the end of the dry season, it resembled an expansive bird sanctuary full of standing reeds and dry seasonal grasses. Egrets and shore birds tracked through the few marshy areas poking at anything that moved, barely wetting their ankles. From there a saddle of low mountains brought me up into Morelia.

The city begins with a broad layer of newer development, much of it nondescript; it's only in the last century that its growth has mushroomed. It's composed mainly of layers of tire stores and auto repair shops, workout studios and small groceries. The traffic was thick but moving at a good pace. Eventually at the crest of a low hill in the distance, the twin towers of the cathedral came into view. What I wasn't prepared for was the large and splendidly intact colonial center I entered several kilometers later. Its ambitious scale feels more suited to a European capital. The seventeenth and eighteenth century buildings are constructed mainly in rose-colored *cantera* limestone, either left rustic and random in profile on the side streets, or finely carved and finished nearer the central Plaza de Armas. The effect is marvelously coherent and continuous; it appears that little has been lost over time, and that the buildings are still occupied and mostly serving their original purposes.

After an hour or so getting oriented to the area around the Plaza de Armas and the grand cathedral of 1744, (late Baroque in concept, verging into Neoclassical over the sixty-four years of execution) I settled under the red awnings at a table in the loggia fronting the Hotel Virrey (Viceroy) Mendoza. Earlier I had stopped for a quick visit to the birthplace of the town hero, Morelos, but found that it was a reconstruction, with all the carved stonework as crisp as yesterday. I left after five minutes. Without the patina of time, it felt like no more than a commercial for Morelia's historic past. Circling back to the Plaza, I stopped at the Biblioteca Pública de la Universidad Michoacána de San Nicolás de Hidalgo. According to a placard on the outside, it's a library open to educators and students. It was founded in 1930 by then-governor Lázaro Cárdenas. The building dates to the seventeenth century and was originally a Jesuit church. The restrained purity of the interior was remarkable, now with three tiers of glass-enclosed book cabinets lining the walls.

The Plaza de Armas provides the focus of café society here, which lives and breathes with the same vitality as anywhere in Europe. Long blocks of arcaded restaurants surround the cathedral and the tree-lined pathways in the adjoining square. The ambience evokes Paris or Rome in the Belle Epoque; it was easy to imagine the men sporting sidewhiskers and boutonnieres, and the women in long dresses gracefully waving fans against the late afternoon heat. None of them wants a tan. In México, skin color of any kind marks a descent in class by degrees.

This afternoon crowds of distance runners were assembling at the edge of the plaza, all wearing an orange paper square giving their number. Some went higher than 2500, so the turnout for the coming evening half marathon was substantial. It looked like an international crowd, with some entrants that might have been from Kenya—lean, angular, and endlessly prepared. Runners were stretching and bending, trotting and twisting to loosen up. In this spirit, I loosened up myself with a glass of cabernet. The excitement was palpable. A rare evening race, it would finish among the lighted monuments of the plaza—I had accepted a brochure on the way in. In the hard-edged glare of the late afternoon sun, I preferred to remain under the stone arches of the Virrey Mendoza awaiting my guest. Above the crowd, red and yellow flags hung from the second story windows on every block.

After the slow rhythms of San Luis de la Paz and Pozos, Morelia pulsed with life. It projected a sense of scale, of magnitude and importance. Watching the traffic on the sidewalks, I saw no expats or American tourists other than a few dressed for the race.

I heard no gun, but the runners suddenly moved out in waves, with little visible space between them. I knew they were ranked in order of anticipated finish times. Once they were gone a silence came over the plaza. The street remained nearly empty as a few officials wandered about near the balloon-covered arch of the finish line. Across the street from where I sat, on the corner of the square, four huge tables were covered with pineapple slices awaiting the racers' return.

I could imagine José María Morelos, a priest, riding out from this plaza and going north to join Allende and Hidalgo to move against the Spanish colonial army in 1810. It would've looked no different then than it did in 1910, when the dictator Porfirio Díaz was overturned and replaced by the first revolutionary president, Francisco Madero, who, even if he didn't last long enough to change the direction of the country, still gave his name to the street at my side. Even now the graceful columns and elegant arches look nothing like the twenty-first century. A moment later, my guest arrived.

I had met Rose Calderone before, on both of my two earlier trips to Michoacán. She is a woman of impressive stature, six feet tall, with her hair done in a pixie cut. For this encounter, she was wearing a beltless *huipil* of native fabric and eight or ten silver bracelets on each wrist. Their collective weight did not bow her presentation in any way. We exchanged the Méxican greeting, a brief kiss on the cheek, and she sat down. The waiter appeared a moment later and we each ordered a glass of wine, the second one for me.

"You missed the start of the race," I said. "It seems like there's so much going on here. Somehow, in my earlier travels I always missed Morelia, I guess because it has a bad press in the U.S. I must have *chosen* to miss it. That seems silly now. If it offers a lesson, it's not to take other people's advice.

"How did you find it?"

Rose leaned back in her chair and put her hands together. "In 2002, in the wintertime, I was asked to host two people from Morelia with a friend of theirs that had previously lived in Chicago, where I lived then. I was asked to put the three of them up, and I agreed to do it. Méxicans are very hospitable and if you show them hospitality, they are eager to show it back. They kept asking me every morning if I had booked my tickets for Morelia yet."

"To let them pay you back. And had you?"

Rose shook her head. "No, I had just started a new nanny business, and I was very busy working all day and half the night. It was Christmas time and I was not ready to book my tickets. But I did come to visit later at the beginning of 2003, and I fell in love with Morelia. I have no explanation for that, really."

"Sometimes we're open to that kind of thing without realizing it."

She was not an old México hand at that point. Anyone who wasn't would not usually choose Morelia as an initial point to take up residence. Rose continues to manage a nanny agency in Chicago, even though she doesn't go back there often.

"I've lived in Texas and in California. The only two trips I ever made to México were to a timeshare with a girlfriend in Puerto Vallarta, and that was a nightmare. Other than that, I crossed the border one time in Texas at Matamoros and I remember eating mango on a stick. It was heaven.

But I had absolutely no other experience of going here, being here, or wanting to come here. México was not on my radar at all."

The waiter returned with two glasses of Chilean red. The streets around the plaza were quiet with tables filling again under the arcades.

"Those guests had nagged me into coming, and then I saw this apartment down here for rent. They asked if I would like to rent it, and I said yes. I went back to the States and I didn't tell anybody what I'd done because I was embarrassed that I'd been so impulsive. I didn't want to hear anybody tell me that I was crazy, stupid or silly, any of those judgments. Now it's been ten years since I did what a lot of people do. I'm in my late sixties now."

"I've seen that before, talking to people who settled down here, and I think of that as the 'falling off the cliff' experience. People wake up on the day before they're supposed to leave and find they're unable to take a single step back into their former life. It's always a chaotic way to disengage, but sometimes it's the only way."

"I know. Some people start coming for short periods, a week or two, soon they're up to five and six weeks. By the time you stay down here six weeks, you're hooked. You just want to get down here again once you're back. I went back and forth like that for eight years. Now I've been here full time for two years."

"But I'm sure you looked at some other towns too."

"No, I didn't consider any other place." The look on her face said there had been no need to. She knew what she wanted. I wondered whether she had the ability to enter into a move like that with such conviction that it didn't seem impulsive.

"I love it that Morelia is popular with Méxicans and

South Americans because of the famous cathedral," she continued, "which is second only to the one in México City. It has a certain grandeur to it. Here, the architecture is all living; it's beautiful. You feel timeless and eternal here. There's something magical that's hard to explain, and you get hooked by the beauty of it. And then, once you discover Pátzcuaro and the Purépecha area, the indigenous villages all around the lake, you're a goner. Because you have your life here in the city, the culture, the nightlife—there's always something happening. Then you can take off for a night or a day and go all around the villages to look at the *tallers* (workshops) of the famous artisans that have been doing this for generations. It's just a love affair both ways, country and city. I think for me, that's the one thing I did choose before I came here, that if I was going to live in the city, the country had to be nearby, within an hour. Pátzcuaro is forty-five minutes away."

"But it can't have been so easy making a change like that after living in Chicago for years."

"Well, I didn't realize until I came here that I was a type A personality. I thought I was normal."

"Normal." I wondered who is normal that moves down here. I had asked this before. People's idea of normal evolves with time. "I think when you move down here the U.S. continues to edge away from you on a different track; moving is a fork in the road. Do you mean type A relative to other expats, or to the way business is usually done here, which is naturally low key? Type M, perhaps, for México. You could characterize the pace here as about halfway down the A to Z scale."

"I'm talking relative to other expats. But it wasn't until the pace of México showed me that. Americans would say things about it, but it didn't really register. Eventually I saw how super-charged I am. So that was an interesting observation. I'm a driven person, but I enjoy life more. My family and my parents worked until they died. They never stopped because they loved what they did. What I'm doing doesn't seem like work. It's just my passion, what I love to do. The pressure seems off somehow."

But that wasn't how it still felt to Rose in the States. She is fond of her ongoing nanny business in Chicago, but it has a more intellectual tone to it. Business is different in the States, more *businesslike*. She does not feel there the creativity that has become part of her daily life in Morelia. Of course, any business involving other people's children and their daily care has a critical element to it; it's more exacting than many other businesses.

"There's no room for error when I work with children. I have to be impeccable in my choice of nannies and in working with them and listening to my clients. It's a straight tunnel; you always have to be careful what you do. I love it because I love children, and there's joy in my work, but the whole thing is different down here. I went to a doctor once and he said to me, 'It looks like your problem is stress related. Do you have any stress in your life?' I told him I had a nanny business and I felt like it was life or death 24/7. Here, it's about enjoying art and people, and being in the business of welcoming people to Morelia. You're always fresh in that conversation about what's new and wonderful, like when you have visitors."

Rose operates a small bed and breakfast called Casona Rosa. It occupies an old building three blocks from the plaza, on Calle Galeana. She had never been in the hospitality business before she moved to México.

We finished our wine and walked along the plaza in the direction of the Casona. The café crowd would probably increase again as the runners headed back toward the finish line. The adjacent streets were lined with memorable façades, molded cornices and doorways, elegant carved doors. Many displayed red awnings on the second floor windows. We passed diverse restaurants, a *fruteria* with gazpacho, and a chocolate shop, a small open-air market under a loggia.

"Tell me about your building. I think I can see it about half a block down." It was a less formal two-story front than those on the square. The trim was all elegantly carved, but the walls were more rustic. Delicate scrollwork in wrought iron screened the windows on both floors.

"What I know is that it was built in the 1600s. The people across the street that helped me find it know the family who lived here for seventy years. That's only one incarnation. I had an architect look at it to describe to me what has happened there. Originally in the back it had a barn, and the three suites in the front part, the formal dining room, the community room, and the Colonial Suite, were all bodegas for storage of grain, hay and corn. So at one time this was their original homestead."

She let us in through a large stone-framed opening, now covered by grillwork, steel panels, and frosted glass. It was sheltered by a red awning. Inside, a long and narrow patio extended deep into the property.

"This space was obviously for the carriage," she said. "The upstairs was added. I am at least the fourth serious incarnation of this place, but there are no records and I'm waiting for the people from Guadalajara to tell me about it, but they're very elderly and they haven't made the trip."

"Are they the people you bought it from?

"No. It was purchased from them about five or six years ago and given as a gift to a brother and sister, who know next to nothing about it."

The open space we stood in was four times as long as it was wide, framed by two-story walls on three sides. On a blue and yellow tiled floor stood several small tables, one cast iron with an umbrella, and numerous plants and ceramic statues with spherical bodies with small heads and arms. The angular sun blazed off the stone and stucco walls. Rose told me she leased the property with an option to buy, but the current owners were reluctant to sell until after the passing of the people who had given it to them. We sat down in the shade of the umbrella.

"Other than the nanny business, what kinds of things did you do in the States?"

"I've been doing the nanny business for fifteen years. Before that I was a teacher. I also had a catering company, Rose Petals. I'm willing to take risks."

"And you're able to make changes consistently."

"When I was younger and made changes, it wasn't cool. I was accused of being 'unfocused.' That was the assessment then. Somewhere along the line they've said now that people have three careers in a lifetime, but that's rather recent. But when I first started behaving like I do, it wasn't really normal. When I graduated from college, you were supposed to get a degree, get a job, and stick with it. I just never did."

"Depending on who is looking at you, you're either a renaissance woman or a rolling stone."

"Precisely. I try not to invest too much in what people think about me, because you have to do what your heart tells you to do. Otherwise you're just run all over the road by people's assessments of you."

"Is that also the kind of person you attract as a guest here? Independent minded, careless of other people's opinions? Michoacán has its share of bad press, as I'm sure you realize. Some travelers get dissuaded from coming here."

"You know, I would say that I get travelers more than tourists. I get backpackers, or people who will take off for six weeks and go throughout México and South America. I've gotten retired people who have no home—they just travel. So I would say that my people are more or less adventurers. As time goes by I'm getting more Méxican people, which is exciting to me because I just had a couple from Dolores Hidalgo, and somehow they found my place. For many people it's all about Michoacán art. The Méxicans say they appreciate it because it allows them to see México differently. I think, just like any place, you don't see your own culture sometimes. For us Americans, we don't see our own indigenous people respectfully. It's often the same way here."

Rose has five suites totaling nine rooms. This was determined by the way the building was laid out, the way it had evolved over the centuries. She also has an apartment in the neighborhood that she rents out. I asked what her guests were looking for in Morelia, and did they come prepared.

"Honestly, people do their research. I find they leave in their rooms reams and reams of paper. They research their vacation for a year. They know all the highlights, the cathedral, the architecture, the aqueduct, the Tarascan Fountain. They know about the villages on Lake Pátzcuaro, and some people will have an obsession for silver or copper. They're expecting to be directed to the best artisan of the particular art that is their passion."

"Some of them are collectors, then."

"A lot of them are collectors, and as my reputation solidifies and increases with networking, I get more of them all the time. That's fun, because they'll say, I want this or that, and if they describe to me what it is, I know exactly where to go, because I've been around long enough. It's a thrill for them to get something unique, and it's also great for the artisans to be able make an income. For me, I'm personally concerned that with the diminished tourism the artisans are suffering from it. Everyone suffers, but the artisans especially, because they often have only subsistence living. They've been doing this for generations, and by now the masters are in their seventies or eighties. They have children and grandchildren who are either going to practice the trade or not."

"Subject to whether it can be a viable living."

Rose would like to have a folk art gallery next, but only after taking a year off to relax. The Casona Rosa project has taken her four years, the early phases of which she had to handle partly from Chicago.

"I notice you have a lot of folk art yourself." We stepped into the dining room, which was entered from the midpoint of the patio. The walls were hung with paintings and needlework from the villages. The buffet displayed hand-made glass pieces. In the adjacent sitting room I was struck by a finely hammered copper vessel slightly taller than a wine bottle. It was faced with a stylized frog figure on four sides. The humor and whimsy of the piece were irresistible.

"This is a copper piece from the *taller* of Jesús Perez family in Santa Clara del Cobre. He and his extended family of sons, grandsons and nephews have been producing artistic pieces, one of a kind, for years. Jesús is now eighty-seven years old and taught himself to do this as a young married man to support his family. He and his wife have fourteen children."

"Do you ever get out of the *casona*? What happens when you do?"

"When I'm not here I'm typically traveling to Pátzcu-aro and the villages on the lake. I have events I go to, as well as the chores of running this place. The movies are two blocks away. On Sundays I love to see the artisans on the plaza and the Conservatory of the Roses. They restrict traffic at the pla-za then because everyone bikes. Saturday night they close the streets because everyone walks there for the lighting of the cathedral and the fireworks. But touring the villages is creative inspiration for me, just to see what the people are making with their hands, because if you locked me in a room and said you can't come out until you've created something, I would starve to death."

"So you miss nothing here."

She laughed in surprise. "Well, that's not quite true. I miss T.J.Maxx and Marshall's, and the Tuesday Morning stores."

"When I try to think of San Miguel expats here they just don't fit in. I wonder if Morelia expats don't fit in Pátzcuaro and vice versa, because that's my next stop. Maybe each place attracts its own variety, as if there were different species. I'll tell you when I finish these conversations. Right now I'm not sure."

"Well, I'm not sure either in terms of knowing them. I know there's a phenomenon that people who go to Pátzcuaro fall in love immediately and begin to make plans to move there. There's something very engaging about it, but it seems like Morelia is a slower cook. I'm unusual in that way. You don't meet too many other people who say we came here and we liked it and said yes to living here in the same day. But that seems to happen frequently in Pátzcuaro, and that's the only real difference I can say. No, there's one other difference. This isn't really a character trait, but expats from Morelia go to Pátzcuaro all the time and hang out and spend the weekend, but people from Pátzcuaro come here and go to the big box stores and then leave. They say, 'Oh the traffic is too much,' or 'We don't like downtown.' I can understand not wanting to drive at night. The cows are very dangerous. These are silly little things, just traits; I don't know that they're character-defining things. In Pátzcuaro you can't help but run into your friends all the time. That's not true of Morelia. You have to organize. It's too big to be a village."

"I can understand about the driving. I wouldn't come into this city at all until I got my GPS. Last time I came I didn't know anything about navigating here and it brought me right to your door."

Morelia shares a trait with most of the cities in México; signage has been slighted to the point of disappearance. Of course, a few of the largest intersections have a sign overhead, as one would expect in the U.S., but other than that, the street names are written on tiny signs in a cryptic script and irregularly fastened to buildings, or nonexistent. If you are driving and closely watching the traffic, which I think of here as 'free style' driving, you will never find your way through. In México, a greater number of emotional breakdowns occur among strangers driving on city streets than in divorce courts or at funerals. The secret to maintaining your sanity is to wear your GPS like a pacemaker, but in easy view.

"I don't drive at all," Rose said, as if the idea were simply impossible. "I have a great driver that I use for myself and my guests."

"What do you think is the size of the expat community here? Is there any real cohesion in this group?"

"I don't know all the expats here. There's a reading group I'm not part of, a hiking group I didn't join, a bridge group, and probably others. The lady across the street has a lot of friends who I don't know. I've gone to parties there."

Rose gave me a classic Méxican shrug: eyebrows, shoulders, elbows, mouth, and hands all in motion at once. It expresses every possible degree of uncertainty, and uncertainty is part of the psychological climate here, one that Rose had already absorbed.

"Would you call yourself a nonjoiner?"

She flashed me an ironic smile. "I was a single mom, and I've always worked hard. I'm driven. Basically I *am* a nonjoiner, not so much as a declaration, but from lacking the time. Doing anything takes a commitment. I have a group of friends that live throughout the city, expats. I definitely feel that it's a strong group. It's also held together by a great organization called Michoacán_Net, which is a Yahoo chat group. A thousand people are on it, Méxicans, gringos, people that live here, visit here, or want to live here. It's incredibly helpful. People will write about anything. Anyway, I run both this place and my business in Chicago, as opposed to other people who are retired and can make those time commitments."

"I was wondering about that. Are a lot of the people you know here still working?"

"Everybody I know loves what they do, so it's hard to think of them as working. I would say that if you're an expat and you live here full time, you're usually retired."

"It sounds a bit like heaven. Is that what it is to you?"

"No. But it's not Chicago either. Or Detroit."

"Do you ever stop and think what you'd like to change about Morelia if you could?"

"I think it's fine just the way it is. It's beautiful, comfortable, warm, and the people are great. Having said that, I'd like to see Michoacán arts promoted more. I've been working with David Haun's chat group and with the Michoacán Net on Facebook. That page as gotten almost 2,000 likes in the last two months."

"And do you feel safe living here?"

"I do. I have two guests here now who are runners. She's from Ecuador and he's from here. They have lived in the U.S., but they're living in Toluca right now. They're running marathons, like the one tonight, so they travel. We were talking earlier about the safety issue. I laughed because I'm from Chicago. It's all relative to what you're used to. My family is Sicilian, so there's the Mafia. I'm not in a beach town here. They have a lot of pickpocket type crime, credit card crime. We don't have that. The narco stuff affects us in a big way that we don't see on a daily basis, so it may seem as if it doesn't affect us. It's not something that's in your face where you feel physically threatened. It hurts your reputation, and your family and friends are saying, are you OK? Then there's a decrease in business because it affects the economy. As far as feeling personally safe, I do. As a matter of fact, when I first moved here, I noticed right away how much safer I felt than in Chicago. For the most part, there's a respect for women here, and there's definitely a respect for older women. You can see whole families out with grandma."

I had difficulty seeing Rose as "grandma," and I didn't believe for a moment that she saw herself that way either. I glanced around for a rocking chair or a knitting basket and saw none.

"You have a son. Does he come down here?"

"He does. He's coming again in June for two big parties I'm having. There's the Summer Music Series, and a friend of mine has written a book about the artisans of Michoacán and we're putting a show together for that. It'll be in Pátzcuaro at the Museo de Arte Popular."

"Maybe he'll move down here."

Rose shrugged again. That was hard to know.

"What does it cost to live here? This town looks pretty good to me, especially the old central part, and what you're saying hasn't put me off in the least. What if I was a retired couple? How much income would it take to settle here?"

"I'm not a good person to answer that, since I'm running a business here and I had to build this place up from nothing. I also have the other business in Chicago that provides an income. I don't live on social security, and everything I had for four years went into this building. I can't be a good judge from my example. I've heard people say you can do it for $2000 a month. It depends on whether you travel, how much you go out. You can have *comida corrida* (a mid afternoon principal meal) for between twenty-five and seventy pesos. ($2.15 and $6.00) It's more reasonable than the U.S. by far in terms of housing. Food costs are going up but they're still a fraction of what they are in the States. Naturally if you want American-made things, they cost more. Costco is not a deal here. They mainly have things you can't otherwise get."

"Do you have a car?"

"No, I don't need one. I have that driver we talked about."

"I'm still trying to sort out this issue of the role of the expat community in your life. How much of your social activity is centered with that?"

"I know more and more Méxicans as time goes by. I would also say that a lot of my social life is with my guests. I also like to put people together with other people."

"Are there any group expat activities that you participate in?"

"I give parties. The Summer Music Series starts on the summer solstice. I'm having a band here on the 21st called Equinox. Then there's a woman coming from Chiapas who has beautiful fabrics."

"So you don't really need a lot of expats in your life."

"I need them to come when I entertain."

"In all this, with a business especially and other activities as well, how is it dealing with the government?"

Rose's face fell. When she started explaining I could see the Sicilian gestures chopping out the concepts. "It's super tedious, but I have a good lawyer and a good accountant, and the doctor across the street helps me navigate through the system. He's not intimidated by them. He tells me it's all patience and paperwork. I muddle through, but it's time-consuming and very expensive. It's irritating that things take so long. I've waited now seven weeks for something that was supposed to happen in two weeks. You learn to turn it over to lawyers and accountants you can trust who will help manage it. To get the papers to open up here it took six weeks of full time work. You have to get one thing before you get another, and no, that's not the right order to do it, so you do it over. It's much easier in the States, where things are on computer. As a person essentially visiting in this country, I have to do everything exactly right."

"Aside from dealing with the bureaucracy, how is it being a single woman in business in México?"

"It is rather odd being a single woman doing business in México since it is such a macho culture. Thank goodness for the sweetness of the Virgin of Guadalupe to lighten things up and show some respect to women in general. I think that if one is kind, yet firm in one's requests, and clear in making sure you are understood correctly, then all that is fine.

"I'm rather imposing I guess, being six feet tall. I tower over most men here, so some may want to please me. I simply show respect. I don't demand things and I don't expect that people are my servants. I give respect and so it is returned."

Rose Calderone is no pushover, no baby shrinking before a well-established but confusing bureaucracy that operates in a language she doesn't always get on the first hearing. Neither is she young, but she has been honed and burnished by her extensive life experience. All of the ways she's changed her life in the last ten or fifteen years have not done her any visible damage, and she would never be anybody's victim. I concluded that she was an excellent student of the lessons life offered her. I'll never forget what a Méxican friend once said to me when I still lived in Minnesota: "The life, it is a school." Rose Calderone is an early graduate.

Indeed life is a school, especially here, where we cannot put down roots in quite the same way that we did in Iowa or Indiana. I had one more thing to ask her, a question right out of that school of life's exam book.

"What has living in México taught you?"

Rose drew herself up as if she knew she wouldn't be spared this either, the demand that she sum up all this great variety of experience that she had never been ready for, had always handled *alone*, and was perhaps no more ready now to distill it into a coherent thought than at any other time. Her lips opened and came together again several times before she spoke.

"I think it's taught me to appreciate the joy of life and the wonder of life. People here have less than what we have in the U.S. for the most part, yet they're happy, they're smiling, and they're kind. They spend a lot of time with their families. Being here has taught me the preciousness of life, rather than merely struggling to get through from one day to the next. It's to experience and really *feel* the joy in every day. With the Méxicans and the Day of the Dead, it's not a macabre perspective on death. You know that we're really not going to be here forever, so let's enjoy this trip. That puts it into perspective. Rather than a fear of death, which I think Americans have like a resistance or a denial, there's something here that's an acceptance of it. They say, 'Well OK, so that's the end of the road. We always knew it was coming. Let me enjoy this trip right now.'

"Looking at it like that brings some peace to the process of living, and when you have that peace, you're able to live differently, to listen differently, to be with people in a different way. It's kinder and more tender to your own soul. I feel like that's the gift México has given to me. And that indescribable thing that's taken me so long to learn from so many people here is what I want to impart to my guests, if I can, even though some of them are only here for two or three days. How am I going to convey that magic to them when I have so little time?"

We sat there silently for a while in the long patio of the Casona Rosa. What I did not know was where all this left her in the delicate and often contentious balance between the U.S. and Méxican relations and perceptions.

"In all this," I asked, "is there an element of giving up on the U.S.?"

She didn't have to consider her reply for long. There was no hostility in what she said; it sounded more like resignation.

"Yes, I about have. I am older now, and I am settled in Morelia. I am running a business here, and anything you want to do well takes love, time and attention. It is expensive to travel and I'd rather spend that money right here in supporting art and music in Michoacán. I am involved with projects I love and I feel are essential to moving Morelia forward in the local, national and international eye. I see my friends and family as they come here to visit.

The following Sunday I had coffee at the Café Europa and watched the vibrant promenade along the loggia. If a table had six seats and only one or two were occupied, I was invited to sit down and share. Judging from the way they were dressed, many people were coming from church. The wide street between the arcaded cafes and the plaza was filled with people on bicycles. Cars had been banished again. The air was clean and bright and the quality of the light invited an artist's brush.

I was scheduled to have a conversation that morning with Charles Dews, who had lived in México for years, not only in Morelia, but in México City and the Pátzcuaro area too. I had never met him, but we'd exchanged a battery of emails and I know he wanted to talk, promising to pull no punches. That suited me, since I had never pursued conversations with people who were in any way reluctant to tell their story. After a while I rose and strolled through the Plaza de Armas, savoring the flavor of weekend Morelia. Near the center stood a huge white tent with banners advertising the 32nd Annual International Book Fair. Inside I found numerous stalls from publishers and bookstores. In the center, photos were displayed of all the winners of the Nobel Prize in literature. It looked like men outnumbered women by two or three to one. I wondered what kind of bias this represented on the judging committee over the years. The women and the men were arranged in separate groups, as if to emphasize this.

I didn't thumb through many books; it is the practice in México to wrap each one in cellophane. It keeps them fresh, but it also makes for a more abstract connection with a volume you're thinking of buying, and I've often wondered whether sales suffer from it. Books have a tactile quality that you don't want to mask. As a writer I always feel that the perspective reader looks at the first paragraph in most cases and makes her decision. This is the system I use, too. We have to be able to open the book to do that.

Outside near the bandstand, under a crystalline sky, a trio of guitar, bass, and violin had set up with four dancers. They all wore bright serapes over loose white tops and trousers heavily embroidered at the sleeves and ankles. From the dancers' straw hats fluttered long yellow, red, white and blue ribbons as they moved. They carried bamboo staffs and wore clogs. The sharp slap of their feet on the pavement provided percussion.

These were *los viejitos*, the little old ones, and while

their masks made them look in their eighties, their movements were the essence of youthful enthusiasm. A passing of the hat followed each dance.

I found my way to Calle Aldama, a street whose name celebrates two brothers from San Miguel, Juan and Ignacio, who were early leaders of the revolt that grew into the 1810 War of Independence. A block down, Charles Dews opened the door to me as I approached. The timing was precise; he had warned me there was no doorbell, no way to ring him inside, and I never carry a cell phone.

Dews is a man in his late sixties with white hair and a short white beard. His build and height are average, and that day he wore a bold plaid shirt in Méxican colors with jeans and a belt that looked like either a Oaxacan weave or beadwork. His manner is forthright and friendly. We entered an unadorned courtyard of informal layout where five townhouses of various designs had their entrances. He led me to one near the far end, where we went upstairs to a small covered terrace on the third floor. The stucco was painted a dark red, and it was furnished with a day bed covered by a quilt and a table with four chairs where we sat. On the wall above his head hung an elaborately decorated plate that I wouldn't mind owning myself. The view framed a building of no great interest across the courtyard.

"Rose told me you have a long and elaborate history with México," I began. "I had initially wanted to talk about Morelia, but I think it makes more sense to sketch in your background with the whole area, because context is important, and I'll be moving on to Pátzcuaro and Eronga in the next few days." He nodded as if he could well understand.

"What brought you down here to begin with?"

Dews took a deep breath. "My partner and I lived in Austin, Texas, and he had been diagnosed with Parkinson's

Disease fifteen years before we retired and moved to México. I had lived in México before in the 1970s. In 1974-5 I lived in San Miguel de Allende.

"When we were leaving Austin, I had the idea that San Miguel was still the beautiful place for artists and writers that it was back then. We knew David had only a few years left and he wanted to spend them down here. He was a strong México fan like I am. So we moved from Austin to San Miguel in 1996, and I guess the main reason was that we were completely and utterly in love with México."

"You didn't choose Pátzcuaro at that time."

A little less than an hour west of Morelia, it is higher in the mountains with an official population in town of 51,000.

"No, we thought San Miguel was going to be the place. I had gotten a job as the editor of *Atención*, (the weekly bilingual paper) and David worked as the lead writer. In those days it was actually a newspaper. There were two people associated with us, Susy Bier, a wonderful, lovely woman, and her husband, Peter Olwyler. They wanted *Atención* to be a real newspaper, and so did we."

Dews took a long drink of his water and gave me an ironic smile. It almost reminded me of the typical Méxican shrug, except that it was more cynical than resigned. Cynicism is the tone of people who once believed in the system. Few Méxicans ever have.

"So something must have driven you from San Miguel to Pátzcuaro, since you weren't there that long."

As it happened, the editor job proved unsupportable, since it placed both men at the center of a series of ongoing conflicts. One particularly nasty dust up was between two groups of animal lovers with conflicting agendas.

"I'm sure you know what San Miguel is like."

"It can be scrappy," I said. "As in any small town, conflict can be an amusement."

"As the editor, I was always on the hot seat. After a year we decided we would leave. We came here to be in México, and that was not like México, although San Miguel in itself is precious, beautiful and exquisite." His voice expressed no irony, and I assume he referred only to the physical appearance of the place.

"So when it didn't last you went on to Pátzcuaro at the end of 1997. (He had furnished me with a timetable when we sat down, correctly guessing that just telling the story would leave me fumbling for dates.) What was that about?"

"The trees, the climate."

"I always feel like it has an Alpine character."

"That's exactly what attracted us. We looked everywhere. We looked in Toluca, in Puebla. We wanted coolness. We looked here in Morelia, which turned out to be way too hot for David. Finally, on a lark, we took the bus to Pátzcuaro and found an apartment immediately. It was the trees, really, that and the cool air, and the fact that it was a real México city. In those days—this was in 1998—there were very few Americans there and so we decided it was possible to have a genuine México experience."

Their sojourn in Pátzcuaro didn't last long either, since after about a year a job offer in México City appeared. Charles could be the proofreader on an English language daily. They discovered a lovely apartment in the old village of Coyoacán, the area where Frida Kahlo and Diego Rivera had lived in the del Carmen neighborhood, on Londres Street. But once established there, the job fell through and they were left in a penthouse apartment scrambling for an income. A period followed where they worked for a magazine called *Latino Leaders*, which was produced in México City but aimed at a U.S. market. Eventually they worked for *Mr.NewsMx*.

"This was an online daily and we were the culture and travel editors. We went everywhere in México City, walking or taking the metro or taxis. Then we moved back to Pátzcuaro in October 2001, and seven months later to Eronga. The reason we moved back was that David had an operation on his brain to stop the tremor in his hands from the Parkinson's. The operation was not a complete success. They had told me at the hospital that he was just going to jump off the table and walk away down the hall. Well, it didn't happen that way. The surgery paralyzed his right side completely. We were trapped then in that apartment in Coyoacán like prisoners; I couldn't leave him. We had friends in Pátzcuaro because we'd lived there before, and we decided it would be a lot easier to find somebody to help us there, rather than in the city. It's very difficult to find help in México City, and the air isn't that good, although I do love the place."

"Now it's the period immediately following 9/11. You wouldn't have felt it in the same way living in México. Instead, something about Pátzcuaro and Eronga captured your fancy. What was it in particular about those towns? Aren't there a lot of other charming places in this state?"

Charles sighed as if this turn in the conversation had brought him back to reality. "The people there are so lively, so down to earth. Pátzcuaro, to me, unlike San Miguel, is a place where Méxicans are the people who do the business. They're in charge, and it's very mercantile. Back then it was a bustling little city with few tourists. The ones who came wanted to see the craftspeople (*artisanias*) on the lake. That's one of the things that attracted me too, the different little villages with all their crafts. I began reading up on the first Bishop of Michoacán, Vasco de Quiroga, and found him an enticing personality. Yes, he was the bishop, but he also had a vision that was mainly informed by, of all things, *Utopia*, a book by

Thomas More."

This is a sixteenth century work that depicted an ideal society.

"That was one of his main influences for what he tried to establish there in the Lake Pátzcuaro area. I can imagine how beautiful it was then, with all the trees. Of course, the villages were all right on the shore at that time. We had moved to San Miguel in the first place not only because we wanted to be in México, but because I had memories of it being a place full of artists and writers. And it didn't turn out to be that way. Everything had changed. This was in 1996. When we first went to Pátzcuaro in December of 1997, I thought we'd have more time and impetus to do our own creative work. David was a wonderful writer, and I was writing and taking pictures at the time."

"Could David still speak when you returned to Pátzcuaro after 9/11?"

"Barely. You could hardly hear and understand him. Parkinson's diminishes the voice. People who have it also lose the ability to transmit any kind of emotion in their faces."

A brief silence followed. I think we both must have been picturing this in our own way, his more vivid and emotionally charged than mine. I felt like it was time to move on.

"What makes Eronga the place that it is?" Here we were getting into the villages that surround Lake Pátzcuaro, a large body of water a little more than thirty kilometers wide north to south and fifty east to west. Eronga is really named Erongarícuaro, which, as a place name containing six syllables, no one cares to pronounce, and many visitors don't try. It is about the third or fourth village going from Pátzcuaro along the western shore of the lake, and like many others, it no longer edges the receding water.

"It's just a beautiful town of about 3,000 people. A lot

of them at that time were working in the States, so it was a bit of a ghost town. When we got there, things really perked up. We opened a little restaurant and had tremendous success, not monetary success mind you, but really good reviews, and we had a ball doing it.

"The interesting thing was when we moved to Pátzcuaro that second time after being in México City, the very next day the landlady of the house we rented asked if we would like a young fellow to come and help us, to rearrange the furniture. I said we did. She sent a young man who'd been working for her in a foundry. Poor kid, his face was all burned from being in front of the fire. He was eighteen at the time and his name was Juan. David and I both saw something in him. We asked him the second day when he came if he would like to work for us full time. He said yes, so we stole him from the señora. To this day he's still with us, building a house in Eronga. He married a beautiful young woman and they have a nine-year old kid. He went with us to Eronga when we left Pátzcuaro. We looked at a house there that Juan checked for us and he said, 'Oh my god.' It was a great big house right on the plaza. Somehow I saw some possibilities in it, so we rented it and moved over there. We got it spruced up and turned it into that restaurant."

"Living in a town that small in size you must have gone without a lot of things."

"People always ask me what I miss living in México. I miss México food, because México food to me is Tex Mex. The food here leaves me cold. *Corundas*, give me a break! I love good Tex Mex, not the yellow cheese kind. Austin is full of it, hundreds of fantastic restaurants."

Corundas are the local variety of tamales, triangular in shape, sometimes stuffed with meat, and steamed. Usually they're served with red salsa and *crema*.

"What did you expect to find in Eronga? I can imagine that it must have appeared at the time to be a stopping point for David, somewhere calm and supportive. Perhaps it looked like a safe harbor."

"It was that, but I was also looking for something interesting and fun to do. The restaurant filled that need. I wanted the place to be beautiful because David was going downhill rapidly. I wanted a place where he could have a happy death. But for a long time he was able to come downstairs and have coffee with everyone, visit a little bit. He almost couldn't be heard. Some of the people would shout at him as if he were deaf. His hearing was perfect, he just couldn't communicate very well. Finally he got to the point where he couldn't type. He had written some short stories that were published as a book titled *The Essential David Everett Reader.*

"After that he stayed in bed and watched television. At one time he had also been a classical and jazz pianist in Austin. He lost that ability fairly early in the process. I remember the day he had to sell that piano—it was heartbreaking. A woman came with her 12-year-old son, and the boy was looking at the piano and putting his hands on it. David said he knew at that moment he wanted that boy to have the piano, and even if the mother didn't have any money he would've given it to them. Eronga was a wonderful place to be, with fresh air and beautiful people. Juan was there to help."

"For the length of time you've been here, you probably didn't pay much attention to the expat community in Eronga."

"They're there, of course, and we had and still have many good friends among them."

"How many are there?"

"I think there might be a dozen. Maybe fifteen."

"And more part-timers?"

"There may be a few, but mostly they live there full time. Another thing that attracted me about Eronga is its history. It has a fantastic background in the arts. It was a place where there was an Italian countess living. Her house is still there and one of my friends has it now. She attracted the Surrealists from all over the world. Remedios Varo, Frida Kahlo and Diego Rivera. I think Trotsky was there for a time, and André Breton."

"Someone told me you started a theater there."

"A friend of mine, Susan Steiner, from New York City, moved to Pátzcuaro. She and I got together and she said, 'Why don't we do a play?' So I said, 'Why not do it here in our living room?'"

"Did you have a theater background?"

"No, just television and film. In television I was a producer. I hosted some programs and produced some series. I also did some acting, but nothing on a grand scale. I loved it, and I love acting. So when Susan suggested we do a play, I said, fantastic. I knew she had a theater background. We started with a two-person play called *Love Letters*. It was a huge success. We did it in the living room of our big house on the plaza. We had about forty people. The room was filled to overflowing. After that we decided to do another one, so we chose one called *Luv*. The next one was *The Last of the Red Hot Lovers*. You can see the theme developing. After that we abandoned the theme and went on to *The Importance of Being Earnest*, and we did one called *Sylvia*. A beautiful woman plays the part of a dog. We had a huge success with it. Now we have our own theater in Pátzcuaro at Posada Yolihuani, a beautiful bed and breakfast."

The small scale of this theater felt to me like a metaphor for the downsizing of Charles and David's lifestyle as his illness advanced.

"You're also a painter?"

"Yes, although I haven't been painting lately, I still think of myself as a painter."

"What kind of painting was that?"

"I'll show you some of them downstairs. Someone told me at one time that I was a primitive. I don't know if that was a complement or not."

"It means loose brushwork."

Dews laughed and poured us another round of water.

"I love painting, but photography is my real love. In the past I've used my photos to do paintings from. But I wanted to tell you something else about Eronga. Surrounding the town in this beautiful location are eleven volcanoes. And the town used to front right on the lake. Now it's two kilometers away. There's a canal to get to the water."

"What kind of shape is the lake in?"

"Horrible. I think that for all practical purposes it's terminal."

"They're not fishing there anymore."

"Some people still fish in it. I'm not a scientist, but the lake is apparently polluted with heavy metals and raw sewage. Some people still scratch out a living, but it's bad and it's receding tremendously. But the setting of Eronga is so exquisitely beautiful, and all through the mountains are trails, paths and little country roads to walk on through the forest. I did a whole series of photos of the wild flowers. I had at least seventy different varieties. When I could get away from taking care of David, I walked everywhere. It was my only release."

"Why did you leave Eronga?"

"I haven't left, actually. I live here mainly with Erwin, my new partner. He's from Irapuato, and we decided that Morelia was a halfway place for us to be. We divide our time, but here mostly. We go to the gym every day."

"Do you think that Pátzcuaro and the lake region draw a different kind of expat?"

"I do. I'm convinced that's the reason it appeals to me, because it's a place that is really México. It's not Disneyland." I was tempted to read an implied comment about San Miguel in this.

"But still different than Morelia."

"Definitely. It's cooler, for one thing. The air is much fresher. I don't know that many people in Morelia, maybe a dozen, and a lot of them are still working. To me the people I know in Pátzcuaro are mostly retired. A lot of them are artists, painters, writers or actors. It draws a much more artistic crowd. I don't know this for a fact, but from what I've seen, the expats here in Morelia are not as involved in the arts."

"The people in San Miguel are different still."

"Yes, I haven't been there in many years so I can't speak authoritatively about it, but it seemed to me then that they were mostly retired and interested in drinking. Of course, we went to some wonderful parties there. Being the editor of the newspaper, I was invited to everything. I'll never forget the first time we went to a big party at a very wealthy Texas woman's house. All the waiters were dressed in tuxedos. We were sitting next to the hostess at the main table. She said to David, 'Well, David, what are you doing in San Miguel?' He said he was taking classes in Spanish."

"'Oh, really?' she said. 'I've been here thirty-seven years and I haven't had to speak of word of Spanish yet.'

"David said, 'I thought I might like to meet some Méxicans and get to know them.'

"She said, 'My dear, they really aren't very interesting.' Like how would she know? At that moment we both had the suspicion that we might be in the wrong town."

"I suppose every place has its downside. When some

of the people here found out I was thinking of doing a section of this book on Michoacán, I received some rude emails, as if they didn't trust anyone from San Miguel to tell the truth about it, or even be able to see it clearly. But on that issue, how have you learned to survive in the climate of violence that's said to exist in Michoacán?"

"Here's some background. This young fellow, Juan, that we adopted as a son, had developed several businesses which we helped him start, and as a result he became very prosperous and he got involved in politics, local *municipio* politics. (The *municipio* is like a county in the States.) Actually he's working now as the treasurer. There are a lot of problems in Eronga, but nothing overt. He told me once that the way I should deal with this is not to think about it, not to talk about it, and don't worry about it. By that he meant that it doesn't involve me (Charles) in the least, being a foreigner. I don't have anything to do with it. I don't use drugs; I'm not involved in the drug trade. Other than that, I guess I've become like a Méxican in the sense that you know it's happening, you do your best to not get involved accidentally or any other way, and life goes on much as normal. I think that's the only rational way to deal with it."

Yet, I suppose that's still a degree or two off normal, if it's at the back of your mind a good deal of the time. Maybe it's something you just get used to, like the water shortages in Pozos, a shadow on the landscape of daily life. You focus on other things.

"I read not too long ago," Dews continued, "that Michoacán is completely out of the control of the government, except within the army bases. I don't know if that's true or not, but that's what I read. To be honest, the people who are involved in it say they believe they're involved in a revolution. They think the government is not working, which it obviously isn't, and they are trying to provide safety to the people, which they charge for, like order on the plaza in Eronga, for example. There are no more drunks late at night hollering and screaming and carrying on. There was a fellow who was habitually breaking in and entering people's houses, and the cops said to him, 'We know you're doing it.' He said, 'What do you mean, I'm not the only cat burglar in this town.' These people who are in charge behind the scenes have done away with a lot of that. But if you deal with the authorities about problems like that, you can have a big hassle. If somebody does something to you, if you want to sue them or charge them with a crime, you have to have witnesses. There are very few witnesses to a house burglary."

"In your restaurant was dealing with the authorities a problem too?"

"Not at all. We had no trouble dealing with them. They wanted us to be there because we were promoting tourism in the town. People came from everywhere: San Miguel, México City, Guadalajara, Pátzcuaro, of course, and Morelia. I called the menu we were serving *fusion*, a fusion between French and Méxican."

"How do you handle the poverty here?"

Dews got up and stood at the edge of the *terraza* with his hands in his pockets, looking down into the gated courtyard.

"This is another thing I learned from Juan. I used to hand out money to anybody who came by looking pitiful. He told me once, 'Don't give those people money. You're just perpetuating it. They should get a job.' Of course, old ladies probably can't get a job, but it's like a business for a lot of other people. There are still a few that I give a little handout to. The thing is if you want to help somebody it's better to pick someone who's doing something you appreciate. For example,

Juan's a brilliant kid and he's a hard worker, but life hadn't given him a chance. He was dedicated, absolutely enthralled with the idea of working hard and making money. David and I decided when we first met him that we were going to do all of our social work with *him*, somebody who was doing something positive, and we would reward that. I think that's how you deal with it."

"One case at a time, one person whose life can be changed with a little help." I had made choices like this myself. Like so many other things in Méxican culture, charity is best done on a *personal basis*, where there are no administrative costs.

"Exactly."

"What importance did the local artists and artisans have in your decision to locate in Pátzcuaro?"

"They were really important. As I may have said, we were fascinated by the idea that every village would have its own wonderful craft. When we first got there we went to all the villages and began to buy things for our house."

"That's a real part of their economic base."

"It is, and at the moment it's suffering terribly."

"Because of the travel and tourism dropping off."

"Absolutely. And that was another thing that appealed to us, a way in which we could promote the arts, rewarding people who were doing things we thought were excellent."

From something he had said in an aside, I had gotten the impression that politics were an important part of his life, and I asked him to tell me about it.

Charles Dews has always been comfortable with left-leaning views. He's a fan of the President of México best known for initiating large-scale land reforms, Lázaro Cárdenas (President 1934-40). I was immediately reminded of his interest in *Utopia*. Dews thinks of himself as a 'red diaper baby,' one whose parents had communist leanings, even though his father had come from an aristocratic family. The elder Dews had been captured in Europe and spent the rest of World War II in a German POW camp. In May of 1945, he was liberated by the Russians.

"Your dad stayed in the Army after his release from the POW camp."

"Yes, and he was later killed in a plane crash at Boeing. They were testing a new plane and it went up and then went down into an apartment building in Seattle. It might have been 1951. My mother remarried almost immediately and my stepdad took us to Japan."

"Michoacán is one of the more left-leaning states in México, and it was the home of Cárdenas. This is no news to you."

"Yes, and he used to come to that house we later rented on the plaza in Eronga. There were two young beautiful and talented women living there in the family home. They were named 'the singing Rodríguez sisters.' Cárdenas would come to Eronga and listen to them in what became our living room, and dance with them. There's a story that General Mujíca, his great Communist general and left-hand man, was frantically looking for him all over town, and someone said, 'Oh, he's over there at the Rodríguez house dancing with the girls.' He came frequently. They were part of a traditional family, and their dad was the great power of the house. Cárdenas offered to get the girls a scholarship to study at the Bellas Artes in México City, but the dad said, 'Sorry, the place for a woman is in the home.' They were pretty famous locally. They did concerts and had a radio show. I knew both of them much later as old ladies. They used to come to parties in Pátzcuaro, and in their little old lady voices they would sing their traditional songs."

I tried to picture this in detail, but I hadn't seen Eronga yet. "How has living here shaped your view of the United States?" I could almost guess what was coming.

Charles made a dismissive gesture. "I never had a very favorable view of it. I grew up in Tokyo. My stepdad worked with the U.S. government there. We lived right in the middle of the city. He worked as a bureaucrat downtown in the Meiji Building, the headquarters of the Occupation Forces. Growing up in Tokyo makes you realize that all the baloney about how we're #1 in the world is crap. We left there in 1957. I'm sixty-eight now. I remember on May Day the huge demonstrations—the whole city would be paralyzed by the parades of people carrying red flags. That stuck with me. When I say I'm a Red, I'm not a party member. I don't proselytize, but I don't pull punches, either."

"I wonder if you've given up on the U.S., especially now that everything has come out about all the domestic spying." Even years before, his departure from Texas would've left no trail of tears. But neither was I surprised to hear this. After all, I was talking exclusively to people who had chosen to leave the States and live in another country. Some might be looking for climate, culture or economy. Some had left with a smile, in anticipation that they would miss babysitting their grandkids. Others might have become expats without meaning to, but there were also those who had political reasons, people who had left with a grimace and wouldn't be looking back. I was not talking to Charles Dews with the expectation of hearing a set of moderate and well-balanced opinions. Perhaps I'd find more finesse and moderation in Pátzcuaro, where I was headed next. Still, I never flee from controversy.

"I *have* given up on the U.S. I see it as a blight on the earth and the cause of the majority of the problems we earthlings suffer. At its base, of course, is the insanely unsustainable economic system of capitalism. If the U.S. would ever wise up and legalize gay marriage I might consider returning for the economic welfare of my partner Erwin, but I doubt that my meager pension would support us without him working in some slave job as an illegal, and I doubt even more that the powers that be in that country will ever allow such a miracle to happen. Here in México it looks as if the movement in that direction is stronger every day, but I do not doubt that the power of the Catholic Church can manage to thwart it somehow. And, after all, this is my adopted home."

Charles Dews was able to say this with a smile, and there was not a trace a rancor in his voice.

"Should retired people think about coming down here for the cost of living?"

"My cousin, who travels a lot, says that the cost of living here is approximately half that of the States. As you well know, you can live in a beautiful home here without a lot of money. I'm living in this gorgeous house and it costs 4,000 pesos a month in rent. ($320) I think that if you don't live extravagantly, you can do very well. You can eat well, too. The markets are full of fabulous food, as long as you don't spend your money at Costco or Wal-Mart, where they serve processed food. I think you can live well, if you're careful, on $2000 a month. Health care is also an area where you can save money. There are plans that allow you to have complete medical care, medicines and everything. But the truth is it's also inexpensive to go to a primary care doc. It's almost cheaper, if you're healthy, to go to a doctor like that than to be in a plan. That's my experience. One of the drawbacks is that a lot of the doctors own pharmacies, so you may be suggested to take three or four different meds. There may be a conflict in that, you never know. At one time, I had a hernia. It was from doing the play, *Sylvia*. I had one part when I had to get down on all fours during a dramatic moment, and all of a sudden I felt this zip! I went to my doctor in Eronga. He took me through the whole process of getting an operation and it was very cheap and professional. I've never had even a minute problem since. That's something that should attract people. The frustrating thing here is that any time you deal with a traditional society you have to come to terms with the idea that people don't want any change. Things are slow. People here have an Eastern sense of time; they live in the moment, and the past is important, but the future is not very important. I find this fascinating. It's a wonderful way to be."

"What is it like to be part of a Méxican family?"

"Wonderful. They treat me like a respected elder. That's Juan's family in Eronga. Maybe I'm a little crazy."

"But there's a tolerance for that, too."

"Juan, from the beginning, knew that David and I were gay, and he never had a problem with that, then or ever. There's not a gay bone in his body. We've always been completely open. His family also knew that we were gay and they had no problem with it. Here you are completely free to do what you do as long as it doesn't scare the horses."

During this trip I was planning my next murder mystery to take place in the equestrian community of San Miguel. Clearly, this was a phrase I would need to work into it.

"Was hard it to live as a gay couple in Michoacán with David, and what about now with Erwin?"

"With David it wasn't difficult for a moment. I think that here in Morelia today, because we're expats, there's a lot of leeway. Also because David was quite a bit older than I was, I could walk with my arm around him. We never had a problem, not in San Miguel, not México City, not anywhere. I think Méxican society is really tolerant, despite the Church. There is a kind of machismo here that you have to be aware of. I think because of our privileged position as outsiders we are allowed more latitude. With Erwin, which is lovely, we sit on the plaza. I put my arm in his arm while we walk. Morelia is really liberal. It's not like México City, where you can walk hand in hand anywhere, but up there in the plaza…It's been a learning experience for me and Erwin, since we're from different cultures."

"Is that what living here has taught you?"

"That and patience, which is the biggest thing, and tolerance. It's also given me something in an artistic sense that I don't think I ever could have found in the U.S. It's opened my view to what art is. I've always been interested in the arts and always studied them. I've done my best to create what I think of as revolutionary art. In México the atmosphere is pervaded with art. Even in the humblest homes you'll see some attempt at making the place beautiful, even if it's only a few plants in a tin can. People here have a totally wonderful sense of beauty. You'll see it almost anywhere you look."

Charles Dews and I said our goodbyes and I went back out onto Calle Aldama wondering whether the art of living might be in that same category. Patience was a word I'd heard before, and one I expected to hear again.

CHAPTER 4

PATZCUARO AND THE LAKE REGION: AN ALPINE RETREAT

About 250 kilometers southwest of San Miguel lies the town of Pátzcuaro, also in the State of Michoacán. It's not quite an hour west of Morelia, the state capital. With the blessing of more rainfall and an altitude of 7200 feet, it departs from the high desert ecology of San Miguel, Pozos, and San Luis de la Paz, and feels almost alpine, graced with tall trees and sloped red tile roofs. It's only 900 feet higher than Morelia, but it presents a different ambience altogether. It's more mountainous and wooded. The population, according to the book, is 51,000 in the city itself. These numbers can be approximate, since many Méxicans shun official measures of this kind. I've thought this before, and I had this sense again as I drove through it, that the countryside I was seeing was not immediately identifiable as México, which might have been anyone's third or fourth guess. Some would have started with Switzerland, but I was thinking Croatia, one of the most beautiful places I have ever visited.

The predominantly four-lane highway is modern and well maintained. I had been warned in Morelia to watch for careless farm animals wandering into my path, since rules about fencing were not rigidly observed, but I was not traveling at night, so I wasn't worried. What I was not prepared for, however, was to look up onto one of the yellow steel overhead pedestrian crossways and see a lonely horned steer casually moving along from my side of the highway to the other. Having had the car washed just before I left, I shifted lanes slightly to avoid passing directly under him. I slowed down, and soon I could see his placid image in the side view mirror as he sauntered slowly down the ramp on the other side of the road. At times I've struggled to define the "Méxican workaround," the manner of finding a way to make things work in any kind of circumstance, even without the proper equipment or tools. This may have been the perfect example to use.

Approaching Pátzcuaro, I saw dozens of A-frame buildings. It does resemble the lower regions of Switzerland. The air was moist and cool. Soon after entering the city I found myself driving on Lázaro Cárdenas, a long boulevard lined with enormous trees. Dozens of furniture workshops occupied the shade beneath, their wares exhibited in front.

In the central district the buildings are all painted blood red to about chest height, and white above. This is the traditional colonial México pattern. In contrast to San Miguel, with its lower level of rainfall and flat roofs, here the roof tiles usually slope out to cover at least part of the sidewalks. The only way to tell the difference between homes and businesses is the painted signs on the latter, all modest in size and with similar lettering. Otherwise the façades don't vary much.

This was not my first visit to Pátzcuaro, and it had taken me a second trip some months earlier to begin to appreciate the subtle charm of its appearance. Charles Dews had suggested that some people are so struck by it that they had to move here immediately, but that was not my take on it, although I could appreciate what I thought of as its somewhat severe integrity. I was used to the more colorful variety of paint colors in San Miguel, and the bravado of its Independence-era history. Now, on my third visit, I reconnected more easily with the understated charm of the town.

I passed the Plaza Grande, with its statue of Bishop Quiroga, a man who had made a unique contribution to Pátzcuaro and the lake villages on ways he never could have imagined. Tall trees provided cover everywhere. Two-story buildings rose on all sides, many with long arcades. There wasn't much car traffic, and the feeling was relaxed and laid back. The town is full of small shops selling the crafts from the lake region, fabrics, pottery, basketwork, copperware, and furniture. It looked like a place where the word *industry* referred mainly to what went on in your own house or backyard workshop. The people on the streets looked more ethnic than where I came from in the state of Guanajuato, and initially I saw no expats or American tourists. As I drove I couldn't help but ruminate on my conversation with Charles Dews. One question I had forgotten to ask him was whether he thought Pátzcuaro had changed even less than some other places in México, a country where, as a rule, change comes slowly and often grudgingly. It wouldn't surprise me if that were the case. One of my earliest impressions of México after I moved here in 2007 was that in many places, while time had not stopped completely, it was certainly dragging its feet.

The town had obviously begun at the lake, where it had been the Tarascan capital for more than 200 years before the arrival of Europeans, the seat of the Purépecha culture. As the city grew, it climbed the slopes of the basin where it was born. Now, on one of the second-tier rises, I pulled up before the house of Rick Davis, another person I had met on a previous trip. In a general way, his looked like every other casa on that block, and on nearly every other block. It reminded me suddenly of the uniforms we wore as school children. The reason for them, we were told, was that the poorer students would not have to feel bad about being less well dressed than some others. The reason here, I suspect, since the colonial rulers of México didn't care much if anyone felt bad, was more likely based on simple tradition, and the designation of Pátzcuaro as a Pueblo Mágico some years before, may have had something to do with it as well.

The uniformity of the design lends the streetscapes a sense of privacy, inwardness. It's a pattern that goes back hundreds of years and reinforces a further tradition in much of México that façades often give nothing away about what you will find inside, should you be asked in.

On an earlier visit I had met Rick in his gallery, the *Galeria el Manantial*, and we'd had a preliminary conversation about my journalistic wanderings in search of expats of a more independent frame of mind than some of those in my own base of San Miguel. He was the one who convinced me then that what was happening in Pátzcuaro was worth a look.

Rick Davis is a man of average height and build, and he looks to be in his late fifties. His restrained manner suggests he may have a great deal to say about this area, but he might have to be drawn out by the proper questions. To some degree his taste is displayed by the objects that greet you coming in. He met me at his front door wearing jeans and a blue shirt in a small-scale checked pattern. We walked through a living room decorated with regional crafts of striking design, and out to the courtyard, which was surrounded on all four sides by the house in its extensions. A large carved stone fountain dominates the center.

Although the eye did not readily pick it up without a little study, some of the rooms I saw were old and others were recent. Rick pointed out the ones he'd added as we sat down. His Chihuahua, a *chica* named Ruby, sat on his lap and listened quietly as he began to tell me about how he came to discover Pátzcuaro.

"My ex is from Michoacán, near La Piedad. He said he wanted to visit Pátzcuaro because he had fond memories of coming here with his grandfather when he was a child. As a result, on our first trip to central México, in 1988, we came to Pátzcuaro."

"You had never been here."

"No, and we stayed at Los Escudos on the Plaza Grande. We arrived late and were unable to see much the night we got in, and in those days the plaza was absolutely bereft of life once the sun went down. The next morning I decided I had forty minutes to find a cup of coffee while he showered. In that time I was able to cover most of Pátzcuaro Centro and the market. Since I wanted something other than Nescafe, I came back to the hotel without coffee. As well in those forty minutes I fell in love with Pátzcuaro. Instantly I decided that this is where I wanted to end my days, but almost as quickly I realized I wanted to get here soon to enjoy it before I croaked. I was thirty-four years old at the time. We traveled that August to México City, where we visited family, and then off to Puebla and Oaxaca. We came back through Morelia and to La Piedad where there was yet more family. Our departure was through Guadalajara. In those travels I was convinced of the wonderful art and *artesania* (crafts) that México had to offer and determined to import my finds to the U.S. I also did not find one town or village that held a candle to Pátzcuaro, in my view."

The city offered no buzz or bustle as a background to this conversation. I couldn't help but contrast it with Morelia. It was clearly a different kind of destination.

"That visit must have started a long process."

"Exactly. Upon returning to the U.S., where I had a high-end home furnishings store, I made up my mind to make Méxican products a large part of the mix. Because of that I was able to travel here more frequently. Each time I came to México over the next six years I put Pátzcuaro on my agenda to confirm that I felt the same about it. Each trip here, about five per year, I felt even more strongly that I needed to live here. In 1994 I bought this house. I was one of the first expats to buy in the old center, and I am so happy that I did. Properties were cheap at the time and the area was much more run down. Within a year of my purchase, Pátzcuaro was declared a Pueblo Mágico, and funding was available to tone up the infrastructure. My 1775 adobe structure and gardens needed a major remodel and update. We started the remodel in 1999 and it was two and a half years in construction. Once it was done I sold my business and my house in California and headed down here permanently."

Rick Davis's delivery was measured and calm as he talked about this period, but I can imagine that supervising construction from a different country was rarely simple or relaxing, especially since he was still operating a business there. My impression was that he is a reasonable man who could make decisions at arm's length and still live comfortably with them.

"What is it about Pátzcuaro, what makes it go? I sense a real integrity here, but it has such a different feeling from Morelia."

"Pátzcuaro is simply a small to medium-sized Méxican town. There is little industry here, and the main economy is tied to agriculture, forestry and its products, and tourism. In terms of choosing this to be a Pueblo Mágico, the 'magic' in that decision is mostly in its history and architecture, but for me the real magic is in its people."

"What were you expecting to find here?"

"I was expecting to find here an honesty to life that I felt was missing in the modern U.S. On my travels here I grew more and more disenchanted with the way things were going up north. Honesty to me means human values and the honor of family, appreciation of friends and of the tangibles one has, as well as an entirely different way of looking at time. I had no rose-colored glasses, and I was well aware of the poverty, the sometimes odd work habits, and many of the unusual customs here."

As I sat there looking at Rick Davis I could easily believe he wore no rose-colored glasses. The man sitting across the table from me was not easily fooled, and certainly not more than once. *An entirely different way of looking at time* was a key phrase, and I had often felt this myself; in fact, I was feeling it as we sat there. I usually had a lot going on, but I never felt I was *rushing* toward anything. Projects were finished at their own pace, and didn't suffer from being pushed too hard. "What do you miss here?"

"Corned beef and rhododendrons." He said this with a precision I had not expected. Since no response was required, Davis went on to describe his business.

"I'm in partnership with an architect from Canada. We both enjoy Méxican *artesania*, and with my years of importing I had developed lots of contacts down here. We thought we could do an attractive store in town reflecting this, using his designs, with unique product ideas. Our main customer is the new middle and upper class Méxican visitor to Pátzcuaro. Mainly coming from México City, Querétero, and Guadalajara, we find that they desire designs with three qualities: made in Mexico, handmade, and having a contemporary flair. Of course expats are an important ingredient in our sales, too, especially those coming up from the beach areas. (Ixtapa and Zihuatenejo are less than a day's drive away.) Not as important now are the international travelers, since because of stiff airline regulations, those tourists can buy and bring back less and less."

"Where do you get your merchandise?"

"All of the merchandise is Méxican. We have items from all over the country with about 60% of the inventory coming from the Guadalajara area. In the future we hope to travel far and wide to collect an even greater mix."

"So you're drawing heavily on your experience in the U.S. home store." The picture I was getting was of an expat in México doing something very close to what he'd done in the States.

"My biggest career was having that business, similar to the store I have here now, but much bigger, in Woodside, California. I was lucky because I got into Woodside when it was a little one-horse town. While I was there it became the wealthiest town in the nation. It exploded around me. Not in overall growth or size, but in per capita economic terms. I had one of the corners in only a block and a half of businesses. I was able to rent for twenty years on that one corner. It was a good deal."

"What would you be doing if you weren't doing this?" I already knew the answer.

Rick Davis put his hands over his face. "I couldn't even wrap my mind around that."

"No options."

"Not really, none. This is exactly what I want to be doing. Imagine! When I found Pátzcuaro, I thought to my-self, this is where I want to die, but I want to be here a long time before that happens. I basically worked twenty years in ten years to get here. I worked twelve- to sixteen-hour days; I worked seven days a week, just to do it. Fortunately for me that coincided with the height of the market, both in home sales and business sales. So when I was ready to sell out, health-wise I was exhausted."

"But the California market was ready for you and that was when you were ready to come down here."

"Right. It coincided with the height of everything. I'm not wealthy. I would rather be economically challenged here in México than wealthy in the U.S."

This was an interesting thought. In a less consumer-oriented society money matters less, and is therefore less *defining* to those who have some, as well as those who have none.

I expected Rick would have become a Méxican citizen by this time, but it hadn't happened because of some bureaucratic mix up that he dismissed with a tolerant expression. He'd been here too long to expect everything to come off as planned. Each process has its own pace and measure. I asked him how the Pátzcuaro expats compared with those in Morelia.

"The expat scene is a new phenomenon in Morelia. It was not nearly as popular with expats until recently."

"No one there could tell me how many there were."

"And I couldn't even come close to answering that either, but only in the past five years have people coming from the north started to discover Morelia as a place to live. I imagine it's still evolving what kind of people want to move there. What I find is that it tends to be expats who are often involved in the arts, because there's so much going on there."

"I didn't see many galleries, although I know the music scene is hopping."

"Not private galleries, since nobody has any money to buy pictures right now. The government funds a lot of things there, as well as the Ramirez family, who are the owners of Cinépolis, the large movie chain. Los Ramirez are wonderful in supporting a lot of art activity. In Morelia it's free. Then there's the movie festival. The Fiesta de Cine in Morelia is the second largest in all of Latin America. The type of gringo I see going there is more cosmopolitan than one who comes here. That's what Morelia offers."

"Then what is the Pátzcuaro expat looking for, when Morelia offers so much?"

"I think it's a combination. I for one am happier in a small town. I love the sense of history and the indigenous culture. I want to live in México, and I get that from Pátzcuaro. But I also don't want to be out in the boondocks. I'm able to run to Morelia for whatever I need."

"It's no hassle, but you wouldn't want to live in Eronga, for example."

"No. Pátzcuaro is fine with me. The population is around 75,000. The newer *colonias* may not yet be included in some counts of the city."

"Are you close to the other expats here?" Clearly they had played no role in his settling in Pátzcuaro.

His face took on an expression of *com si, com sa*, which is French, not Spanish, meaning so-so. "I know they're here, and they know I'm here, but I don't really socialize with them. That's more about me than about them. I come from a family that didn't socialize much. It became the way I am here, too. I can count on one hand the number of close friends I have here, where you'd go out to dinner and so on." I heard no regret in his voice. Whatever it was, that number was just about right for him.

"Do you have some close friends among the Méxican community?"

"Definitely, Pátzcuaro is like a big family, and I don't say that lightly. That's one reason people's seven and eight-year-old kids can leave the house and we don't worry. We all look out for each other. Yes, friends among the Méxicans, but not extremely close. As I say, that's me, and it goes back to my upbringing. But to say hello, to chat a bit, it probably happens a lot more with Méxicans than expats. The Americans that live here, I love them all to death. There are very few that I can't speak highly of. It's that I'm not that sociable myself."

I wondered for a moment whether it was unusual for Rick Davis to even be having this kind of conversation. He knew this would be part of a book. Yet, if he was measured in his responses, he didn't seem at all shy.

"I enjoy the young people here. They're fascinating. The ones that don't have any money need to go to public schools, and that's a pet peeve of mine. So I have about four or five kids that I help out. One is an adopted son, and he'll turn twenty on Saturday. He's been with me since he was fourteen. There's another one here, Ricardo, who works half time for me to save money for college. It's a three-ring circus, this house. I had a rock band going last night, and the computer room was filled with kids. My son was having a pre-birthday party. That's what keeps me going, but I'm not a cocktail party person, going out to dinner every night."

"Are there things you'd change about this town?"

"Basically the main thing I'd change is what you'd want to change in every town in México and the U.S.: the local government." Rick sighed deeply and shook his head. "I really like a clean and tidy town, and I wish that people would get it through their heads to be more ecologically aware. Just the cleanliness factor in maintaining the city is something I'd change."

"As a business owner, what's your relationship with local government?"

"None, they don't pay any attention to anybody."

"But they're not hassling you, either."

"No, in fact, on the surface, they've been very nice to me. But when it comes to issues, they're like the upper class

Méxicans: they appear to be very polite, and then they completely ignore you."

"On those issues like cleanliness."

"That, and one of my pet projects is tree planting in the new areas and *colonias*."

"What's the condition of the lake?"

"Horrible." He folded his arms and shook his head.

"Can it be saved?"

"I don't know. I've not read anything that has proven to me that they know where the water comes from; they have no natural river that feeds it. There's been study after study that I've seen and the lake still remains a mystery. And it's been steadily going down. It was much higher when I first saw it years ago. I think it can probably be maintained at a certain level, but I don't even know that for certain."

"Is sewage the issue, heavy metals?"

"Sewage is a large part of the issue, and then the runoff from agriculture. The government has put millions of pesos into water treatment, but I'm in not in a position to know how well it's working. Honestly, when you live here, the lake is not as big a part of your life as you might think." He pointed over the roof at the front. "The lake is down there somewhere. Pátzcuaro comes up here in a bowl. I see the lake from a distance a few times a week. That's all it means now."

Of course, part of this growing distance is from the recession of the lake itself. All these surrounding towns grew up directly on the shore.

"But historically," I said, "the lake must have once been the whole point of settling here. Fresh, clean water, sources of the food supply, reeds for baskets and other containers."

"Sure, and fish has always been an important part of the local diet. Pátzcuaro itself has mostly been its own little burg, more dependent on agriculture."

"How is it doing now economically?"

"I don't think it's very good."

"Is it the decline of tourism?"

"That's part of it, and if you have to depend on agriculture alone without it, we don't have any large scale operations here. It's all small farmers, who have to live at subsistence levels. There's a whole traditional culture around it, but if you're looking at it as stimulus for a city center, it doesn't provide any. I feel for the hotel owners who have to depend on tourism. They're really going through a tough time. We had a problem last fall and winter with these idiot *normalistas* over in Morelia…"

"I don't recognize that term."

"It's the kids who go to normal school (the old term for teacher's colleges in the U.S.), and there is a branch of these schools that is very radical and they're demanding certain rights and conditions that are outside the sphere of education. There's an extreme one outside of Morelia, and they block access to the city periodically."

(Shortly after this conversation eight *normalistas* were killed when a truck on the toll road had a brake failure and blew through their human roadblock near a toll station.)

"Was this the highway problem here?"

"Exactly. They stole buses and burned them. For those of us who live here it's merely an annoyance. But it also gets on the news in México City and other parts of the country, and all the viewers see is the burning buses. They're terrified. The combined message they get is that burning buses are linked with Michoacán. I've been coming here since 1988 and even at that time the Tierra Caliente (the hot lands in the southern and western parts of the state) was the place you were warned about, and now we've had another resurgence of the Knights Templar, or whoever they are. Again, the traveler from México City or Guadalajara sees violence and Michoacán. So even though we're as peaceful as can be here in Pátzcuaro, we're not getting the tourists that we should coming in from other parts of the country."

"Has the faltering economy affected your business, the absence of tourists?"

"Sure. Our big target customer is the new middle class in México, upwardly mobile. We get plenty from the gringos, but they are people who live here generally. Anybody who comes to México by air is so limited now in what they can take home, and it's become so expensive. Ten or fifteen years ago you showed up at the airport with extra boxes and you just carried them on."

When the question of nightlife came up, Rick went on to explain that few people realize Pátzcuaro has a substantial gay population. No one seems to know how it became a subtle magnet, but with no fanfare, and over a long period of time, it has. This group includes both Méxican nationals and expats. They are mainly in their fifties and sixties. As I've encountered again and again in México, they're not flashy or ostentatious, but living their lives in a new culture and climate that suits them better than some others may have in the past.

"Often a person or a couple will come down here and fall in love with the place. They decide that this is where they want to be. Thank goodness, I've found it, they say. And they'll rent long term, or they'll buy a house. They have no idea that the town is full of others like them. Only after they've been here a while do they go, oh, my gosh, what's going on here? It's not something that's advertised as some mecca, but we do have a disproportionate number here."

"And is there an easy relationship between that group and the straight Méxican community?"

"Absolutely. It's very interesting. For instance, all the kids here in this house are straight, and they know I'm gay. That'll tell you something."

"What else are you doing here when you're not in the gallery?"

"Well, this property takes a lot of upkeep, as you can see. But I really like to go on day trips. Part of the excuse to have the gallery, both for myself and my associate, is that we both enjoy *artisania*, and working with the artisans, so I like nothing better than to jump into the car and head out to some little village. The gallery gives me a perfect reason to do that. Then there are the normal life tasks, like restocking at Costco. The garden is another thing I really enjoy. It's a quarter acre."

In the back corner of the courtyard a stone staircase leads upward level by level through a terraced garden. It is wild with native plants of all varieties; both potted and planted in the ground. We left the courtyard and scaled the slope, pausing at each tier as Rick pointed out his favorites and talked about his near-term plans. Oh, this is nearly finished, he would say, or, I have a batch of this or that coming in to replace it. Would you like a cutting of this? I realized I should've brought a basket.

Near the top level we paused to look out over the rooftops, starting with the quadrant opening up past Rick's own house, then farther over the city into the distant mountains edging the lake, which was not itself visible. Perhaps at the top of the slope as it continued behind us it would be. I was silenced for a while. Here not the slightest sound of the city rose to invade the calm. Indeed, there's not much traffic in Pátzcuaro anyway. I thought of Morelia, where I had caught the city in its relaxed, weekend mode, but I knew the drumbeat of traffic was a more familiar mode there. I saw the serene look on Rick's face. He very well knew what he had, and what he had made of this property was no accident. He had said he'd come to Pátzcuaro to die, but after a long run of vibrant living on his own terms first.

In that spirit, this was a space that invited reflection, almost required it in a gentle way, not only about the present or the future, but also about the past. I had sensed the same thing myself in other secluded byways in México. Where had we come from, and where were we going? This was a point in the road where it was easier to make an assessment about those issues, which differ for all of us. I have speculated on those matters elsewhere in print, and I was certain that I'd revisit them again because they fuel a variety of open questions. Méxicans are not usually defined as easily by the goods they possess. When they are reflective at all about such matters, they need to come up with other answers for why they live the way they do. These speculations offer no closure. That was what led to the next question.

"Has living here over the last twenty years affected your view of the U.S.? I look at all of this and I wonder whether you even realize how remote you are? Yet, you made this happen."

"But I do, very much, because coming here I was thinking of the materialism of the way people live their lives, my family included. I think of what's important to them. México is a place where you stand back and look what's going on here, and how your life was there. I haven't been back for six years, and I have no interest in going back. It's a whole different world. In the U.S., when you're living there, that place is the focus of everything; it's the all-important center—the culture, the economy, the world presence. But when you're outside it, as we are here in this moment, you feel like, well, OK, that's nice for them if that's what they want, but this is a different way of life that I much prefer. There's a strong attitude of self-importance in the U.S. that is, I think, quite false in any larger sense."

As if to emphasize this, he broke off a sprig of something I didn't recognize and pressed it into my hand. "Here, plant this when you get back, it's amazing." We started back down.

At one time I used to think I wanted to live in Luxembourg, where one branch of my family came from, because that nation didn't have then, and could never have, any pretensions on the world stage whatever. It made for a different national psychology, one on a scale you could relate to.

Yet the compact size of Pátzcuaro meant it was incomplete as a marketplace. "How often do you go to Morelia?"

"Two or three times a month. Often it's for a quick stop at St. Costco, or Home Depot. Other times it's to go shopping downtown."

"Do you ever get up to San Miguel?"

He shook his head with a smile. "No. I only go through there on my way to Dolores Hidalgo, that's all." I assumed he went to Dolores because it was a center for many ceramic workshops.

"Any concerns here with personal safety?"

"No issues at all."

I began to understand that the issue of risk was not going to be easy to deal with in these pages, even as it was unavoidable. Living in México, the State Department hammers us about it mercilessly. Because those bureaucrats have a lower level of credibility than our own experience, yet a broader overview, it's still possible to shrug it off if you're an optimist. After all, aren't they sitting in Foggy Bottom writing these dour dispatches? The problem exists at the back of your mind, and it affects the tourist trade that fuels people's income.

That's a base line reality. Yet, if you never come face to face with it, what reality does it have beyond its negative PR, which everyone feels? Perhaps it's like the fear of death. We all know it's waiting for us around some unexpected corner, but until we see it up close, why worry, as the old comic magazine says. As often as I asked this, I was never going to get more than one person's highly individual response. As I have learned to do here, I shrugged and moved on to other issues.

"How much does it cost to live in this town?"

"If you're a homeowner, I always ask how much are you paying in property taxes? I was paying on my house in California $14,400 a year. (This was twenty years ago.) Here, for this enormous thing where we're standing, the taxes are $120 a year. That gives me about $14,300 in money that I don't have to spend on property taxes. If the price of chicken is forty cents a kilo higher here than in the U.S., I'm still coming out ahead. Medical costs are a big deal. I don't even carry major medical. In a few years, I'll be covered by that. I pay out of pocket now and I have had a few serious things. One involved an ambulance trip and a hospital with numerous doctors. It was still only a thousand dollars. Pátzcuaro has a hospital that I wouldn't use. Morelia has a wonderful hospital, and more than one. We have a few very good doctors here. I had an incident where I needed an IV for a week, medical care, etc. The doctor said, with the staff and cleanliness you have at your house, you're much better at home. I'll come twice a day, which is what he did. He came for about forty minutes morning and afternoon. The difference in the medical care here is that they care, they really do."

"I've seen that too. It's in their nature to care."

"Yes it is."

"As you know, I live in San Miguel, quite a different kind of place from this. I've visited here a few times, but I've never stayed long. What am I looking at in Pátzcuaro that I don't fully understand? I'm sure there's a list. Maybe I should do more homework, but I prefer to have someone with your insight tell me."

"You're seeing a very historical town. It was more than 150 years old when the Spanish arrived. It was the home of a lot of wealthy people from the 1600s through the early part of the last century. Many of those families are still here. Yet overall, it wasn't a wealthy town, so what happened was that, say unlike Uruapan up the road, where there was more money, farms and an industrial base, in the 1940s, 50s, and 60s they looked at those 'awful' old adobes downtown and tore them down to put up aluminum and glass modern architecture. That's part of why that town is so hideous now."

Nothing dates faster than being cutting edge, I thought.

"Poor old Pátzcuaro didn't have the money to do that. When I bought my house here in '94, this street was mud, and you could hardly walk up it during the rainy season. It was no more than a donkey path. No one wanted to buy in *centro* because it was a mess. The few gringos all bought up on gringo hill. I still thought I wanted to be in *centro*. Anyway, I found this house. About six months later, they made Pátzcuaro a Pueblo Mágico, and all this money came in to fix things up."

We reached the bottom of the stairs, crossed the lush courtyard, and began to walk through the house, room by room. The art was exquisite, and the artisanal wares, the pottery, the glasswork, the furniture, was all what you would expect from someone who had exercised his pick of the local and regional offerings for years. It was predicated on Rick having an eye for furnishings and accessories in the States for a long time before his arrival in México.

"Historically, what do you know about this house?"

"When I bought it from a professor in Morelia, he said, 'I'd like to get you a gift.' But I thought, I don't need a gift. What I'd love for you to do is check the records in Morelia so I can find out about this house. It was built across the street from what was then the convent. In 1775, that was this part here where we're standing. Later, in the 1820s, it became a posada, serving the pilgrims going to the basilica. (This focal church is two or three blocks down the street.) It had a ramp from outside that took the animals up to the back of the property. It functioned that way until the 1940s, when it was divided into three parts that were walled off from each other. In the 1980s the professor bought them one by one, and then later brought all three back together again by opening them up."

This made me appreciate why the remodeling had taken two and a half years.

"What has living in México taught you? This is my favorite question."

"While I still like my possessions and comforts, they're not all-important. I have certainly calmed down in what I think I need. I've learned patience, and I've learned a lot of admiration for young people. They were always in my way before. I really think the young Méxican is a different animal from the American teenager."

Patience: there it was again, an idea I'd been hearing a great deal about in these conversations. It was essential to the process of unwinding the tightly stretched coil that we Americans and Canadians walk around with inside our heads. We usually are not aware that we have it until we settle somewhere else and it feels like it's suddenly wound too tight to bear. We don't have to be a self-admitted type A personality, like Rose Calderone, to have this be true.

"How is the Pátzcuaro expat different from the San

Miguel expat?"

"I sometimes hear remarks about San Miguel that are not attractive. Even though that place is not my thing, I thank goodness for it. I really love it that people come to central México, because this *is* México. It's not the tourist resorts on the beach. To me the beach has no culture, nothing. I want people to come to central México. But if you speak no Spanish, if you really need that Italian restaurant, if you need French wine, San Miguel is there with open arms. Of course, you're going to pay triple for any of those things you buy in the stores. It's a wonderful place for people to feel comfortable. I want people to come to central México and travel around, but then they might think it's almost like a hospice to go back to San Miguel. They spend a week or two driving around, then get to San Miguel and chill. They can go to the spa."

"It probably won't surprise you that I encountered some hostility in the earlier preliminary conversations because I was from San Miguel. There were some unwelcoming emails as I was setting up this trip."

Rick gave me a patient smile. "I think they were being protective of their town. They might have had the feeling that you're trying to promote Pátzcuaro to gringos."

I was about to respond to that, but I think he already knew that promotion is not my game.

After I said goodbye to Rick Davis I crossed the Calle Lerín and entered the old convent. It had also been a hospital at one time. The style was seventeenth century. Now it's called the Eleven Patios, and it shelters a number of small shops and studios that specialize in a variety of local crafts: ceramics, metal work, and weaving, each employing a retail space in front and a workshop in the back. It's a vast rambling space full of twists and unexpected corners, overhangs and Juliet balconies, privacy grills and tiny windows that remind me of the ancient monasteries in Coptic Egypt. And everywhere are the small angular, echoing patios. The stone stairways are framed by weathered wooden beams and railings painted black, their cracks and fissures whispering subtly of the ages. The buff-colored limestone of the arches is softened by time and mellow under the hand.

The paint colors are the same as in the rest of Pátzcuaro, but for an added red stripe meandering over the lower base line. One small room holds a stone basin for bathing. I have trouble putting into words what it is about this place that I find so moving. The shops are not substantially different from those in other parts of town or out along the lake. Is it the unique sense of space that frames them? Is it the aura of utter peace, the unyielding past fused with the accommodating present? Every time I've been there, few other people were visible. Most of its courtyards are empty. If I spoke, which I'm not inclined to do there, my words would echo before they were lost in silence. Its look is never pretentious or gaudy; in fact, it has little adornment of any kind and offers no fanfare at all. It started as a utilitarian building; whether to house nuns or the sick, I'm not sure which came first. Over centuries it evolved into the spare commercial relic it is today. But its soul is unchanged for all that. Nor will the next reinvention of the coming year or century dislodge it from its deep anchorage in another time, another way of life, another mindset altogether. As I stood there for a long moment listening to the voices of the distant past, their muted whispering did not die away. As much as I enjoyed the grand public structures of Morelia, the arcaded cafes, the stunning neo-classical cathedral of 1744, this plain, humble, yet venerable refuge remains my favorite building in all of Michoacán.

Of course, as Rick Davis made clear, Pátzcuaro the town is not the lake of the same name. I headed out that afternoon around its curving western shore looking for a restaurant on the way to Erongarícuaro, which the locals like to call Eronga. I had reread my notes from my conversation with Charles Dews before I left.

My mind was already running ahead as to the way this story was developing. Continuity had been abandoned for variety. Location and setting were everything. Pozos, San Luis de la Paz, Morelia, and Pátzcuaro had no intimate relationship and no obvious connection beyond inhabiting the same country: a slender thread of contact at best. Think of Selma and Seattle, Missoula and Miami. Where's the link? They use the same currency, listen to the same news, receive the same junk mail. But after that is said, they all go their own way. Writing a conclusions chapter for this saga now looked like the biggest challenge of all. Shaking my head, I studied my sketchy map and hit the road.

When I first glimpsed the Restaurante Campestre Aleman fourteen kilometers out of Pátzcuaro, I thought I'd made a wrong turn and ended up in Bavaria. It was clearly time to break out the GPS again. It looked like the perfect Alpine South German inn, with steep red tile roofs and white stucco walls, varnished pine casement windows with flower boxes below overflowing with geraniums. I was disappointed to find no hunting horns painted on the awnings, but the weathered antlers over the entrance suggested a welcome for the Teutonic Knights, lances up as they returned from a campaign in Poland or a sortie into the Baltic States. The building rambled on wing after wing. It had to be drawing a huge clientele to justify so much capacity, yet I hadn't spotted a single person dressed in *lederhosen* anywhere in Michoacán.

The interior was all red gingham and unabashed *gemütlichkeit*. Polished pine furniture and red tablecloths, red checked curtains over the windows, carved wooden posts.

Beyond, acres of outdoor seating was arranged around a great pond where tomorrow's dinner sedately swam in family groups. The place was known for its trout.

It was a Monday at two in the afternoon, and only one table in the entire space was occupied. A man came in immediately after me and I turned to introduce myself to David Haun.

Haun is a trim fellow in his early sixties. He wore a red sport shirt and jeans. We sat down at a table overlooking the water three feet away and down a step or two.

"I don't understand this place," I said. "The weekend traffic has to be terrific, otherwise there's no reason whatever for it to exist."

"It is. People are coming from all over, not only on the lake, but Morelia as well. Then there are the folks shopping in the villages. The Campestre Aleman is well known to all of them."

I had come across David Haun when I discovered he was behind the chat group called Michoacán_Net that Rose Calderone had mentioned, and one I had joined several months earlier, about the time I started planning my tour of these less well-traveled roads. It's a group similar to the one we have in San Miguel, where issues are aired and announcements offered. Most of the thousand or so members of the local version are residents of the area served, but others live everywhere else and participate because they're interested in following the news and getting to know at arm's length some of the local expats. Although all of these lists degenerate into bickering and trivia now and then, most of the time they act as real community resources.

"The restaurant must be well known," I said, "because I can't imagine that anyone ever found this place by accident, and serendipity could never be the main force beneath the success of a business of this size. That must be partly true of Eronga too. You had to have known what you were looking for when you settled there."

"Not really."

I thought immediately of the careful preparations of Rick Davis once he had zeroed in on Pátzcuaro as he looked for a good cup of coffee.

The waiter came by and we started with drinks. I ordered a Negra Modelo dark beer, and David had mineral water.

"I actually didn't choose it myself, my friends did. I was a good friend of a woman named Carolina when I was living in San Cristóbal, in Chiapas, when Carolina moved to Eronga, here on the lake. When I came to visit her, I caught a bus to Morelia, then to Pátzcuaro, and then caught a cab to Eronga. I only came here the first time to visit a friend."

This reminded me of Ron Austin and Lamar Strickland's introduction to San Luis de la Paz.

"When I first saw it I was so surprised that I hadn't ever been to this area, because I'd traveled all around México. But that was my first visit to Eronga, in 1998. It was an interesting time, and I stayed with Carolina. My mother was quite ill in a nursing home when I arrived. On my last day in town, I wanted to go into Pátzcuaro, because I hadn't seen much of it, but Carolina was busy with some things she had to finish, so I went in by myself. The last thing she said was that I should not miss the basilica at the top of the hill, where the statue of La Virgen de Salud is, the Virgin of Health. Carolina told me that she performs miracles."

David paused for a moment with a vague backward look, as if reliving that day, fifteen years ago now. A white farm duck swam slowly over in our direction, cocking its head as if to catch more detail of this story. The water was almost green, but quite clear, and I could detect flickers of other activity beneath the surface.

"So I came to Pátzcuaro, walking around the market, having a day on my own, just for myself. As I was ready to catch the *combi* (the van shuttles that serve the villages on the lake and Pátzcuaro itself in lieu of any full-scale bus service) back to Eronga I realized I had forgotten to see the basilica, so I walked up there. I'm a fallen away Catholic, but I never mind walking in and genuflecting. I love to say prayers and watch all the quiet goings on. I knelt down and (here Haun paused for a moment and looked away), all of a sudden, my mother visited me."

Having no logical response to this, I took a long draft of my beer, looking out over the pond. I had written about such moments in my fiction, and although I had never experienced one myself, I knew they did happen.

"It was really weird because I'm not a spiritual person. But my mother was next to me in the pew telling me goodbye, and I'm not sure if I was gnashing my teeth and flailing around yelling, 'Wait, don't leave, because I'm coming home tomorrow.' And she was saying, 'No, I've got to go now.' And I was crying, saying no, don't go. I couldn't see her, but she was there. I knew for a fact that she was saying a final goodbye to me. All of a sudden she was gone. After a moment I got up and walked out of that church totally stunned. When I got back to Eronga I found Carolina crying. She said, 'David, your mother has passed away.' The first thing I said was, 'When did she pass?' She said, 'At two o'clock last night.' I said, 'No, it was two o'clock this afternoon.' Immediately I got on the phone and called my brother, and it was exactly at that time when I saw her that my mother passed. Since then I've gone to that basilica numerous times hoping she would show up again, and that's the only kind of experience like that I've ever had in my life. But that was also my first experience with Pátzcuaro and Eronga. It was the day that my mother came here to visit me."

The waiter started to move in our direction to take our order, but I sent him back with a subtle gesture. I wasn't sure whether to regard David's mother's appearance as her invitation to him to settle on the lake, or as a pure coincidence because that was the moment of her departure from life. David offered no more insights or detail, and after a few moments of silence as he composed himself, we put in our order. The couple at the other table got up and left.

"After that, what were you expecting to find here? Did that experience color your expectations?"

"Not at all. I was only expecting to find my friends, and that's who were here. I didn't expect anything else. I was on vacation." He shrugged.

David Haun has a manner of delivery that is disarmingly direct and clear-eyed, even cast in a fairly vivid emotional pitch. Although it was a deeply spiritual experience, the appearance of his mother in the basilica seemed to include no omens and summon no other links to the beyond. I didn't get the sense you could easily draw him into a séance.

"So far this story has a serendipitous quality to it," I suggested, "an unplanned, but life-changing move. Was it the character of Eronga that brought that about? I feel like there's a link I'm missing." Was it some kind of supernatural tipping point?

"Eronga is one of the few villages around Lake Pátzcuaro that really welcomes gringos. It has always been an accepting town, even in the Frida Kahlo days when she came here to paint, and it is documented that she was here. The Beatniks showed up after that, and then the hippies showed up. I don't think any hippies stayed, but the expats remained around this area after that."

"An accepting town in the sense of different values and lifestyles, yet it's situated in a place so remote and even unthought of. Until I started this project I had literally never heard of it."

"Yes, that's the history. Although I came here because of my friends, and many have since left, I remained here for the peace and quiet. But not solitude! I can easily exist in both worlds of Austin, Texas, and Eronga because I can freely leave both and arrive at either. I have neither spouse, children, houseplants, nor pets. I travel well, and I can easily transport myself from one world to the other. It's never hard for me to fall in step with the beat of a different drummer."

"What do you do when you're in Eronga?"

"I relax. When I'm not there I am a silversmith artist. I travel around the U.S. doing art festivals, covering between three and five thousand miles a month at juried shows. My business partner and I have developed a line of jewelry, but since jewelry is such a fashion industry, we're always coming up with new designs. When we have a new design, we make that line and we have no one helping us. It's just the two of us. We take it out on the road selling it at art festivals. We don't have a gallery and we don't sell online. For each person who has bought my jewelry, I have put the piece on her to see how it looks. I like the personal contact of actually telling them it's the right earring, or as is often the case, telling them it's the wrong one. Many people have a habit of buying the wrong thing."

"If you let them." Just then the waiter brought in our midday lunch, our *comida*. Mine was the biggest piece of pork shank I had ever seen. David had half a trout boned and grilled.

"In a market that must be a little different, I suppose,

in each town, at each show, how do you get a sense of who your target customer is? You must have learned that quickly. For me, I don't write a sentence without knowing who my target reader is, who would care enough about my subject to buy the book."

"That's a bit easier for me. The target customer is the person who walks up to the booth. We're selling at juried art festivals. We have to apply to get in with four slides of artwork and one slide showing our booth. There is a jury of three to five people, or even as many as ten professionals in some cases, who look at the slides and grade them, based on the presentation. For instance, the big Uptown show in Minneapolis will have four to six thousand applicants. They will allow as many as seventy-five jewelers in, and seventy-five potters, and so on. So the top seventy-five in each category get invited, and the next ten to twenty go on the wait list. They always make sure the show is full when it opens. Getting into these shows is both a matter of luck and skill."

"And experience, I'm sure. It must depend to some degree on the jury's taste as well."

David paused for a moment to slice into his trout with a fork.

"Yes, and that varies. That's why there's never any guarantee, because on some festivals the jurors will like contemporary jewelry and are looking for very sharp designs. Those are the shows I like because I do contemporary jewelry. Other jurors may think that everything must have gemstones set in it, or diamonds, or it must be gold or it doesn't count. Those are the shows I don't get into because I don't set stones."

"And you're working in silver."

"Yes. I also do surface decorations in solid gold, and I do a lot of mixed metals. When I graduated from college I taught elementary school for a couple of years. Back in the 1970s I didn't mind working a second job to keep my teaching career, but when I had to work a third job to keep teaching, I decided I could do anything on earth that would be easier and provide more pay. That's when I started making jewelry as a job."

"What would you be doing if you weren't making jewelry?"

"Heaven forbid. I'd probably teach school again."

"Charles Dews told me about the glory days of Eronga. It must draw a completely different kind of person than Morelia does."

"Exactly. And to go even further, Morelia draws a different crowd than San Miguel or some of the other large gringo enclaves, like Lake Chapala. I think it's that people who stop in Michoacán have their choice from this area of the big city—the state capitol of Morelia, or of going to Pátzcuaro, which is the magical village with small businesses, and with a small expat community. We do have our Bodega (Bodega Aurrera), a discount market chain owned by Wal-Mart, but it's on the outskirts. The center of the city is historical and will always be beautiful. Or you have the choice of living out around the lake, and that's what people do who want an even smaller community, with no Bodegas, just tiny little shopping venues. They find the quietness and the lack of things to do very appealing. People who want the absence of noise and traffic, that's the crowd that comes to Eronga. They want to get even one more step beyond getting away from it all."

Two large trout drifted past our table, narrowly eyeing, perhaps, the plates they were destined to end up on another day. I tossed them a couple kernels of rice, which they snapped up. "Live in the moment," I said to them.

"Do you think they feel it's a more authentic Méxican

experience here?" Not referring to the trout.

"I think so. Yet that's so relative, because even in a town with a large American population like San Miguel I think it's easy to have your best friends be Méxican, if that's what you want. And that's also quite common in a small community like this, since it's mostly Méxicans around you. It's also easy to have all your friends be expats if that suits you better."

"Are you close to the other expats here? Does it feel like a community?"

"Extremely close. I know almost all of them."

"Would you say there are fifteen? Someone suggested that to me."

"I'm sure there are more than that. I don't know that anyone has actually ever counted. We have a Sunday brunch club where a group of as many as ten to twenty will meet in Oponguio, which is the next town on the lake. They have a lot of good restaurants on that part of the shore. Only the Eronga people are allowed to attend those affairs. I'm very close to the expats here."

The town names around the lake, including Pátzcuaro, reflect the Purépecha language, so distinct from other languages in México. The major exception is Quiroga, named for the Spanish bishop who introduced the *artisania* way of life to the villages.

"What would you change about Eronga, or was it just right as you found it that fateful day in the basilica?"

David's face took on a nostalgic look and he set his fork aside.

"I'd like to see it go back to the good old days when Charles Dews' Red Star Restaurant was here. I'd like to see the days when Testorelli's Italian Ice Cream was here with their delicious hamburgers. I'd like to see the days when Ivo's

Pizza was still here. Right now there's virtually no place to eat when you come to Eronga. Fortunately, on market day, there's a lady named Silvia who does comida-type cooking at the market. She'd like to open up a restaurant. A lot of the gringos bring Tupperware-style containers and take the food home to eat later. That's about the closest thing we have to a restaurant. There's no coffee shop, either."

"So every time you need something that's other than pure peace and quiet or a social day in the markets, it's a trip to somewhere else."

"Exactly. I go into Pátzcuaro about every other day, and I don't think anything about it."

"How is the lake doing?" The pond we sat next to was not connected to it.

"It's pretty bad right now. I remember when I first went to Lake Chapala, years ago. You had to stand on the dock and then climb down to catch a bus to take out to the lake. That was only ten years ago. Now their lake is lapping on the old shoreline. Of course, the gringos in Chapala take all the credit for it, but it was the government deciding not to take all the water out any more. No matter how bad our lake is now, there are many people who are working on it to return it to good condition. With all the crafts here a lot of the residue from the lead-glaze pottery was washed into the lake. There are organizations that are currently working on getting the lead out of it now. There is another story of the earthquake that hit México City that was so bad, and we feel all of them here, but not that badly. The rumor is that it cracked the basin of the lake and it started draining. I drove around it in 1998, and all that way from Pátzcuaro there was water near to the road on the entire route, which means it's really low now."

As he finished I was thinking about all that lead in the lake. Naturally it sank to the bottom; you could never skim it off. How could it ever be removed? The issue of the lake's condition seemed cloaked in layers of vagueness that varied with each person you talked to. The government was not very forthright about what it was doing, but then governments are often veiled, here and anywhere.

"How often do you go to Morelia?"

"Since I moved here three years ago, my goal every time I come down is to spend more time in Morelia, but I just can't do it. It's too big, and if I can't be comfortable driving through it, I don't want to go there. But this year, I use the *collectivos*. It's like a taxi van, and they charge thirty-five pesos to take you to Morelia."

The meal was spectacular and we drove off toward Eronga with David leading the way. In less then three kilometers he turned in at a dirt lane that soon became steep and rugged. We pulled up at the back of a recently built two-story house with a third floor roof terrace. From the back, the design was crisp and contemporary, done in a dark red at the base, and sunflower yellow above.

From inside, the view embraced a broad bottomland valley from a hundred feet up the slope. The soil was turned and mostly waiting for planting at this time, mid May. The strategy was probably to plant and catch the start of the June to September rains. Beyond, the string of dormant volcanoes Charles Dews had mentioned defined the near horizon like ancient sentries. The house wound along the hillside to include a view of as much of the scene as possible, including a large slice of the town of Eronga. Everything was about the space, and the house was as much a part of the valley as the valley was part of the house. The furnishings were not elaborate, even spare. As we walked through I noticed immediately that there was no jeweler's tool in view, neither work-bench nor cabinet, and no scrap bowl of silver trimmings. No display of finished product. The house held no single hint of the owner's business. Living there was about something else entirely, but I realized that without going to a show in the U.S., I was not going to see David Haun's work. As an artist, this would have told me things about him that our conversation did not.

"I'm now getting the picture of you making jewelry and attending shows in the States for six months, and then what follows is this quiet time where we're sitting now. It's all about silence and the absence of movement. No traffic, no turbulence. You don't have any materials down here, and you don't have a single tool. There's no inventory and you're not selling anything to anybody. It looks as if you pull a switch when you cross the border, and the position of that switch always reads *off duty* when you're down here."

"Exactly, and to me that's very easy. I've always taken a vacation away from work and I've never brought my work along with me. It's the same when I'm traveling those three to five thousand miles a month; that's work, and it's no vacation. We do not stop at my family's house in Houston to say hello. We're on business all the time. I think of myself as an entrepreneur. My work when I'm here is promoting the Arts of Michoacán. Beside the forum, Michoacán_Net, I also have the website www.LakePatzcuaro.org. With the new Facebook page for Michoacán_Net, I'm occupied full time."

"Now I'm thinking about what the transitions must be like between this place and that. This is why I can't live in two places myself. I don't have anything left in the U.S. because I don't want the disruption of going back and forth. But, aside from magazine pieces, I work mostly on book-length projects, and I need more continuity of place, so I'm trying to put myself in your shoes. As you approach your return to the U.S. in the fall, what kind of feeling does that bring on? Isn't it apprehension? Disruption? Or are you eager to get back to being on the road?"

Haun shook his head slowly. "I always feel like crying when I shut the door to this place and leave. But I also feel like I'm blessed because wherever I am, I'm happy to be there. I love driving too, and I could spend my life solo driving because that's what I like doing. When I get to Austin I love living in Austin. I also miss Eronga when I'm there, and I miss Austin when I'm here."

"But how does it work to have one leg here and one in the States? What does that do to your view of both México and the U.S.? Does it give you a special perspective that people who are in México full time may not have?"

"I think that it probably should, but what it does is give me more of an acute love for being in Austin when I'm there. I'm a big bicycle rider. I ride thirteen miles every other day in Austin around the town's lake, and downtown. But I can't do that here. So when I'm here I get those same endorphins, the same high, from walking around that big cornfield down in front of my house."

It seems that David Haun is not given to generalize greatly about trends or contrasts between the U.S. and México. He is more focused on being where he is at that moment without a lot of concern about overriding meanings.

"Do you feel safe out here?"

"I really do, even though I'm sort of an afraid-of-the-dark kind of person. I do get a little scared at times living here alone, and I've thought about getting a dog. But it's not a high crime area. Juan is with the municipality here, and he's my next-door neighbor. (This is the Juan that Charles Dews spoke of.) No one is bothering people around here at all. I think I'm extremely safe in this house. I always feel that when I'm traveling around México, if I were to leave a suitcase somewhere on the street corner I could probably come back on my next visit and it would still be sitting there. I just feel like I don't attract any problems, so I don't have any issues with security."

Aside from the regular expat brunches, Tuesday is market day in Eronga, and in the tradition of market days everywhere, much of the town turns out. David Haun spends most of the day in attendance, chatting, eating, and exchanging news and views with his neighbors. It's little changed from the thirteenth century. On every third Sunday there is also an alternative fair, where some artisans bring in homemade beer or soap, and a large variety of produce from organic gardens.

"Other than those occasions, I'm getting a lot of reading done. As a matter of fact, when I rent this downstairs area again I'm going to bill it as an artist's retreat, a get-away-from-it-all kind of place. If you want anything to do, this is not your destination. But if you want to write or paint, this is the place to go. That's the angle."

"Have you learned anything from living in México? I can imagine you sitting here up on the slope watching the corn grow. On a quiet night you can hear the ears squeak inside the husks as they stretch the leaves around them. If there is something to be learned from this experience, you can be wide open to it with the expectation of having no distractions whatever."

I felt like my excursion into Michoacán was a descent by degrees from the throbbing heartbeat of Morelia, into a middle zone of sociable calm in Pátzcuaro, to a kind of retro Méxican minimalism in Eronga.

"What living here has done is it has helped my understanding of human nature. A few days ago we celebrated the battle of México when the U.S. took half the country away and turned it into Texas, California, and the other states of the Southwest. Yet the Méxicans are still speaking to us. Why is that? To me, as strange as this is, that's my example of how the Méxicans are. It's that they're such a loving people. They don't hold grudges. I think the immigration policies of the U.S. are confusing to everyone, including myself, and that doesn't help anything, but there are no jobs up there right now anyway."

"How do you feel about the impact of regional violence on the economy of Michoacán?"

"Awful. They don't know the exact percentage, but the tourist industry is a major part of the Méxican economy. But thinking of the economy taking a hit reminds me of one more story I can tell you. Sometimes we don't get into art festivals and sometimes we can't pay the bills. The fact that I've been able to build this house and live here is a miracle in itself. I realized that with my low Social Security, if I could have some kind of income property somewhere, that would help. I thought about doing a garage apartment at my house in Austin, and I thought about building something in Oaxaca, because I love Oaxaca, and I was looking around thinking about what I could do. At that point I got this email from Charles Dews one morning saying that Juan had found this old abandoned development outside of Eronga and they had bought a lot and wanted him to build them a house. I emailed him back immediately and said, 'You're living my dream, that's what I want to do.' He wrote back that the lot next to it was available for $3,000.

"I responded and said I had some money in a savings account where I was getting almost zero percent annual interest and I wanted to get rid of it. 'Let me just get out $3,000.' I bought this property sight unseen within five minutes of hearing about it. Next I came down and started buying the different adjacent lots. Juan would email me and say we need $5,000 to start the foundation, so I'd get a credit card loan, one of those with 0% interest for some period of time. Well, then we'd need another $10,000. Pay that off, get another one. This entire house was built with 0% credit card loans. At one point I had $20,000 for one year at 0%. That's how desperate they were."

Perhaps those dollars had also been desperate to find a loving home anywhere, but David Haun in this house they had built was not. His needs were specific. For others they may have been inflating the housing bubble in the U.S. Nothing about it suggested desperation—its focus was peace. A kind of quiet seeped into the room as we stared out over the valley when the conversation ended. I felt I understood what this was about. This country place possessed no grandeur beyond the view, which was unforgettable, and even as it offered no luxuries, it still provided everything its owner needed. It might have been one of many possible metaphors for the expat experience in out-of-the-way places.

Perhaps in some ways David Haun is the ultimate off-the-beaten-path expat. He had come down here and created a kind of void, into which he drew none of his U.S. life. Instead, he filled it with México in its simplest and most abiding and timeless forms.

Almost with regret, I said goodbye and drove into Eronga, which began about half a kilometer beyond Haun's driveway. Coming in it resembled the other lake towns I'd passed through that day, but I knew it was different in subtle ways. I went by a white church with a single tower, where two young laughing priests struggled across the parking lot balancing a large bag of ice between them.

I parked on the plaza. It was not large, but elaborately landscaped nonetheless. A big circular fountain occupied the focal position, flanked and approached by paved paths winding among the raised and fenced plantings. All the surrounding shop fronts were protected from the weather by the deep overhang of the sloped roofs behind. The color design was the same as in Pátzcuaro, bull's blood red to the elbow, white above. The businesses were basic: an Internet café called "El Centro," the quesadilla shop, "Yosy," and Plasticos "Nico."

I stood there for a while searching for the ghosts of the Red Star Restaurant, Ivos Pizza, Testorelli's Italian Ice Cream; all images of a lost era. And not only those most recent phantoms, but those of Frida Kahlo and Diego Rivera. She had died in 1954, he in 1957. Somewhere in the tailored shrubs of the plaza lingered the shade of Leon Trostky, Frida's doomed lover, who had been murdered with an ice pick in México City on Stalin's orders in 1940, not too long after his own visit to Eronga. Now, nothing moved. If time had not stopped, at least it was moving far too slowly to observe. But for a few cars, it could have been any day in the past 200 years.

But wait, that was not quite true, because wasn't that el Presidente Lázaro Cárdenas over there near the corner, knotting his tie tighter and pulling his mustache straighter as he approached the front door of the sisters Rodriguez for an evening of musical entertainment? One of them would soon greet him in her filmy, flapper-inspired, but still modest, frock of the 1930s. His bodyguards followed him three paces back, narrowly scanning the streets, the plaza, thinking of Emiliano Zapata or Pancho Villa, and the violent ends they had met—the penalty for coming in second or third in this cradle of revolutionary contests. From beyond the red and white anonymous wall, the tinkle of piano keys can now be heard on the evening air. But where was Remedios Varo? Where were Andre Breton and the Surrealists? Ah, that was an easier answer. The place itself was surreal and timeless. It was their legacy that was most intact and palpable today in Eronga.

CHAPTER 5

PUEBLA: UNDER THE VOLCANO

The last time I visited Puebla, five years ago, I drove from San Miguel and ended up lost like a microbe in the uncharted bowels of México City. In Spanish the word for lost is *perdido*, a term hellishly close to perdition, and for good reason. Sometime later, when I quite serendipitously emerged and found myself high in the mountains above the main highway into Puebla, I was able to peer down on the place where I urgently wanted to be. But I had no idea how to get there as I dawdled behind an overloaded furniture truck at twenty kilometers per hour on a tiny road with no shoulders. The next level place was a thousand or more feet below. Or above. This was a juncture in life where I had been before. I had the idea then that I might never be heard from again, and I was glad I had written as much as I had, leaving behind some small record of my own unique set of myths and misconceptions, if only so others could avoid them.

Since that trip a new bypass has been built around México City. In the past there had been none, unless you hugged either the Gulf or Pacific coasts. All roads in México lead to México City, as if people really want to go there. I'm sure some do.

I enjoyed watching the freshly paved bypass unfold under the bus wheels, relishing the clear new signage. Here is the way to Puebla, it proclaimed; stay the course. This in a country that is generally not clear on why anyone would need road signage, since long-distance drivers here tend to be guided more by fate. Road maps are a subtle form of insider humor. Paying to be misled is a common, if unintentional, practice among gringo travelers.

Now my first class Volvo bus went around—instead of through—the mega city and pointed me toward Puebla without mishap or argument. I am more than willing to pay for someone else's driving expertise because I have learned that ignorance is much more costly, especially in a country where I am not a native son.

Although the Spanish language offers four names for seasons, Central México responds to only two, neither of them on that list: brown and green. It was the fourth week of September, when the rainy season normally draws to a close, but tropical storms buffeted the country like angry intruders on both coasts.

We drove through broad plateaus of dense green, fields in strips divided by rows of spiky agave or dwarf trees. Some fields were spotted with rose-pink or yellow flowers. Every scene was made up of corn, goats, cattle, sheep, and more corn, backed by low-rise mountains. Overhead, the sky expressed a pent up violence that threatened to erupt at any time.

The bus I rode that day offered reserved seats and cushioned footrests, shades on the windows, video monitors showing movies, and lunch with a beverage. It had a bathroom aboard, and it lacked only a masseuse and queen size beds for perfect comfort. Traveling with me were only three other passengers, and the movie was, as always, forgettable. I reclined my seat to the maximum and pulled out my book.

When I had spent a few days in Puebla five years before, I realized that this city must be México's official auto horn testing station. Back then, every driver was required to rest both hands on his horn for at least twenty percent of the time he was in motion, no matter what his speed or how thick or sparse the surrounding traffic. It was a strategy that worked brilliantly, because I never detected a single car whose horn faltered in any way. Now, that test period may have been waning, or even transferred to another town. The streets were still noisy, but I also felt a sense of restraint that I'd missed before. Perhaps not being behind the wheel myself helped.

As the fourth-largest city in México, Puebla is hardly off the beaten path to a larger world. It has a substantial contingent of Europeans in residence, mostly for business reasons. In some schools the second language taught is German. Yet, if I asked a group of 100 Americans or Canadians who soon planned to move to México which of them had chosen Puebla for their expat home, I suspect I would raise no response. While there is no good reason not to move there if you wish to live in México, the reasons for choosing it are clearly not obvious to many outsiders, either. My task on arrival was to dig them out.

To do this I chose to interview two expat women who were married to Méxicans. Both of their husbands are *poblanos*, which means from Puebla. Both of the women are Americans. At the time I made this selection I didn't try to imagine what else they might have in common. They presented an apparent symmetry, yet beneath, I knew their differences would make the story just as contrasts among characters make a work of fiction.

In the old historical district I settled into a hotel that had begun life in 1593 as the convent of the Concepción. It was an odd choice of name perhaps, for a cluster of determined virgins, but I doubt they had seen much irony in this.

The interior was spare but ample in dimension, as was appropriate. The Romanesque arches in the vast courtyard were plain and uncarved, but for base and capitals, yet direct and forceful in their architectural character. It was a no-nonsense building then as now. Its charm came from its age and its scale, the texture of its walls, which in various places had been left unrestored to reveal the ancient faded stenciling. Overhead, the sky was shut out by a translucent sliding cover of a kind you might see only on a minor baseball stadium in the U.S. I welcomed it now, since the rains had followed me off and on from San Miguel.

On the following day my first conversation was to be with Rebecca Smith Hurd, who lives in Cholula. When Puebla was founded in 1531, it was not built on the foundations of an earlier indigenous town, unlike so many others in México. Instead, it was a planned link on the road between Veracruz on the coast and México City, which might then have still been called by its Aztec name of Tenochtitlán, or as some say, it was in transition as México Tenochtitlán. Cholula is an ancient site that still prospered at that time, but at a twenty-kilometer distance from the fledgling Puebla—then nearly a day's journey. It possessed an enormous pyramid, the grandest in the world, far surpassing in size those in Egypt or any in the Mayan territories. It was so overgrown that the Spanish invaders may have mistaken it for a hill. No surprise, since when they turned around, what they saw was the smoking cone of the Popocatépetl volcano at 18,000 feet, and this sight must have set the tone, then as now.

Atop this vast pile of ancient stone stands a lovely church dedicated to the Virgin of los Remedios. First built in 1594, it's been damaged by earthquakes and reconstructed several times over the years, the last quite recently.

I was well prepared to get to Cholula, setting out that

following morning as I stood in downtown Puebla on Calle 7 Poniente. I had an Internet map of my destination in hand to show the cab driver. All was well, and planning matters here.

As the cab threaded its way through the continuous urban fabric on the way to Cholula, the streets were so full of pot holes I was reminded of spring in my native Minnesota, another place said to have only two seasons: winter and road construction. The cab swerved through the perforated pavement like a minefield in Sarajevo. The city was immense, mostly laid out in one- and two-story buildings, and we alternated between fifty miles an hour on halfway intact side streets to a crawl on those paved mostly with holes. I began to realize that what I was seeing was negative paving, something like roadway antimatter. The constant acceleration and deceleration set up an abstract pace that interfered with my own biorhythms and blunted my nerve endings. I suspected I'd be stuttering freely by the time I arrived in Cholula to sit down with Rebecca Hurd.

Not that there was any way to know when we did. The cab driver didn't appear to care. The ancient indigenous site is now three towns that have effectively merged with the modern urban outflow of Puebla, and aside from the pyramid, which was not in view from the back seat of this battered black and gold Nissan, it looks no different than its larger neighbor. After a ride of nearly fifty minutes, I decanted myself onto the street, somewhat shaken but not yet stirred. Twenty seconds later I was standing in Rebecca's living room. I had never met her before. After a brief introduction to her husband, Pablo, he then vanished into the bedroom with Lucy the cat, who had offered to participate in this conversation, but found no eager takers.

Rebecca is an outgoing woman in her early forties with shoulder-length blond hair. Her look is frank and self-assured, her gestures expansive. My first impression was that she knew who she was and lived comfortably with that knowledge. She had been on a journey to get here, one whose milestones she had not forgotten. For our conversation she wore black, which may have underlined her seriousness for the occasion, but it in no way dampened the liveliness of her responses. To tell the truth, she was fully prepared and she didn't mind showing it.

We chatted for a while off the record. My initial task is always to make people comfortable and ready to tell me everything about their lives, or at least to try to make me think that they have. That works just as well, because the knowledge of what people would like to be is as useful in seeing them as the understanding of what they really are.

The apartment was in a two-story building with eight units. It seemed typical for the area. We sat in the living room, rising to avoid the leather sofa, which tended to squeak as I moved on it. My recorder is often too sensitive. From a series of emails that had led up to this visit, I knew Rebecca had initially come down to Puebla to learn Spanish, but I didn't know much more about her than that.

"Why did you choose the city of Puebla as a place to settle? Was it mainly the school connection, or did you already know something about this town beyond that?" How much research people do in advance of such a move can be revealing. Rick Davis exhibited one extreme, David Haun the other.

"I knew about it before I came down here, although the reason I chose it *was* for the school. Before I came to México I was a working journalist, and I still am, in a way. I chose it because I wanted to learn Spanish. The school, the place, and the price were what brought me here. I picked Puebla because México was affordable, the city was beautiful and safe, and when people talk about the kind of Spanish that's spoken here, they generally speak highly of it. The accent isn't strong, so the formal Spanish here is solid 'King's Spanish' in the sense that you can speak it and be understood in most places in the world. From my traveling I have found that to be true. By brother-in-law is Argentine, so I have that as a comparison. My sister lives in Buenos Aires, and I knew I didn't want to learn Argentine Spanish. The other choices were Spain, Colombia, or México, and in terms of being an American and wanting to learn to speak the language, México made the most sense."

"How long have you been here?"

"I've been here a little more than six years."

"Was there something about your job in the States that was part of your reason for moving? Or was it primarily learning Spanish?" I often wonder whether behind the official motive lurks another set of reasons. I had learned in earlier conversations with expats that such a move can be either a cure or an escape. Not that either of those is a bad reason in itself. Crossing a national border to live in a different country has parallels with the concept of drawing a line in the sand.

Rebecca told me she had been in journalism since the age of sixteen, when she got her first staff job at a newspaper. It was twenty years later, when, after a series of career advancements in that field, she came to Puebla.

"I was completely burned out. Before I came here I was working for a major magazine in San Francisco, as assistant managing editor, and I had huge responsibilities. I had gotten to a point where, for a variety of reasons, I needed a break. I decided to take a six-month sabbatical, but feeling like I couldn't just do nothing during that time, I decided to learn Spanish. As a word-nerd I figured that speaking Spanish would help keep me employed as I got older; it just made sense. My original plan was for a stay of sfour months in Puebla. I studied first for ten weeks in Monterey, California, at a major translation and linguistic grad school, and then I was going to spend four months in an immersion program here in Puebla. I lived with a retired couple that didn't speak any English. Toward the end of those four months I met my husband, who is a graphic designer and was working at a magazine here in Puebla. At that point I realized that six months of combined study was not long enough to become as fluent in Spanish as I wanted to be, so I decided to stay a little longer. That 'little longer' has turned into six years and change."

I looked at her for a moment, reading the subtext.

"The developing relationship with Pablo had to be part of that."

"Yes."

"After those six years, what is it that you like best about this town?"

"My answer to that question changes all the time, but more generally, it's that I learn something new every day. That's partly Puebla, partly México, and partly just living in a foreign country. But Puebla is an amazing city. I think part of that view comes from the fact that I grew up in California. Things that are old there are 300 years old. There are a few exceptions, but the oldest buildings in California were built by the Franciscan monks who came from México."

"Father Junípero Serra, who put up a number of churches in central México before he went north to what was then Alta California." His earlier efforts were in the neighboring (to me) state of Querétaro.

"Right. All of California was still part of México then. To me, living in Cholula, arguably the longest continuously inhabited city in the Americas—there've been people living here for more than 2000 years—there's something magical about that. For somebody who makes a living by being curious, I haven't even scratched the surface of all the things I could learn just being here. So for me, that's really what keeps me here, other than my husband, obviously. We both free lance, so we could work from anywhere. The reason we choose to stay here, other than personal connections, is that Puebla offers this richness that you can't find in a lot of other places."

"But it's not perfect; no place is. What would you change about it?"

Rebecca laughed in a way that suggested long familiarity with that subject. "As the founder of the website *All About Puebla*, I feel I ought to be politically correct in my answer to that, but at the same time I have to be honest."

I dismissed this with a wave. "This book is going to have a bias toward honesty, not that we don't all have our own truth."

"Well, honestly, then, I think if I could change anything about Puebla I would make it less provincial."

"Even though it's the fourth-largest city in this country."

She gave me a wry smile.

"Yes! The irony of Puebla, from an outsider's perspective, is that although it is the fourth largest city in México, people here can be very provincial in the way they think. Even though a lot of the business people seem to be international in their outlook on one level, they don't always follow through in their actions. For me the most frustrating thing about being here is that because of my website, and my family being *poblano*, I feel like I bend over backwards just to understand not just the language, but the culture here."

"It's their turf. That comes with a certain proprietary air anywhere."

"Yes, it *is* their turf. However, I feel like sometimes there is *zero* attempt, even when I'm doing business with people, to understand my foreign point of view." Her gestures could have been Italian. She got up and began to move around the room as she spoke.

"For example, the biggest cultural barrier is 'honesty' in the way I would define it, versus what people here would define as honesty. There's one subtext in California, but there are *forty* subtexts here. People will tell you to your face that they're going to do one thing, and then they do something else entirely that is completely unpredictable from an outsider's cultural reference.

"So on one level, while I want to be respectful, I always remember that I'm a foreigner in a foreign country where I have to play by their rules. The problem is that after six years, even having *poblanos* in my family, I don't always understand what those rules are. I feel like when it comes to business, and not personal things, from an American perspective we put all this emphasis on our word, and here that is totally not the case."

I had an idea or two about this based on my own experience doing business here. The idea of giving your word about something is not regarded in the same light as it is much farther north. It's part of a dance that includes some degree of improvisation. Business is structured around a *series* of negotiations. To start, you make your initial deal. Once you have put a deposit down on that transaction you have entered a second phase of negotiation, where the terms of the first no longer matter. Northerners are often surprised by this, and may easily feel misled. The issue, I believe, is that there has been a shift in power.

You have fulfilled one side of the deal and the other party has not. He has gained power over you, and your subsequent negotiation is hampered by your weakened position. Your next goal needs to be to add more power to your side of the balance. If you have not considered this in advance, you remain at a disadvantage. On the surface it looks much like an issue of honesty and integrity, which is the way we would interpret it in the U.S. or Canada. But México has a long history of the advantage always being with the one who has power, and power has always been poorly distributed here. So when you get some, you are damn well going to use it. There is another aspect of this too, and I raised that issue.

"Do you think it would be correct to say that it is merely being polite for them to tell you what they think you want to hear?" In San Miguel, entering any Méxican's personal space evokes a zone of politeness and formality. Greeting each other within this closer range, we exchange courtesies, and the formulae are clear and nearly inflexible. The same person will later stop his car in the middle of the street and enter a store. He blocks all the traffic in doing so, but at least he is not parking there, because it is a no parking zone. Later, leaving town, he throws his bag of car garbage out the window onto your doorstep. This is all consistent—it's about proximity, which governs degrees of politeness. Beyond a certain distance, other people's faces blur and they lack basic qualities of humanity. Within a closer circle, you are nearly family, even when you have never met.

"Yes. That *is* what I mean. It's a very cultural thing, and it's rude to say no. That makes it hard to feel comfortable doing business here, for me. Because I'm a journalist, and because journalism in the U.S. is so different from the media here, it scares me a little to do business in Puebla because I never know what I'm going to get. For example, I never know when I'm going to get paid. Those are risk factors too in the U.S. as a free lancer. I outsource myself, working remotely via the Internet, so I still work almost full time. I don't have to put in crazy hours like I did in California because it's so affordable here. But almost all my clients are in the U.S., so I am remote, but they're almost all there. I pay federal taxes in the States. I also occasionally work for people in Puebla. I worked for six months for the international affairs department for the State of Puebla. I've done minor translation work for other agencies. I've always worked legally. I am now a permanent resident of México, and I have the right to work here. When the state wanted to hire me, everything had to be above board."

"My objective in these conversations is to think about what kind of person comes down here and doesn't need much other support. Why do you think that is, and does it take a different kind of expat to do that? Can you define what that means for you, given your personal history?"

Rebecca shrugged at first, then sat down again. I sensed that we were entering a stretch of turf that was less emotionally charged.

"I don't know. I may stray here a bit. My experience may be different from many other expats." I already knew that it was. Although I was writing a nonfiction book, I don't generalize much on these conversations.

"I think it changes," she continued, "when you have internal support, like in-laws, although it's true that I came down here by myself without anyone's support initially. But in one sense I have always had support. I didn't come down here and find an apartment and start to make my own way. I came down as part of the Spanish Institute of Puebla's academic program, and its director took care of everything. I paid the equivalent of my apartment rent in San Francisco, just my rent, for an entire month of living here, which included all my classes, room and board, and two excursions, which was one of the reasons I decided to come. But the school was incredibly supportive, as was the family I lived with. In fact, I house sat for them when my classes were over and they went to the

U.S. to visit their son, which also convinced me to stay here longer."

"You didn't come down here with the intention of being an expat. You just grew into it."

"Yes, I did. I didn't plan to stay more than four months. I tell people that I fell in love with Puebla, and with a *poblano*, and I decided to stay."

I love these tipping points. I have written in other places about the moment when people come to México, stay for a while, and realize on the morning before they're scheduled to go home that they cannot possibly return to their former lives. I have called this the 'falling off the cliff' experience. Rebecca's process sounded more gradual, but the outcome was the same.

"Can you recall the moment of that decision? What was it like? Was it a big thing, like changing the course of a river? Or a small, subtle thing, a tipping point that was mainly recognizable only later?" Sometimes you have to look back over your shoulder to see them.

"I think there were several moments, but initially it was thinking, really, why not? I had spent six years working for *Wired Magazine* in San Francisco. During that time we had preached a sort of unplugged, outsourcing, you-could-be-anywhere in the world sort of 21st century style of living, and I drank the Kool-Aid of that message, so to speak. I'd been talking about this lifestyle from a journalist's perspective, writing about the possibilities of it for so long, so why not live it myself? Why not outsource myself, because while I was here, I had taken this sabbatical and met Pablo. I wish I could say it was this grand plan I had made that worked out perfectly."

"But you can't."

"No."

"It so rarely is." But it also doesn't need to be, I

thought, although I didn't voice it because she had experienced it that way.

"A lot of it was only a happy accident. While I was in Puebla I started getting emails from former clients and colleagues saying they wanted a writer or an editor. Can you help? I said I was living in México, and they replied, 'We don't care where you are. Can you meet the deadline? So I thought, why do I need to go back to San Francisco and pay $2,000 a month for rent when I can work remotely and have a much better quality of life? That was what sealed the deal."

"So the answer to this question is that you didn't consider yourself an expat who came down here and didn't need a support group; you simply didn't consider it at all, and you still had the implicit support of the school, that structure, at least in the beginning, so you didn't have to ask yourself that question. That simply flowed into what developed."

"Yes, and after I left the school I had my boyfriend, (now husband) and his family. But all that being said, after being here for a couple of years, and not having an expat support group, I began to look for one. I couldn't find one, so I started one." She shrugged.

Although I hadn't known Rebecca even an hour, this seemed absolutely typical of her. "And because of those efforts, do you now have a sense of how many expats live here?"

"I still don't have a sense of that. When I worked for the State of Puebla, I asked that question a number of times, but I never got a definitive answer. Through my website I have a mailing list, and that's how you contacted me originally. I have nearly 300 people on that list. They are from all over the world, not just the U. S. and Canada, and they don't all necessarily live here, but many do. I organize get-togethers now and then."

"Would you call that group a community? Or is it

more a random collection of people living here for diverse reasons? Sometimes they're in contact, and at others, not."

"Yes and no. I think the problem with Puebla, and maybe it's not really a problem, but the difference between this town and a community like San Miguel or Ajijic (on Lake Chapala, directly below Guadalajara), is that they're both very small cities, and when you have a critical mass of foreigners, it's apparent. Here, it's not. Puebla also isn't like México City, which is much larger and is home to so many foreigners that you can find formal groups, such as the Newcomers Club and the Alliance Francaise, even a Korean community.

"Here I think it's in between those two points. Puebla is such a huge city. The population—2.6 million in the greater metro area—is the same as Chicago, I think. There are so many foreigners, but the city is also so huge and sprawling that we don't necessarily run into one another much. We live in different neighborhoods, and we're from a lot of different countries. For example, there's a big German population here because of the Volkswagen plant. But that working community and the English-speaking community are two completely different entities. The English-speaking expat community here is essentially British, American, Canadian, and Australian, plus any countries where English is a dominant foreign language, like China, Russia, and India. We've had gatherings where people spoke four different languages. A lot of that group speaks Spanish too because many of them are married to Méxicans.

"So when you talk about the expat community here— I can't speak for a lot of other cities, and I only know what I've heard, but I think the biggest difference between this expat population and that of other places is that it's incredibly diverse. We're united only in being expats, but there is no newcomer's club. As far as I know, I'm the only one actively trying to bring people together here. My goal in doing that is to provide a forum in which other people can actively network. I don't try to hook people up, and there have been a few somewhat unsuccessful attempts by others to start singles groups. I think the hard thing is that a lot of the expats here are transient, and the diversity includes a large range in age. We get people in their twenties who are in college, and we also get some who are retired. It's been difficult for some people to make close connections."

"Their main point of commonality is that they all live here."

"Yes, and that they're foreign—living outside their own cultures."

"So let's look at the other side of that picture. What are *poblanos* like?"

"It depends on the *poblano*! Just like anywhere else I can generalize, but people still run the gamut from open and friendly to stuck-up and closed. I've met some great people here. My husband and his friends are very similar to my old friends in the U.S.—middle class, artistic, somewhat rebellious, and educated. They've been very accepting of me and that may be because I'm married to a *poblano*. I haven't had many negative experiences. Also, because of my website, I've received a lot of moral support from the city tourism board, plus many local business owners and chefs. That's partly because when I worked with the state I met a lot of people. In general everyone has been, at least on the surface, open and friendly with me."

"You've developed a good working relationship on both sides."

"I do have a good relationship with the director of the city tourism office. He's a great guy and he's supported me a lot by providing me with information. As for the State of Puebla; yes and no. I worked with the international affairs office, not tourism, for six months and then resigned after the project I was working on was finished. It was the International Mole Festival (mole is a classic sauce typical of Puebla, and has nothing to do with short-sighted animals that live mostly under ground), so I did some media work for Puebla and negotiated contracts with some of the chefs, like Rick Bayless; that kind of thing.

"I still keep in touch with my colleagues from the office, and when I reach out to them they're happy to help me. The state tourism board, however, has been hard to penetrate. Even though there are expats on its staff, my repeated requests for information have either been ignored or denied. So I've stopped asking. I always hope that when tourists walk into their office they are more helpful than they have been with me, but based on the comments I get from readers of my website, that may or may not be the case. I have sometimes walked in there and found very helpful people, and once I even got a tour of the Cathedral, in Spanish, but the staff who does media relations ignores me, which is frustrating. I don't know why they do that."

Privately I wondered whether her energy and get-things-done attitude might have been intimidating to a state mid-level bureaucrat. Rebecca has the latitude to do about whatever she wants, and because she's an individual, and owes her job or views to nobody, she also needs to accommodate no encumbrances from colleagues or hierarchies.

"Do you think your connection with Pablo replaced your need for more of an expat support group here?" I didn't feel like we'd exhausted the support group topic yet.

"It didn't really replace my need, but in basic terms, day to day, like where do I find a dentist, where can I buy curry powder; if I have questions of that kind I just call my mother-in-law. Also, my ability to speak Spanish eliminates some of the need for a support group."

"Of course mother-in-laws everywhere are the archetypal support group in themselves, or the opposite. That leads into the question of what kind of relationship you have with your husband's family."

"I adore them. They've been great. From day one I've always felt welcome and accepted by them. I particularly bonded with my father-in-law, who passed away in 2009. I'm a Californian and I like my wine—it runs in my veins—but he was a huge wine fan, and my mother-in-law is diabetic and doesn't drink. He was very sweet. My husband has two younger brothers, and they've been great too."

"Is this a reinvention of yourself that you could ever have foreseen?"

"That's a great question."

"Can you see the lines leading back through your life that provide some continuity with this moment?"

"Yes and no. I feel like those are two slightly different questions. I don't think I've reinvented myself, but I do feel I've expanded my world view. I've become a much more aware person from living in another culture, in a way I never would've understood before I got here. One of the things that led up to me coming to México was that I got divorced in 2005, which was a bit of a personal crisis, as it would be for anyone. The following year I went to visit a friend in Madrid, and I spent an entire week of that time alone driving through northern Spain along the Camino de Santiago. I'm not very religious, but that road is the third-largest Christian pilgrimage site in the world, after the Vatican and Jerusalem. My friend had walked it. I didn't have time for that, but he kept saying it was so beautiful that I had to see northern Spain. 'Go, I'll help you,' he said. I didn't speak any Spanish at that time.

"So I spent several days driving that route. I decided to go out to the very end, which is in Galicia, and it's called kilometer zero, the point that the Spanish and Portuguese believed was the end of the world, when they still believed that the world was flat. It was to them the westernmost point in Europe. In fact it isn't, but that's what they thought at the time."

"Kilometer zero. That sounds much like square one in English."

Rebecca nodded as she went on. "While I was sitting out there on a rock looking at the sea, it reminded me a lot of Northern California. After visiting Compostela and spending that time reflecting on faith, I realized that faith is a very open-ended thing. People have faith in God, in each other, in themselves and in the planet, so faith manifests itself in all these different ways. It occurred to me that there was something admirable about those Spanish sailors who stood on those same rocks and looked out at the sea, back when the world was still 'flat,' and decided to set sail anyway. They had to have faith that something else existed out there. And it was only the people that took this massive risk—that they were going to sail off the edge of the earth—who found these two whole new continents. That became the metaphor for the rest of my life. It's only the people that have the courage to venture into the unknown that discover this new world out there.

"In hindsight, I suppose that metaphor is how I really feel about being in México. Learning Spanish has opened this whole other world to me that I didn't even know existed. If I spoke three more languages—Chinese, Arabic, Russian—how much more of the world's literature, architecture, thought processes, and media would I be able to understand? Speaking Spanish, there's an entire hemisphere that speaks this language, and most of us north of the U.S. border with

México don't. How could we not want to know what they're talking about, what they're thinking, and how they think differently from us?"

This was a bit of a long speech, but it came from the crucible of her experience at a critical time and was obviously heartfelt. It was one of those unconsciously eloquent moments when it all spills out. This occasion in particular, at kilometer zero at land's end in Northern Spain, had launched a turnaround that Rebecca did not herself think of as a reinvention, but it fit my definition without qualification. She was a different person when she rose from that rock.

We both got up and stretched for a moment or two. She seemed still immersed in the recollection. I wanted to lighten up, to bracket this comment with a subject that would provide it with emphasis by going in a completely different direction.

"What do you do for amusement here?" She grew more composed and focused again.

"There's so much to do I feel like my list is never-ending. I love exploring new things. I would rather go to a restaurant I've never been to than one I've eaten at six times. What I love about Puebla is that, even though it can feel like a small town, it's a massive city. And not only does it have all the amenities, but it also has all the artistic, colonial, cultural, and architectural aspects, the depth that comes from more than 2000 years of Cholula and nearly 500 years of Puebla itself. Puebla was founded less than fifty years after Columbus discovered the new world. The first block to be laid out was the *zócalo*, (the main plaza), and it's still there. It's changed over the years, but it still survives. Every time I go downtown somebody has a door open and there's something behind it that I've never seen before. Again, it goes back to learning something new every day. What I do for fun is explore new things. Yesterday we ate butterfly larvae."

"Good for you." I probably showed too many teeth as I forced a smile. I don't eat bugs, myself, if I can help it. This did indeed present a change of course from the life-changing pilgrimage road.

"A friend who's a translator in town invited us. He and a friend of his have been doing get-togethers for thirteen years. I can't say they were my favorite things, and I still prefer *carne asada*, but it was a good experience. I wrote a blog post about it."

She waited for my response, but I only cleared my throat and drank some more water. With the tip of my tongue I checked the back of my teeth for foreign matter.

"How has your family reacted to your relocation down here? Do they come to visit?"

"Yes, they've been really good about it. Occasionally my extended family will give me the 'México is scary' comment, but my immediate family is incredibly open-minded. My sister lives in Buenos Aires. When I was in college my mom lived in South Korea for two years and taught at the International School there. My parents are hip about these things. They're from a tiny farm town in southwestern Pennsylvania, but in the end we moved to California and they became very open-minded. They travel a lot, both of them. They're divorced, and each of them has come to visit on separate occasions twice. My sister hasn't been here yet, but we met her and my brother-in-law in Puerto Morelos on the Mayan Riviera last year to celebrate their anniversary. So, my family has been very supportive. My mom is my 'accountant' in the U.S.; she manages the financial aspect of my business, or at least anything I can't do remotely from here. For the people who can't pay me electronically, I have a post office box in her town and she goes there once a week. She's my support network in the

States, because she manages the financial aspect of anything I can't do here."

"Do you go back up there very often?"

"I do try to go as often as I can because I miss my friends and family, and I want to shop for things I can't get here. We were just in California for two and a half weeks, where we went to a wedding and visited friends. I was at my mom's for a month in January helping to move my grandparents to a retirement home. I'm going back with Pablo for Christmas."

I was a little surprised at all this travel north, since her engagement with Puebla was so deep, but family has different meanings to different people. "Has living here affected your view of the U.S.?"

"Definitely. Not to sound negative but it has made me understand how arrogant and ignorant we are as a society. There are exceptions to that. But it's shocking to me how even many Americans *living in México* still buy into the stereotypes perpetuated by the U.S. media about this country. I still don't fully understand all of the issues, but I can see how we have based our perspective of México and Méxicans on the narrow demographic of people who emigrate to the U.S. They are the poorest of the poor, the people who can't get jobs here, who would rather make seven or eight dollars an hour picking vegetables there than fifty pesos a day ($4, the minimum wage) here. I think that we are not good neighbors to México. I really hope that will change."

"If it does, and I wish that too, it won't be because of any pressure from the American media. They make a living from negativity."

"You asked me about how and why I started my website. Part of it was to combat those stereotypes and to provide information from a foreigner's perspective, mine, but one that aims to be culturally aware. The biggest compliment I've ever gotten about *All About Puebla* was from a friend of mine who is *poblano*. He said that what he liked about it was that it was honest and not condescending. I work very hard at that, presenting information about only Puebla. I refer to the site as *A Gringa's Guide,* because I want people to understand that I'm foreign, and that I'm coming at things from an outsider's perspective. At the same time, because I'm married to a *poblano* and I live here, I try to explain why things are the way they are, in a way that visitors and other foreigners can understand. What a Méxican tourist looks for in terms of information is extremely different from what a foreigner looks for, and that's the hard thing here, particularly with the state tourism people, since they don't get it."

"They don't distinguish between the two."

"Right. The American comes in and says, 'What is it and why should I care?' That's not something a Méxican tourist typically asks. They already know some of the answers. I give food tours for a friend of mine who has a company, Eat México, that specializes in that. Almost all the visitors are foreign, but I have given tours for couples from México City. I realized then that I can't give the same information to them that I do for foreigners. They already know, for example, what *poblano* means, whereas most English speakers don't. So it made me understand the difference between presenting tourist information to domestic tourists versus international tourists. That's what I'm trying to do with my website is to give an insider's look but from a foreign perspective as to what's happening here."

"Is our conversation today part of that process too?"

"In a way it is. It's the same reason I started my website. I want people to care as much as I do about Puebla and to try to understand it. That's why I posted a piece about eating butterfly larvae, and I also posted some things on Facebook."

"Are there any safety issues here?"

"Another question I get asked constantly."

"You can imagine that I'm sick of asking it, but my readers who don't know México intimately want to know this about each place. If I don't bring it up they'll think I'm hiding something."

"Then I'm glad you did. A friend of mine in México City wrote a great piece recently about trying to pitch a story about our volcano, Popocatépetl, because all of the *narco* stuff aside, we live next to an active volcano on both sides, México City and Puebla. So he wrote this wonderful piece about how he lives in México City, he loves it there, but he's not against using the stereotype to sell a story. The piece is about how his story turned into a nonstory because it's one of the least dangerous volcanoes in North America. It goes back to all the stereotypes there are, the volcano, the *narcos*, the emigrants. Yes, there are places in México that are extremely dangerous, especially for women traveling alone, or for people who don't read the news. But here in Puebla, in terms of it being the fourth largest city in México, in the six years I've been here I haven't had anything happen to me that couldn't have happened to me anywhere. I lost my wallet with my credit card. But that said, when I lived in the Bay Area in California, my front door was the crime scene in downtown San Jose when a policeman was shot in the head with his own gun. In San Francisco, a friend who I was having a drink with before I left had her purse stolen from between her feet, and neither one of us saw or heard anything. I've witnessed bank robberies and shoplifting, too. So yes, things happen in Puebla, but they happen everywhere. However, unlike an increasing number of places in the U.S., you probably will not get shot going to church in México, or to the movies, or to school."

"And you won't be killed in a drive-by shooting. Why is it better to live in Puebla than in México City, for example. Or is it?"

With a grin, she ticked off the reasons on her fingers. "Smog, earthquakes, prices, traffic. I love México City, but I don't want to be there when the next earthquake hits. Here in Cholula I've only felt one small one in six years."

"What has living here taught you?"

"Patience." Rebecca laughed and I did too. That was almost the only answer I ever received to that question. "I used to joke that patience was not my virtue," she continued, "but since I've lived here I've become much more patient."

"Are there some issues here that are particularly relevant to women?"

"There are a couple different ways to come at that question. One is that I don't think México is much different from most countries in the world when it comes to women. If you come from the U.S., you're used to being treated more equally, particularly in the workplace, which is great, but that's not *always* true. I spent my entire career in California being one of the boys, working in music, business, or tech journalism."

"Let's take a look at that phrase—being one of the boys. Doesn't that suggest you had found a way of fitting in well and playing by their rules, rather than your own?"

"Yes."

"Interesting that you expressed it that way. When I was in business I was always a small-scale entrepreneur, so I never became an expert in corporate culture on a serious scale, although I was aware of it through some big companies I dealt with, like a couple of major banks and Weyerhaeuser."

She nodded slowly. "I don't think I ever would've said it that way until now. I never looked at it in those terms. In the States we have a strong legal system that has virtually leveled the playing field. Here in México that's not the case at all. One of the reasons I left my job with the State of Puebla was that they hired me as an expert and treated me like a secretary just because I was female, or so it seemed. They paid me less than any of my other clients, so one of the reasons I left was economic. I realize that's a huge cultural thing, but fundamentally that's not something I ever want to be forced to adjust to. Here in Puebla a woman who is raped and wants an abortion needs to get permission from a judge. It is incredibly backward."

"But abortion is legal now in México City."

"Yes, but you still need to have the money to travel there and pay for it. There's all that economic disparity in the background of this issue. Just from a woman's standpoint, people talk here about girls always looking for the rich guy with a nice car and a good job, but that's the only way they can ever get ahead if they have no money to start with, and few of them do. They still make thirty cents on the dollar to what men make here. Imagine the worst-case scenario in the U.S. and it's five times as bad here in terms of the workplace.

"In the home, it varies widely. I think there are some progressive people here, and just like in the U.S., there are backward people. On the flip side, from a safety perspective as a traveler, you can put yourself in dangerous situations, but in general Puebla is respectful toward women. It's contradictory; women and mothers deserve respect, but you don't have to pay them much in wages. Respect takes a different form.

"From the viewpoint of a woman traveling solo, I lived in a very urban neighborhood in San Francisco before I came here. I lived alone, and if I was bored I could go out to have a beer and watch a game, or have a cup of coffee and work on my laptop. Here, if you go out as a woman alone, you are seen as looking for company. No one does anything alone here. Part of it is that if women feel unsafe in México it's because they're seen as misbehaving culturally, violating expectations, which still doesn't make harassing them right. Still, why shouldn't I be able to go out at night and do what I want? It's because *that's not what people do here.* Single people go out in packs. They don't go out alone because that's sending the message that they want to meet someone. People you encounter feel sorry for you if you're alone. When I first came down here my host family would apologize to me for leaving the house and making me be alone on the weekend. But personally, I was relieved because I was used to being alone and I needed my own space."

Although it clearly could have gone on, at that point we both sensed we were finished. With a release of some tension in her shoulders, she leaned back on the sofa and smiled at me. We might have just returned from a long and intense working lunch. But it would never have been as personal or revealing.

I felt Rebecca had been a perfect person to talk with for this exploration of the less well-traveled roads of expat life in Puebla. Her perspective as a woman in this macho culture was essential to the thread of this tale, and I knew she saw further milestones ahead of her. She had put down deep roots in Puebla; she knew where she was and what she was doing. Despite some experiences that had made her stop and reflect deeply on her life, she had not come to México to disengage from the past in any way. Most of all, she didn't mind discussing her experiences with someone she had never met until I rang her doorbell. I was not a total stranger, of course, since about a dozen emails had paved the way for this conversation.

Sensing a pause, Pablo emerged from the bedroom with a smile on his face and the cat in his arms. He must have heard some of our discussion. With a firm handshake, he told me that I reminded him of his father, a great tribute I'm sure, since he had recently passed away and was much missed. I, however, saw myself more as cast in the mold of Roland Hedley, cartoonist Gary Trudeau's much younger crusading journalist. Even so, I knew Pablo meant to flatter me, and in that light, I took his comment in the spirit it was given. Between them, Pablo and Rebecca had earned a solid place in the story of expats living and thriving off the beaten path in México.

The long cab ride back to the main plaza was cheaper than the one outward bound. I've been told that's normal here. Being denser, perhaps the historic central district has greater gravitational pull, and therefore the cabs use less gas on return trips. My mind, as we swung back and forth over the pitted pavement, was occupied sorting through Rebecca's thoughts and ideas. I was happy to have met with a journalist on my first encounter in Puebla. People who have been around the block a few times in that dicey trade and can still preserve some integrity in their ideas always earn my respect. It can be a rough game, and the sad example of the downward spin of much of U.S. journalism is always before me as a cautionary lesson.

The remainder of the day was mine. I never like to have two conversations in one day if I can avoid it; they tend to mingle during the night and confuse my dreams. Because I like to take a mental break from these encounters, I headed for a nearby museum, the Hospital San Pedro, a sixteenth century monument to cutting edge medicine at a time when germs had not yet been discovered. Nor was the role of hygiene well understood yet. I'm sure they meant well, but prayer, leeches, and cold compresses may have been the principal remedy for most ailments. It was not until the second half of the nineteenth century that Joseph Lister realized that doctors ought to wash their hands before delivering a baby or commencing surgery. His memory has subsequently been enshrined by naming a mouthwash after him. Immortality comes in many forms. The diseases summoned to this treatment center were different then, of course. You might have come there to be treated for ague, consumption, plague, or catalepsy. Saints preserve us, I said half aloud, a phrase that must have been uttered many times before within these walls.

From the façade the San Pedro suggests the typical two-story, four-sided plan of a colonial building with arches surrounding a courtyard within. That courtyard was filled with empty folding seats facing a low podium when I came in. Nothing was happening, so I climbed the stairs and paid my twenty-five pesos to get in. Two dollars: the cheapest hospital admission on earth. Logically enough, the first exhibit was the pharmacy. Rows of Delft-like jars in blue and white bore the names of their contents. Mostly they were herbals, although some raw minerals were also offered, such as mercury, once a remedy for syphilis now oddly fallen out of favor.

Another room, configured like a chapel, was hung with devotional paintings of superb artistry, although many needed restoration. I had looked at offerings of similar work all over México, and the finer ones are quite pricy. These were all eighteenth century examples, but from artists whose names I didn't know.

The three largest rooms were devoted to marionettes. Not a medical exhibit perhaps, but surely an educational one. This was a costumed collection, correct in period detail, even to the muskets, devoted to historical events. I understood that the audience must have included adults as well as children, but essentially it was aimed at a non-literate group learning the national story. The animated figures would speak about their role in the War of Independence, the Revolution, the Cinco de Mayo defeat of the French invaders. At the end, as

I emerged, for fun I saw Snow White and Cinderella—dessert after a main course of history.

I wandered back toward the stairs in a more mellow frame of mind. The marionettes had both a distance from my purpose and a particularity that I valued. The small-scale articulation of their joints and jawbones was clear. Woodcarving with mechanical elements. Their speeches were almost audible, and I could easily imagine their rapt audiences as these stories were repeated through the generations.

When I emerged into the courtyard, the voluminous sound of a full orchestra washed away all my other thoughts. I didn't recognize the piece, but it had the style and orchestration of the mid nineteenth century. I sat for a while on a bench on the main floor gallery and listened. México offers many examples of objects or situations where you don't know what you're looking at. At other times, you know what it is but you don't know why. As with today, that's an easier dilemma that needed no quick answer. You sit back and enjoy the serendipity of the moment.

Somewhere across Puebla, skirting the murky borders of Cholula, on the following morning, Monday, a woman named Lenya Bloom was expecting my arrival. It was set for nine-thirty, so she would have a chance to deliver her two-year-old daughter to preschool. I had a street address, a *colonia* (a neighborhood) in hand, but beyond that I had no idea where we were going as I got into the cab.

As we approached twenty-five minutes later, the character of the street was private and quite fresh, although the pavement had some of the same issues I'd seen before. The construction was more recent than much of what we had passed through. We paused at cream-colored gates, and a doorman let me in on foot. He knew I was expected.

The house, one of three in this small compound, was also cream-colored and contemporary—a style I think of as Méxican Modern. It tends to be spare in detail, without moldings or window and door trim. The other two were a good match, of a unified concept, as if they had been built as a family compound.

Lenya Bloom met me at the door with a welcoming smile.

The interior was painted white, with an exposed brick wall in the living room, which also had wood floors, a rarity here. The modern Franklin stove in one corner was fronted by a three-sided glass screen. Sliding doors led to a small courtyard lined with bamboo along the walls.

We sat at the dining table, with a voice recorder between us.

Lenya is a youthful woman in her early thirties. Her tightly curled brown hair was pulled back into a ponytail. She was wearing a polo shirt with a narrow dark stripe over jeans, and a leopard print scarf looped loosely around her neck. Over her shoulder I looked into the large kitchen with dark wood cabinets on three sides, granite counters, and modern lighting. The sink wall was opposite us and the housekeeper withdrew as we sat down.

We chatted for a while off the record. Her look was frank and engaged.

"What brought you to Puebla? Was it simply the school connection?" I already knew that like Rebecca Hurd, education had drawn Lenya down to México.

"Puebla ended up being an accident. I initially went to México City since I'd thought about studying for a master's degree at UNAM (The National Autonomous University of México). That didn't work out because my field was anthropology and they weren't looking for someone with my interests. A friend of mine suggested looking at Universidad de las Americas in Puebla, which I did. That's the big private university here, and it looked like my high school. It wasn't what I wanted. I decided that Puebla was a good place to study because it had many options, and I chose the Benemérita Autonoma de Puebla, which is like the local UNAM."

"How old were you at that point?"

"In 2004 I was twenty-three. So that's how I got here. You're right that it ended up being a school connection, although the school I ended up teaching at was the American School of Puebla, Junior High level."

"Have you been here ever since?"

"Yes."

"What were you planning to do with your master's degree?"

"Oh, I didn't really have any plans. I just wanted to finish it and then see what developed. I wanted to do that master's degree here because I needed to look at México in a different light, and studying here had that effect. That examination probably made it possible for me to build a life here."

"Can you explore that a bit—looking at México in a different light?"

"I grew up in California, where there's a very strong Latino presence, but I don't feel like what people see in the U.S. is an accurate representation of what Méxicans are really like here—things change as people cross the border. I had first come here earlier to do an undergraduate semester abroad, and I did a typical one."

She gave me a smile that appeared to mix fond memories with a hint of regret. "I played and stayed up all night, and went to the ruins and didn't think too much about things until I got back home to finish my bachelor's degree and felt that I had been unfair with myself and with México in terms of how I behaved. There are a lot of preconceptions here about what American women are like, and I lived right up to those stereotypes on my first trip."

"Preconceptions on the part of Méxicans?"

"Yes, because they think we're all fun-loving, silly, up for whatever, which has never actually been true of me, but in that semester I just wanted to have fun, which I did. And then I went back to finish studying in the States and brooded about it. It was always in the back of my mind as I interviewed for jobs after college, and then there came a point when I was working when I would either get drawn into the New York editorial world and stay, or I could leave then. If I didn't go I was just going to get sucked in, which is pretty much what happened to everyone I graduated with. So I saved up my pid-dling little salary from that year. I told my parents I was going to come down here and study and then I did. I think that other light I was looking for had to come from the inside of México, not someplace obvious. Not necessarily Oaxaca again, where I had been before, or even México City. I feel like Puebla is not an obvious starting off point for an American."

"I don't think that has changed since then," I said, "and that's why I'm here. In the frame of mind you were in, perhaps that was part of its charm."

"I don't know that I was really thinking about that so much. I met the guy who eventually became my husband in México City after having been there a month and a half."

"Is he a *poblano*?"

"Yes, he is. He was studying at a university in México City and we had friends in common. He was the one who brought me here to look at universities, and then that con-versation we had on the way down turned into this, into my life. I think that somehow I knew he was my person, that he was my one. While he and I both finished studying, I spent a lot of time alone, not knowing anyone here. The people who were in my program at school came from a completely different background from me. They were from public schools and were there with a grant. Many of them were there *for* the grant, rather than to actually study. At that point master's students were paid 6,000 pesos a month, which was better than their salaries would've been doing other things. As long as they maintained their GPA, they received their monthly stipend from the government to study. It's probably more now because of inflation. I didn't receive anything—I paid for it myself."

"But wouldn't your husband have received that?"

"Yes, except that he went to a private university in México City. I had always gone to private schools, too, I'd always lived in a big urban center in the U.S., and you get self-involved as an American. Since I studied anthropology and eventually sociology for the master's, I felt that the only valid study in those areas was first, an examination of self, and then you have to take yourself out of your comfort zone and out of your context. I ended up learning a lot about what it means to be educated in America, and what it means to be an American, because we tend to take it for granted. When I started my master's program, George Bush was president, and people had strong feelings about him here, especially in this leftist sociology department at the public university where I went, so I got clumped together with him. People talked to me as if I was related to him, but I was here because he was in power. He gave me a good excuse to leave."

"Please tell me more about that issue of learning what it is to be an American. Have your thoughts on that evolved in the years you've been here?"

She nodded vigorously. "Yes, because you end up having to make compromises in terms of your national identity, no matter what culture you've brought with you, and you save only what's essential. The rest you have to give up a bit in order to fit in."

"How do you feel about that?"

"I'm fine with it. I come from a place, San Francisco, where everyone is half something anyway. I'm half Jewish and I have friends who are half Chinese. Everyone was half something and we were all a mix growing up. So I feel like it's OK, I just added another part. It's good to whittle down to what's essential."

"When you're working now, what kinds of things do you translate?" This activity had emerged from our earlier emails. Even with her household help Lenya needed something she could do mostly at home.

"I just started doing it. I translate all the school documents for the American School, where I taught."

"Are you working free lance?"

"Yes, and I've also been doing some work translating contracts and accompanying bureaucrats from the Ministry of Public Education. They're bringing a museum here, a copy of the Vienna House of Music. They just had a Viennese contingent come in and none of them spoke Spanish. I accompanied them and took minutes during their meetings. And that's it so far. I haven't actively gone out and looked for any more work. I don't know if I'm prepared to yet."

"It must be hard with a two year old. And your husband is actively doing other construction projects?"

"Right. He's in Xalapa (in the State of Veracruz) as we speak finalizing plans for a housing project."

"Are you aware of the volcano's presence all the time here?"

"Totally. Should we take a look at it?"

We climbed the steps to the third floor where we stared out the window at a perfect volcanic cone. The upper quarter of it was covered with snow that contrasted with the blue-violet sides. At the top a long coil of vapor poured from the mouth and drifted off to the left. I couldn't help but wonder whether she might lay awake at night waiting for it to erupt. We watched it in silence for a while. In a subtle way it was constantly moving as if it were alive.

"It has a good plume on it this morning. It must vary a lot."

"I grew up with the ocean," Lenya said after a long moment. "I still need some kind of forceful natural presence in my life, and there it is. Originally when we built this house we couldn't see it because we had only two floors. Then, when we had the baby, we added a third because this was not a house for a child at that point. Adding that floor gave a view directly onto the Popo, as we call it. So my daughter says good morning and goodnight to the Popo every day."

Just as my kids had said goodnight moon, this little girl greets an active volcano outside her window.

"We know whether it's going to be cold or warm according to whether there's snow on it. Recently it's been very active."

"Was that in May?"

"Right. May and some of June. I wouldn't change it."

"Is there anything you *would* change about this area if you could?"

She thought about this as we went back downstairs. "I think I would physically take down some of the walls. That's a big one for me. I know I have one myself, as a security issue. But when we were looking for a place to live we saw properties that were built with walls and gates within walls. All of those divisions have a heavy feeling for someone that grew up in the States where questions of segregation are still alive."

"How do you read that in terms of this culture?"

"I'm not sure. I feel like it says that even your neighbor isn't someone who can be trusted, let alone the people who have to go through all of that security to get into your house to work. There's not much public life here."

"By that you mean life in public."

"Right, at least in the social sphere that I ended up living in. People get in their cars and go to a specific place. You don't really go for a walk, and you saw what the roads are like around here. I would focus on enriching public spaces and improving roadways so people could move around without having to close themselves off any further."

This was a message I hadn't heard in any of the other towns, even in Morelia. Perhaps it was just the population density.

"What else is compelling about this town?"

"The food here is so interesting. I started a list ten years ago when I moved here called *Delicious Things*. I still have it in my bedside table, and I add to it occasionally although it's pretty complete at this point. It's about the availability of good food and ingredients and everything that draws people together."

"Do you eat out a lot?"

"We used to."

"Now it's more about the baby."

"My father-in-law is a real connoisseur of regional cooking, and he's taken us all over this area to show us what the food is like. I try everything once. It's very complex. When he grew up Puebla was mostly the downtown area. Out this far, none of this was anything, only a wasteland between Downtown Puebla and Cholula."

"Are we in Cholula now? It wasn't clear to me as we drove out here that we'd crossed any lines."

"This area is borderline. My bank statement says this

address is Cholula and my driver's license says it's Puebla."

"Is there a regional character? What are *poblanos* like?"

"I don't have anything to compare them to. When I was in Oaxaca I didn't get to know people the way I have in my time here, and I don't know many Méxicans from other areas. But it's been interesting because a lot of their religious aspects are still strong in terms of moral ballast."

"Moral ballast?"

"How people make their decisions and judgments. I think there's a very strong presence of the Church here, even if people don't actively go on Sundays. It's deeply rooted in behavior and expectations. You can't get away from the churches here in Cholula, even on top of the pyramid. There's a church up there."

"Yes, la Virgen de los Remedios."

"This is a big city, but at the same time it's really small in some ways. Most families have been here for a long time. They all know each other and each other's stories. This is both an advantage and a disadvantage for me. I don't always know people's last names and I really don't always care."

"It sounds inbred." It also reminded me of Rebecca Hurd's comments along the same lines.

"It is, in a way. There's no anonymity."

"Are you comfortable here?"

"Pretty much, 90%. There's always something I don't understand, or don't want to understand. My Spanish at this point is very good, but there are cultural references I don't get because they may refer to music or TV shows that weren't mine growing up."

"There's a lot of nuance in this language and culture anyway."

"I do my best to keep up with popular culture here so that I can participate in spontaneous conversations. Driving is insane and stressful and the social interactions are too. There's some kind of code among the women here that I don't know how to decipher. I always go into a new social situation feeling like I have my eyes closed. If some type of friendship results from it or not, or I get misjudged, I just can't worry about it."

"Do you have Méxican friends outside of your husband's family?"

"Barely." Her eyebrows went up. "I mean, my husband grew up here, and he went to school here, so he came with a whole social group, which has grown as people have gotten married and moved away or come back."

"Are you well accepted within that setting?"

"I think so, but mostly because he's kind of a leader. It was always going to happen that the woman he chose to marry would be accepted. His name is Manuel. Many of his friends are now friends of mine, much like in-laws, in a way. At least I chose my husband…"

"But then you also got his clan."

"Yes. And within that group I've chosen to become closer to some than to others."

"So, outside of that group, how have you gone about making your own friends here?"

"Just time and seeing other people repeatedly has helped. I have a group of friends that I worked with at The American School who are the ones who stayed. They've gotten married and had children here and are also here on a permanent basis. But those are American girls and we always have in common that we can complain about the traffic or our mothers-in-law. And then, I don't have one, not even one, close friend who is a local Puebla woman where we chose each other. But I feel like that can still happen, even if it hasn't yet. I don't know how much of that is me and how much is this kind of insularity that I already talked about, and the religiousness which is always an issue. We baptized my daughter, but that was because of my husband. I grew up kind of Jewish."

"Is Manuel a practicing Catholic?"

She shrugged as if that was hard to define. "We always go to the weddings of people we're close to, but otherwise we don't go to church. We have other friends who do, but not us."

"Is this part of the question about what of your old culture do you keep when you get here and settle in? Religion had to be an issue at some level when you got together."

"Yes! And even more, I think there will always be this question of why on earth you would leave the States. Why would you leave your family and come down here by yourself? The women here are just never going to understand why I would do something like that. As modern and educated as they may be, there is still some kind of essential barrier there, because it's not something that any of them have ever done themselves. Here they are." Her hands made a gesture of dense weight, of being settled, bulky and unmoving, perhaps like a Henry Moore sculpture of horses or large women. "Many of them moved right from their parents' house into their husband's house. They have never lived by themselves."

"I think that's typical everywhere in México," I said. "Young people stay home until they get married. You don't hear of three single girls just out of college getting jobs in the big city and renting an apartment like you would in the States. All the same, it leaves a void in what I think of as the experience of personal independence, the time when you test yourself and the outcomes of your decisions away from your family. It's another practice period. I just read an article somewhere that said adolescence in the States has been extended now to age twenty-five."

"Right, but not here. Out of all of the people I know

my husband is the only one who studied outside of Puebla, and I probably wouldn't have been able to marry him if he hadn't done that for himself. So there are things those women and I are never going to get past, but they also become a binding point with other American women, even though some of them came as missionaries, and ended up getting married and staying. That impulse to come to México is something we ignore, and the fact that we were able to do it is our starting-off point."

"But not what went before."

"Right."

And this thought was right on the mark. There is no shortage of retirees in México, but they have traveled to survey this location and that, and settled on a spot and moved, luggage, cars, furniture and all. My two new friends in Puebla had fallen through a rabbit hole, like Alice in Wonderland, coming down for reasons apart from reinventing themselves or relaunching their lives into a different kind of orbit. Were they accidental expats? In Lamar and Ron, we have already seen the eco-expats in San Luis de la Paz, where you don't leave a footprint on the culture.

"I think that women here are very different," Lenya went on, perhaps waiting for me to digest this. "I was educated to go out into the world, and told that if you get hurt you get hurt. You are stronger because of it. Whatever may happen to you, it makes you a better woman, a richer woman, a wiser woman. Here, I keep coming across women who, if they have gone out and been hurt, they would rather *hide* that than use it. To them, those types of experiences make them a less valuable woman."

Looking at her, the expression on her face, made me believe that she lived by this.

"Perhaps," I said, "the message here is that, for women, experience outside the home is damaging. There are things you don't want or need to know. I'm sure that can be true in some situations, but not in any general way. It must mostly function as a reason to keep women from making decisions, where their lack of experience makes them unqualified. Like, you don't know the world. My own mother-in-law, who came from Wisconsin, would tell her kids of either gender when they had a rough time, 'Suck it up!' Don't you think you have to own these experiences to learn from them?"

"To an extent. You certainly have to be willing to examine them. You have to be willing to take tools from them also."

Like ballast, this was another one I didn't know. Was the phrase from sociology? Anthropology? The willingness to examine them I took to be equivalent to owning them. The key is to not blame other people for your own mistakes. "Take tools from them?" I repeated.

"As you live somewhere else, as you live in Puebla, every day gives you a new tool to integrate yourself. At this point, people here don't necessarily know I'm American anymore. Just from looking at me, I mean."

"They can see that you're obviously different, but they may not be able to say exactly how."

"And I'm fine with that. I don't want to be labeled as an American, even though there are some things essentially American about me that I can never get rid of, and I don't know that I'm actively trying."

"OK, so there's the expat group of women you knew from school who didn't leave. What can you say about the larger expat group of Americans and Canadians? Any idea about how big it might be?"

"No idea."

"I'm getting the feeling that they're not your community. I've been coming across that in other places too, for example in conversations I recently had in Morelia. People would say, oh yes, there are some, but they can't recall how many, like it's a group, but not a community. It has never coalesced."

Her expression didn't suggest that she cared much.

"I really don't know. I recently signed up for the newsletter that Rebecca Hurd has been putting out, which gave me an instant sense that there are people out there organizing themselves. But up until then, I thought everyone was a bit of a satellite like me. I can see Americans and Canadians walking around, but I don't know what they're doing here."

Picturing this, I could also see the tourists in San Miguel, dazed, looking in turn from map to building and back to map. Often I offered to help, recalling my own confused entrance years ago when I was a tourist in México. Not that I wasn't still a tourist in some ways.

"And you don't particularly miss a community like that. Or is there something…"

"I wouldn't necessarily look for it. I actually don't mind being alone."

"And that was true of you back in the States too."

"Yes, it was always true of me. I have very strong friendships reaching back to kindergarten, so with Skype and email…I'm also in a position to travel frequently—I don't want to sound like I'm going back all the time, but whenever it's really necessary I go, like to weddings or to visit my parents. I don't feel closed off from that, and I don't know how much room I have for more relationships here."

"You didn't tell me how you met Manuel. I know it was at school, but we didn't get into the specifics."

"No, because we didn't go to the same school. We saw each other first at a party in México City before I even started my studies. I guess he liked me instantly."

"I guess he must have. You wouldn't have been the normal enchilada he might encounter."

She didn't respond to this.

"Even though we didn't officially meet at that first party, I remember him, so there was something there. I can still recall what he was wearing. We didn't even have a conversation that night. Later he offered to bring me to Puebla. He was going home for the weekend to visit his parents and he offered to take me along so I could visit the universities. That's how it started."

"What is your relationship with your Manuel's family?"

"Anyone who comes here and sees how close they are says, 'How do you deal with that? Isn't it too much?' By close I mean physically present. I do also have an emotional nearness with my sisters-in-law, my mother-in-law, but I haven't adopted them. They're my in-laws, and I'm happy to have such warm and generous people. For people of my generation it's hard to comprehend why someone would come here. I think for the older generation, like my parents, and my husband's parents' generation, it's even more difficult. That essential barrier that I mentioned before is an issue with my extended family."

"Do you think your husband's parents would have given some thought earlier to the person he might end up marrying? What she might be like? Are they from an upper class or business class background? Class is more rigid here."

"Well, neither of them grew up with money. My father-in-law worked very hard and everything he was able to give us he made in his lifetime. Of course my husband is happy to help grow what he already worked on. But I'm sure that they never imagined he would marry a foreigner."

"I can see that." I had also noticed that she never used the word *gringo*, even though it was in such wide usage where

I came from in San Miguel that it had long ago lost any negative connotation.

"Probably they still hoped he would marry someone who really understands him and would help him to build his ambitions beyond the boundaries that are inherent in being a *poblano*. He was already looking for that on his own, which is what took him to México City. But he could've just come back and married someone from here. Then his world would've shrunk again instead of expanding." Her look suggested he had made the right decision.

"What was it about you, do you think?"

She gave me a wry smile. "Well, I think I just called him out on his bullshit on our first date, and that had never happened to him before."

"And he liked that."

"Yes. He has two sisters and a very strong mother. I think he needed to choose a woman who would be even stronger, which I feel like I have been able to do. Like hold my own, because they would be very influential if I submitted to that."

I could imagine some of this give and take, even if she didn't detail it. "What do you do for amusement here?"

"I used to go to the symphony and art galleries and all that. When you're in New York or San Francisco it's all there and often free, so then it's easy, but I haven't done that in Puebla and sometimes I complain that there's no culture here. But I haven't gone out to look for it. We really just kind of cook meat and drink beer. We invite people over or we go to other people's houses and rehash the conversation from last week." This suggested a routine that wasn't that fascinating on the face of it, yet under the skin it conveyed an engagement that was not easily achieved for most expats trying to connect socially in México. Intermarriage made all the difference.

"How does your family feel about you living here?"

"Both of my parents always say, 'I can't figure out whether I did something right or something wrong.' I have three brothers. For the ones who are old enough to be independent, neither of them are even near San Francisco anymore. My parents felt they chose that location and everyone would want to stay there. But instead, it's a city that teaches you how to be able to live anywhere."

"How does that happen?"

"My family was among those who were willing to make sacrifices to allow us to mature in a liberal capital. We grew up eating and appreciating a wide variety of food, and observing and thanking the people who provided us with that diversity. We ate dim sum, Israeli persimmons, dragon rolls, burritos and tacos, Northern and Southern Italian food, pho and cellophane noodles, Dungeness crab and fried calamari, organic baby spinach, among many other things. Being exposed to so many different foods taught me about being open-minded and nonjudgmental. There were also the elements of universality and globalization in the early knowledge that every cultural group needs to eat, and reveres the process of food preparation and consumption. It made me feel like part of a whole. Also, Thanksgiving dinners, Passover Seders, and Christmas Eve meals all required both a spiritual and an intellectual appetite in addition to an empty stomach. So I guess a deeper, first-hand understanding of how food unites people has allowed me to enter into this Méxican culture and certainly into my husband's family. As a child I just assumed the whole world lived in a place like San Francisco, where diversity (at least back then) was the norm. I didn't actually appreciate the place my parents chose to raise me until I left it to go to college in 1999. My first and only year at BU was an awful awakening to what the rest of the USA is really like: people who hate entire ethnicities and who don't know what a pomegranate is.

"As for me living here now, they're fine with it. It's a difficult trip for them. It's a seven-hour flight to visit my brother in Florida, and a six hour-flight to visit my other brother in DC. It's a four-hour flight to México City, and Manuel and I always go and pick them up. They're both dedicated to what they do and they don't visit us very often. They both love Manuel. On his first visit with me to San Francisco he told them that he really appreciated that they had taught their daughter how to live somewhere else because he really wanted to be with me. He also said he was going to work very hard so that I could visit. My dad is a softy anyway."

"Well, that cut some ice."

"And they're comfortable here They know Puebla."

"And do you go back often?"

"As often as I can. I don't like to go just for a couple of days, especially with a baby. But we do winter holidays and any big event that comes up. There were a couple years when it was three events a year. There's a lot of movement. We try to see them at least every four months."

"Tell me about your name, Lenya." This, from our earlier emails, was a subject we had both been waiting for.

"OK. I think my name is interesting, because Lenya, my first name, is a reference to some reading my parents did about the flappers and Lotte Lenya. It's also a mix of my grandmothers' names, one of which was Greek, Elena, and it's mixed a little with Lena, who was some great aunt or something on my father's side They brought it all together into this name that already existed through Lotte Lenya."

"And they recognized that reference." I didn't want to tell her that Lotte Lenya's real name was Karoline Blamauer. This was an extremely odd coincidence because my last interview in journalism, before I gave up writing entirely, was with Lotte Lenya in November of 1963. She was playing the Guthrie Theater in Minneapolis in *Brecht on Brecht*, a compilation of material from her late husband, Kurt Weill, and Bertolt Brecht. Lenya herself had premiered *Three Penny Opera* in Berlin in 1927, and repeated it on Broadway many years later. Smoking a cigarette in a long holder that evening, she told me how she had just finished shooting a James Bond movie with Sean Connery where she was the villain, *From Russia With Love*.

"Yes, but I wasn't named directly after her."

"Right, but it still hit me like a brick when I saw your name."

"But that's because I know you have a personal connection with her. (From the emails again.) But people who haven't heard of her, wouldn't even think about it. So that first name speaks to my Greek and German heritage, and then Bloom, which comes from the people who emigrated from Poland. They had changed it at Ellis Island. My name gives you my whole ethnic background. It's all laid out there. Here everyone has to have two last names right? Your mother's name and your father's."

"Your parents were working in the theater in Toronto at one time?"

"My mom is a theater person, always was. They were doing a version of *Brecht on Brecht* that my mom acted in and directed while my dad was at a polytechnic university there. That's also how they met. My dad was playing the guitar for some performance. Everywhere they went, as my dad collected degrees, my mom did theater for some time after they were married."

"How has living here affected your view of the U.S.?"

Lenya gave me an uneasy look. "I don't feel all that comfortable in the States when I go back now. There's something different about it."

"I think the crime is there more than here," I said. "I tell people to come down to México if they want to be safe. Or is it the values?" But it was more than that. I felt it too. North of the border something was changing gradually, and not for the better.

"My brother accused me of having latched onto a kind of moral relativity that people have living here. I found that offensive, but on the other hand, it's true in a way. I feel like here you can get or do anything you want if you're convincing and forceful enough. That was one of the first things my mother-in-law taught me. I was going to the grocery store and people were constantly cutting inline in front of me. She told me a nasty phrase to use. And she showed me how it's done. You have to be a little bit louder and pushier, which is a good lesson for me, because I can be a yes man. Her phrase doesn't translate well, and it's very abrasive in the States. The way I drive and maybe the way I ask to have things done reads as abrasive up there. But I can't do things one way here and another way there, especially not with a child."

"You see this question as being about how you've drifted away from certain systems of getting things done."

"I don't know if it's been a drift exactly. I feel like I have to work on those things consciously to be able to maintain the essentials. There are habits that you assume in being here that just help you fit in. My day-to-day life runs more smoothly. It makes me feel less foreign."

"And as those systems get more and more ingrained, they become less like the way you would do things in the States."

"Yes. For example I've seen Méxicans who go to the States and behave differently there than they do here. I always thought that was a weird kind of hypocrisy, because if I'm going to raise a bicultural daughter, I need to have one way of behaving that works in both places, but in order to have it both work there and work here it never works quite right in either place. You sacrifice something."

"Most compromises involve sacrifice on both ends. Do you feel safe here?"

"I do. My behavior in keeping myself safe has changed a lot. I've become more paranoid about everything. I think about the way I moved around México City when I first came, and I feel like maybe my innocence protected me a little bit. I did things I would never do now. My husband has told me again and again, don't do this or that. Do not leave the house without money in your wallet in case you need to pay someone off. Or you can't leave your car unlocked, or you shouldn't pull up to a stop light with your window rolled down. These things are now unconscious; I just do them. But I do feel safe in Puebla. I've never been a witness to anything that would make me feel unsafe."

"Why do you think it's better to live here than in México City? Is the proximity of family part of that?"

"We ended up living here because everything my husband had was here. While their construction company does have a central office in the capital, they've been working to move everything down here. My father-in-law is in México City Monday through Thursday. That's why my husband was able to be here, and he's in charge of the south-central eastern area of México. They also work in Tabasco and Oaxaca."

"Are they building residential mainly?"

"No. Real estate is my husband's specialty. His father is a civil engineer. He does projects like government buildings and roadways. A lot of bus stations and their maintenance all the way down to Chiapas and out to the Yucatán. They also have an office in Mérida."

"What has living in Mexico taught you?"

This was met with a sigh.

"It's been a huge exercise in patience, which has ended up serving me well as a mom too. It also taught me how to shut up and listen. There was a time when my Spanish wasn't good enough and I had to be quiet. That doesn't come naturally to me. It's also taught me a lot about what my own family gave me. I've had to choose what I wanted to maintain from that. That's what I'm ultimately going to contribute to my children. So for them, that's what being an American is going to mean. After all those years, that will be what I've communicated to them, those things that will make up the American half of their identity. If it even gets to be half."

"Have we gotten to the nuts and bolts of your experience here? Is there something else that might help to illuminate it?"

"It's important to say that after a certain point living here stops being merely an experience and it becomes your life. So when I talk to people in the States and say I'm visiting from México, they're confused by that. Like why would you want to do that? Another reaction is, you don't look Méxican. I always say, I'm not Méxican, I just live there.

"Also from my extended family in the States, but not my nuclear family, there are a lot of misconceptions about what my life here might be like. But for me, coming to live in México never meant having to sacrifice my quality of life. Obviously I chose someone who would be able to take care of me the way I would've expected. Having my own house, and being able to send my daughter to a fine school. Also to have my own car, nice things, and I didn't have to sacrifice any of that. It sounds really superficial, but it's about comforts, and it means I don't have to sacrifice on a daily basis. When we built this house I told my husband, I don't want to worry about the gas. And if it's raining I want to be able to still dry the clothes. These day-to-day comforts allow me to forget that this is an experience and let it feel like life. Having these comforts keeps me from having to constantly face the fact that I'm living someplace totally different that I never expected to live in, and just focus on the living itself."

Lenya folded her hands on the tabletop and waited for more, but I had nothing else. In my mind I was already writing the chapter. One unique perspective that she brought to the story was that she had a young child.

I don't often find this degree of introspection talking to people about the expat experience. Lenya was fully as thoughtful as Rebecca, who wrote about the Puebla experience regularly, yet the two women came across quite differently. She gave me a ride back downtown and the conversation returned to more general things. I sometimes wondered whether people looked back on their conversations with me and tried to remember the specifics of what they'd said.

When we said goodbye near the *zócalo* she let me off and I strolled through the streets, looking for a place to have lunch. Puebla has a unique architectural style, featuring decorative brick and tile work, elaborate window surrounds and Juliet balconies. The central district is equally as interesting as Morelia, although it seemed to me a touch less formal. Anyone looking to live in a city that offered those things that México does so well could build a comfortable place here. Without intending to, Rebecca and Lenya had both found their point of engagement and acceptance through marriage. It was a fusion of cultures for each of them. This connection had reduced their need for an expat support group, although this was a bit truer of Lenya than Rebecca, who reached out to that community through her website. In any case, I had no other examples of intermarriage in these conversations, although one or more might be coming up. That fact alone was clearly another way to connect, if not to be completely absorbed by this culture. México has a long tradition of accepting eccentricity, and that would easily include having a point of origin in a different country.

CHAPTER 6

OLD ZACATECAS

In mid October I arrived in Zacatecas on the same day as the Dalai Lama, but with much less fanfare. I was on the first class bus again. He was headed for a sold-out appearance at the convention center and I was going to a one-on-one conversation with a man I'd never met before, Barry Griefer. Coming into town I tried to think who might be the equivalent iconic person for the United States, one who embodied all the aspirations and finer spiritual qualities of the nation, just as the Dalai Lama did for Tibet. All I could think of was Donald Trump.

Once again, this city is an old mining town, this time set in the lower clouds at just short of 8,000 feet elevation, in a district of other old mining towns, most of which have mines that still produce. However, designation as a World Heritage site has its price, and the old Eden Mine at the edge of Zacatecas was shut down with about 40% of its ore untapped. Tourists can still go inside and see the conditions where the miners worked, some of them children, and at night they can rock out at the subterranean disco.

México has no shortage of gemlike colonial towns, and I've visited many of them. Each is different, although they mostly sprang from the same set of desires: to exploit mineral wealth, to subjugate and convert the indigenous natives to Catholicism, and to prop up with massive silver ingots a Spanish monarchy fighting the evil of upstart Protestantism throughout Europe. That is a conflict that has now been mostly worked out, one way or another.

Far down the historical road to the present day, this legacy has bequeathed us a lot of played out mines (remember Pozos), a racially mixed population that straddles two cultures with varying degrees of comfort, and a heritage of ruined or restored townhouses and haciendas from earlier centuries that speak to us of a seductive and nearly irresistible lifestyle now long gone.

A certain kind of expat would like to step in and take up that lifestyle again. The closest we can get to it now is to restore some of the old houses and haciendas. The ancient skills are still widely practiced, and almost anything from the earlier periods can be reproduced or renewed.

I already knew that Barry Griefer, my contact in Zacatecas, was not in this group, since he was renting. I had tried to scrape up a tiny community of expats here without much success, and if there were four or six more, none of them was interested in talking to me. Even Barry told me he had scanned my website to see whether I was the real deal. I told him via email that this was not a tabloid exposé, and I only wanted to tell his story.

We met at the Hotel Reyna Soledad on Calle Tacuba, just two blocks from where I was staying at the Emporio. The Reyna Soledad is a sixteen room building with a yellow façade and a four star rating. Three tall windows framed in stone face the street on the second floor behind a wrought iron balcony, and at the street level, shops selling leather, cell phone accessories, and one simply called *Glow* share the front with the hotel entrance. Barry was waiting for me inside by the desk. He is a man of average height, seventy years old. That day he was wearing camouflage pants, a striped green shirt and a safari hat.

Inside, the rooms are arranged around two small courtyards, and on the second floor we found a table overlooking the rear one farther off the street. Potted bougainvillea and small agave covered most of the surfaces around us. I opened by talking about arriving in the city, how surprising it was as I saw it for the first time.

"For this project I've spent some time in Morelia and Puebla, both cities with great historic cores, but I'm amazed at how beautiful this city is. Because I come from a place that has 10,000 expats, the first thing I started asking myself was why there aren't more expats living here? Is it only that it's unknown to people?"

Zacatecas is not on the great crossroads of north-central México, the principal arteries going north into Texas. Barry settled into his chair.

"Yet, you'd be startled at the crowds that gather here for big events. You might also be surprised at the range of origins of the tourists that come here. Maybe it's only that—and this is only a guess, I haven't given it much thought—that Americans tend to go where there's flash, bright lights and lots of crowds. That's not Zacatecas, except for four weeks a year."

Across the street from my hotel two truck trailers full of equipment were parked along the small Plaza de Armas edging the old cathedral. I think of plazas in México as being huge, like México City or Puebla, or about a block in size, as in San Miguel. The Plaza de Armas was only half a square block. This may be explained by the topography—it would be hard to find a larger level space in the center of the city. My study of the map on the way in had suggested there were numerous other parks spread throughout the city.

"There is something going on here now with street theater."

"I don't know if that's a unique event, but the performances they bring in for this week—it looks like there are about ten events going on today—are all unique in one way or another. I get to maybe two or three of them each time and they all blow me away. I don't get to them all because I'm either involved with something outside of Zacatecas, or I'm just too lazy. In this town it's easy to move around on foot, bus or taxi, but you do need to know where you're going."

"Do you have a car?"

"No, that's one of the reasons I live in Zacatecas, I don't want to have one. Here they speak more English than you might think, but they don't advertise it. So you might feel that if you don't speak Spanish well you could get in trouble, but you're not. If you do as people do in every other city in the world, go where the other people are going and don't wander alone down dark alleys, you're as safe here as you are in Plains, Georgia."

I smiled at the simile. Peanut country in the red dirt versus silver in the rocks.

"What brought you here?"

"I had worked in Saltillo, in 1982-85. During that time we had plenty of vacation, and we got to wander around México." Saltillo is the capital of the state of Coahuila, and it isn't far from Monterrey, in the northeastern part of the country.

"You say we. Were you married at that time?"

Barry gave me a wry look.

"I was married and had two teenage kids. Zacatecas was a place we hit as we traveled, but because of the weather at the time—it was the coldest winter on record, and there was no heat anywhere in town—we spent most of the time driving around in the car with the heater on. It left an impression on me, nonetheless. When I decided I wanted to retire, I wanted a place in México—I had decided that a long time before—but I didn't want it too hot or too cold. I had been back to Saltillo for a visit in the summer of 2000. They used to call it the 'air-conditioned city,' but it had turned hot and humid. I guess that was from global warming, and so I ruled it out fairly quickly. I got to Zacatecas and it was a combination of the place where I stayed, a hostel not more than three blocks from here, and the owner and the people that I met while I was there, from all over the world. The only thing here that's a bit difficult for me is the altitude. Fifty years of smoking, which I quit in 2011, have caught up with me."

We were sitting there in that small hotel at 8,000 feet. I could still feel the difference between that altitude and San Miguel at 6,400, and I hadn't smoked in many years. We make our choices, and timing is always part of it.

"Other than that, it gets a little cold in the winter, but if you go outside on a clear day, the sun keeps you warm. We have people walking outside in their shirtsleeves in the middle of February here. Those are only the natives, though. Weather-wise, this was about as ideal as I could find in México.

"Living in this town, the main things for me now are the weather, the architecture—just wandering through the streets every now and then I come across something I haven't seen or noticed before. It could be simply a business with a different decoration out front. The next thing is the culture, and you've seen that out front with the street theater. There are four specific weeks in the year when culture runs rampant in this town. In Semana Santa (Holy Week), they have a big festival—everything from hard rock and opera to orchestral concerts. Then there's the folklore festival, where groups come in not only from México, but all over the world."

"Dancing and musical groups?"

"Definitely dancing, singing. There's plenty going on,

even if it's only ballroom dancing on the plaza. It's something to go to. I'm not dancer but you get into the swing of things as you watch".

"I've never been in a major city in México before where there's no big central plaza. It's always a focal point of city life. As wonderful as Zacatecas is, it feels to me like there's a void at the center, even though I do realize how difficult it would have been to level a larger area."

"Well there is one, but it's fairly new. It's the Plaza Bicentenario. It's on the main highway in and out of town, on the site of the old bus terminal. The former governor had it razed. They built a big plaza and the municipal market was there for about a year because the old building was just about falling down."

There are also a number of fine green spaces less close in, like the Alameda.

"Where are you living now?"

The topography of Zacatecas is that of a town laid out in terraces along a broad inside curve skirting the slope of a basin. The principal streets parallel each other at successive levels, and while the up and down communicating passages are occasionally accommodating of cars, they are more commonly pedestrian routes with steps or ramps. The effect creates interesting vistas unencumbered by traffic, except at distant intervals. I thought of Barry's earlier statement that he didn't care to have a car, and truly, cars wouldn't always be the best way to get to your destination in Zacatecas.

"I live about four or five hundred feet up the hill. I usually walk down and take a twenty-peso ($1.60) taxi ride back up. The people here are enough accustomed to tourists to treat them with courtesy. They know that part of their financial wellbeing is wrapped up with tourism. The ten or so Americans who live here get to be known, and they're treated like welcome, long-term guests. There's a certain provincial air to Zacatecas and it takes a measure of good luck to become a member of the community here. I've had some luck in that area."

I noted the pride with which he said this. I could easily believe that not everyone got in here.

"So you're in it now."

"Well, not really in it, but I'm on the edges. One of the nicest things that happened to me here is that one night the owner of the hostel where I was staying originally, and rented an apartment from later, called me up and said, 'Would you like to go to a party? It turned out it wasn't so much a party as a small procession of about fifty people from the Plaza de Armas to another plaza on the east side of town. It was really a reception for the mayor of Medellin, Colombia. That's the kind of thing that happens here that would never happen in the United States."

I could believe that. "What did you do for GM here?"

"I was manager of data processing for them at their Saltillo plant until '85, and that's when my association with them ended."

If up to this point I had pictured Barry as working in assembly, this is where the truth caught up with me.

"And you went back to the States from there?"

"Right, and I went into a different industry. Roger Smith was chairman of GM at that time and he thought he was getting screwed by the people in systems, so he bought a systems company, Ross Perot's EDS, and he threw everybody who was in systems at GM into EDS. How would you like to be kicked in the ass like that, when it was like saying that your last twelve years of work weren't worth anything?"

I had no response to this, except to change the direction of the conversation.

"Did you look at other places for retirement besides Zacatecas?"

A sheepish look met this question. "I was going to. I landed here in May of 2008. I fell in love with the place and decided I didn't need to look any further."

I could see this, but think of Barry's background. He had worked for several years in Saltillo, but Zacatecas is a showstopper. The obvious problem is that if you need an expat support group to relate to, it's off the map. It does not exist here. Spanish language skills are a must.

"What do you do here that you couldn't do in the U.S.?"

"Well, I can hobnob with the mayor of Medellin, Colombia."

"That would be one thing."

"I met a lady less than a month after I got here in September of 2008. She's from Zamora and we decided to hook up; that lasted a couple of years."

Zamora is a town about the same size as Zacatecas located in the northwestern part of Michoacán, southeast of Lake Chapala.

"Then we decided that two stubborn individuals of a certain age in the same house didn't work that well, but we're still good friends. Last June she called and said, 'Hey, my sisters and a niece and nephew are going up to the northeastern part of the U. S.; New York, Philadelphia, Boston, D.C., and Niagara Falls.' She hinted around at it long enough that it became a left-handed invitation to come along. It wasn't that I was shepherding those people, it was more like I was someone who smoothed over the rough edges on the package tour we bought. A sidelight, not part of the tour, was one day we went to the place where I was born, Bensonhurst in Brooklyn. And Coney Island for Nathan's Hot Dogs. To see their faces light up when they saw things like the house I grew up in, the primary school I went to, the Brooklyn Bridge at night."

The taste and texture of Brooklyn is still on Barry's tongue and in his mind. I can hear it and I imagine he can still taste it. The original Nathan's, at Surf and Stillwell in Coney Island, became Nathan's Famous and went ballistic.

"It turns out that their first cousin is the mayor of Zamora," he went on. "So we spent the evening of Independence Day, and el Grito, in the enclosure of City Hall in Zamora. After the Grito we attended a reception and supper in City Hall. It was mostly the mayor's staff, friends, and family." His grin recalled the pride he took in attending this event.

El Grito is the annual reenactment of the original call to independence in Dolores Hidalgo. We saw this before when I passed the church where it happened on the way to San Luis de la Paz. Every city in México celebrates its own version.

"How big is Zamora?"

"It's getting close to 200,000 people now. It's growing because of the berry business; strawberries, and blueberries exported to the U. S. In Grand Central station, one of the highlights of our recent tour, the same brand was exported there."

"Did you find that traveling with her reenergized that connection?"

I was thinking that extending her invitation to Barry was not the act of someone determined to hold him at arm's length.

"Yes and no. We're still very close but we're going to be distant again. She's the widow of an American that she met when she was working in California several years ago. Her family has a business there in Zamora, but there is really no place for her in it. She only earns spending money. She decided based on her experiences eight or ten years ago in

California that she could do better up there."

"What keeps you engaged here?" The city of Zacatecas is gorgeous, but a person had to do more than just stroll about appreciating the architecture and the mood—although perhaps not. Retirement means different things to different people.

"That's a difficult one for me, because my objective is to do as little as possible. The kind of thing that keeps me engaged is some new cultural event that I might happen upon. There's a Casa Municipal de Cultura here, and they have events and exhibits throughout the year. I wander by there from time to time. If, for example, there's a sculpture exhibit, I can spend a couple of hours forgetting about the rest of the world. Or they're putting on a modern dance exhibition, or somebody is working in an engraving shop—they have one off to the side—I'll wander in and see what he's doing and we start up a conversation. That kind of pace is the life I was looking for and the one I found here. I spend a lot of time on the Internet with people in México or in the States. People I met in Europe. I get into arguments over politics on Facebook."

"That's easy enough to do."

"I wouldn't say my life is reclusive, since I get out when the spirit moves me. I like a lot of solitude."

This reminded me of the name of the hotel where we were sitting, Reyna Soledad. It meant either Queen Soledad, where Soledad is a woman's name, and a not uncommon one, or it meant the lonely queen, or it may have been something more personal and sentimental to the owner. I missed seeing Barry's apartment because I liked to place these conversations in a context like home, but he hadn't been eager to do that, and I was fine with having it at this small hotel.

"How would you describe your neighborhood?

What's it like?"

"I think you could call it typical fifteen hundreds that has been upgraded to the twenty-first century, but it still looks old. It's pretty typical of the *centro historico*. There are a few houses that are big and obviously well maintained. Then there are medium-size houses that are not so well maintained. The focus of the neighborhood is a large elementary school with a kindergarten behind. There is a big truck body parked against the school that is a lunchroom and school supply store at the same time. Across the street is a guy who specializes in repairing Volkswagen bugs. He does it from his own house. Ten or twenty steps up the street are some little *abarrotes*."

Abarrotes are often hole-in-the-wall groceries that operate with minimal capital, although they can also be larger.

"There are probably a dozen of them within a four-block radius."

"What's your day like in that community?"

"Well, I get up at seven, take my meds, make a little breakfast, check the email to see if there's anything I need to attend to right away, or I may go out to any number of places where I can get fresh tamales, *gorditas*, enchiladas. I also might go to McDonald's."

"What would you change about Zacatecas?"

"I have told some people in government about this idea. I would like to see a single website, in an easy-to-use format, that lists every event that you could either categorize as cultural, touristic, civic, or even a demonstration by a company that teaches gymnastics. We actually hit on that once by accident and it was great."

"So there's no central listing of events."

"There are several websites, a couple of them from the government, and some private ones that attempt to put out a calendar, but they're incomplete."

"You've been here since 2008, and before that you lived in Saltillo from '82 to '85. How do your relatives react to your living here? Maybe by now it seems normal to them."

"They think it's a great idea."

"Do they visit?"

"One did. It's not that far from the border, but it's a little difficult for my kids to schedule time to come here. My younger son does get to work in México from time to time. He's the Latin American manager for a software company that produces equipment and x-ray systems for cancer treatment. He got down here for a few days. Then we decided it's my turn to go up north."

"Do you get back up there much?"

"No." I had trouble reading his laugh. Was it apologetic? Ironic? "My travel is not as extensive as I wanted it to be, and it's pretty much confined to México."

"How has living here affected your view of the U.S.?"

He gave me a careful look. "I'm going to assume you're not CIA or NSA."

I gave him one back. "I don't think you can assume that, but I'm just a working journalist, trying to pay the rent."

"But look at what the working journalists are doing up in the States right now."

I realized that I might have been too quick to identify with this group without some qualification. "I'm a *real* working free lance journalist, even though I write fiction too. But I'm objective, and although I also write feature magazine articles, I'm not affiliated with any news organization."

"Ah, a journalist in the old meaning of the word."

"I hope so. I believe in the writer's ethic. You respect your reader by telling the truth as you really see it." Sometimes, if rarely, the subject of these conversations likes to turn the tables on me and ask a question or two. I don't mind. Barry was ready to move on. I felt I'd been vetted.

"Americans are so damned provincial. They don't know what's going on outside their neighborhood, much less outside their country. The nonsense that's going on now in the United States—I don't care what your political viewpoint is—there's no good explanation for it."

I nodded. "I've searched for explanations too and I don't have one." I didn't know which particular nonsense he referred to, but there was no shortage to choose from. However, there was none that I cared to put into this conversation, although I'd posted a number of blogs about it. It occurred to me that in my main writing, my books, I mostly wrote about México and things that happened here.

"This occurred to me in the last few days because I was down in Zamora visiting my lady friend. Polarization was built into the United States right from the get-go. There were slave states and free states. The Constitution and the organization of government is obviously built to cause gridlock instead of having people come to blows over the polarization and doing any more damage. That's what we're seeing today. That's the best I can come up with."

I had watched the developing gridlock with dismay, but I hadn't thought of it that way, an intentional paralysis. If so, it had worked. Even observing the government with no political party bias, which is where I come from, results in a confusing stew of reactions and interpretations.

"That's an interesting take on it. Do you miss having an expat support community here?"

Barry chuckled, as if I had asked whether he missed Ovaltine or Studebakers.

"Why would I want one? I got here speaking as much Spanish as I really needed. Even if I didn't speak it that much, I could've found people on the street that could help me. I had a built-in support group for when I needed it in the owner of the hostel where I stayed at first. A great guy, and in this size town everybody knows everybody. I needed a dentist and he pointed me in the right direction. At one point I needed a computer monitor fixed under warranty and he knew who to go to. Now, the owner of this hotel is a good resource for someone to go to in you need to get something done, even if it's as simple as putting a zipper on a jacket."

"So, when I write this I'm going to describe you as a sturdy independent sort. It's Bensonhurst Brooklyn meets old México, and they fall in love. That's you here with no problem, and the independence part would be equally true in the States, wouldn't it?"

"Exactly." Barry's arms flew up in an indefinite gesture. "The last place I lived in the States was Las Vegas. I'm not one who roams the casinos twenty-four hours a day. If you're not going to the casinos, there isn't all that much to interest you in Las Vegas that isn't perfectly cookie-cutter, vanilla flavor; the same thing you find every place you go. Here, there are about six different places I can get *posole*." (A hominy stew with pork or a variety of other elements.) "Each one depends on who made it. The same thing is true with all the traditional Méxican cuisine. You can walk into a business and it's a local business. The owner is completely invested in that business, whether you're an American or a German or an Israeli, or an Indian. They treat you like real people. So I can get things done by going to the locals. There is a certain code here, though, and you do have to know people well enough to trust them, and that goes for expat or not." (Barry went on to explain about finding an internist here through the hostel owner, getting an opinion, and then having a second opinion in the U.S., which supported the Méxican opinion.)

"How do you react to the American news media?"

"As for the American media, it sounds trite at this point, but if it bleeds, it leads. They've got to find something they can make look like it's bleeding, even when it's not."

"Would you recommend Zacatecas to other people as a place to retire?"

"I would if they can go into it with eyes open. This is a place where you pretty much live on your own. You make your contacts and your friends, and they're almost certainly not going to be Americans, except for maybe one or two if you happen to bump into them. You need to be ready to take problems in stride, and to work through them. Not necessarily be patient, but be accepting of the way things are. Enjoy the uniqueness that Zacatecas has to offer. The people I know here are retired and loving it."

"Do you feel safe here?"

"Yes, perfectly. There have been a couple of isolated incidents, but they were far from where I live."

"What does it cost to live here?"

"I could get by on $500 a month if I had to."

I struggled to find words. "I'm stunned."

"And that's not bare bones, that's living comfortably but without any luxuries. That's one of the principal reasons I'm living in México."

I sat there shaking my head, nearly mute. I've done enough of these conversations to rarely be surprised, yet this was a stopper. People in Morelia had quoted me $2,000. Later I went to Barry's website and saw that he took several trips a year on average, and not just within México, as he had suggested. This would explain his fiscal restraint at home.

"People say to me all the time, 'Well, you always talk to the rich people. You never talk to anyone who needs to get by on social security.' It sounds like you could cruise along forever without touching your capital."

"My social security would more than cover my expenses here. I also have a private pension. In total I'm living on less than $20,000 a year, because I'm splitting my pension with my ex. I'm not complaining."

"What has living in México taught you?"

"I guess the most important thing I've learned is to take things in stride. If you're impatient, try not to show it. You can stand up for what you know is right, but don't get in people's faces. You can use strong language, but don't insult them and don't make it personal. If you can avoid that you can work through just about everything."

"Any issues with mail here? You're using the regular Mexican mail system?"

"Very little. I don't get much physical mail, hardly any. I even told AARP to stop sending their magazine, because if I want to read something I can do it online. I have a post office box in McAllen, Texas that I'm going to give up at the end of this year, because mail does get to me here, like my telephone bill. Anything that I want to bring into México I do myself physically, because you can't trust to have it sent here."

"How does it come down here then?"

"I go up and get it."

"I'll bet that doesn't happen too often."

"I make about eight round trips a year. I see a couple of doctors up there too. My only fear about medicine down here is that I might get into a situation where I think I understand the Spanish, but I really don't. As far as their competence, I have no problems. I have Seguro Popular (a government health insurance program that's extremely reasonable), and my gatekeeper or primary care physician is a guy who knows his stuff."

"What do the locals do for a living here? What's the business structure of this town?"

"There are people here who are safety managers for mining companies. Tourism is big too, but mining is the biggest industry."

"Any manufacturing?"

"Yes, but I'm not sure where it's centered. There's a company that builds parts for a Brazilian aircraft manufacturer. There are also some auto parts makers that sell to U.S. manufacturers. One makes wiring harnesses for pickup trucks."

"What should people be aware of if they're considering living in Zacatecas?"

"The altitude, the weather. There are good and bad sides to the weather. It has snowed here."

"Would you say it does not snow every season?"

"Definitely not. The last snow was two years ago, and that was the first time in twelve years."

"And it lasted?"

"A day or a day and a half."

"So the real problem is the absence of central heating if it's cold enough to snow." I was also thinking of the 8,000-foot altitude here.

"But you can overcome that with space heaters. The cost of gas is not that high. The altitude can be a barrier for people who are otherwise healthy. The other issue is that you better have survival Spanish if you want to get out and around on your own. That's about it."

"It's a truly beautiful place."

"Right, and it has its own unique character. It's not a Disney World type of restoration. The cracks and blemishes are all exposed."

"So coming here was the right decision."

"For me, yes. I may have to move to a lower altitude at some point, but I would do that very reluctantly."

As I stepped out onto Calle Tacuba outside, my mind was still reeling. The idea that Barry Griefer could live on so little money made me think I had hit one of those places in México that still had Méxican prices. His needs were simple, I told myself. He was an easy-going guy who had settled in a gorgeous spot to play out his retirement on a minor key. I hadn't asked, but I was certain he must have an INAPAM card, a seniors' discount card that got people into cultural events at a reduced price or even free, and gave them half-price fares on the great bus system here. It wouldn't even cost much to go up to McAllen.

I walked back through a maze of graceful build-ings from the Porfiriato, that period between 1877 and 1911 when Porfirio Díaz was a virtual dictator, and imported both his technology (electrical grid, telegraph, phone system, and railroads), and esthetics from Europe, especially France. The Méxican phone system was set up by a consortium from France and Belgium during that period. The architectural style of the public buildings reflected the official taste of academic Beaux Arts France, not the younger whiplash rebelliousness of Art Nouveau. Yet the scale was intimate and inviting, well suited to a smallish city of about 130,000. For Díaz, it must have seemed like having a framed credential of good taste, and it's held up well. Today the city is clean, well maintained, and relatively free of graffiti. My overall sense was that it presented an attractive alternative to San Miguel for someone with good Spanish skills. And it was certainly much less expensive, al-though San Miguel is still only half the cost of living in the United States.

Earlier in the day, back at the Hotel Emporio, I had watched a television clip showing the arrival of the Dalai Lama at the Zacatecas International Airport. It made me wonder about passport control. Take your sandals off and walk this way, please. His sleek white executive jet swept out of the brilliant sky with a weighty and determined grace I would have expected more from Al Gore than the leader of Tibetan Buddhism. Watching it was slightly disconcerting, although I don't think he could've justified this lifestyle by saying you only go around once.

His presence set up a strange counterpoint to old Zacatecas. What did he see when he looked at it? Was it as exotic to him and his entourage as Tibet looks to us?

That evening, approaching the Quinta Real Hotel by taxi to have dinner, I encountered armed guards out front wearing Kevlar vests, and beyond, a metal detector gate. I realized that this was where the Dalai Lama must be staying, and the reception desk confirmed it with what sounded almost like a hoot when I asked. They weren't going to keep from trumpeting that fact just for mere security reasons. The hotel occupies the entire circle of the seventeenth century San Pedro bullring. Situated next to the graceful aqueduct on the other side, some think it's the best hotel and the best restaurant in town. In any case, the view from my table was spectacular.

At the table next to me, eight monks from the Dalai Lama's entourage were seated, and restraint was not on their menu. Apparently the master was upstairs having room service, granting these devout young bucks some slack time. I won't say what they were eating, since I couldn't make it out and I didn't want to guess. But as one of them leaned forward over the table to pass a condiment to another, I saw he was wearing a wife-beater tee shirt under his dark red robe. How disconcerting was that? I understood that he had to be wearing something next to his skin, but like the question of what lies beneath a Scotsman's kilt, it wasn't necessarily anything I needed to know, even though I try to be an unbiased (and unflappable) observer. When you cultivate an atmosphere of serenity, you need to maintain it. Witnessing this scene felt to me like Zen Buddhism meets *Streetcar Named Desire*. So be it.

Zacatecas may be, as Barry Griefer suggested, a provincial town, but it's not entirely *out of the map* either, as people like to say here. After all, the Dalai Lama saw a good reason to stop there, and so had I.

CHAPTER 7

RETURN TO OAXACA

I have seen Oaxaca with its hair on fire. Late in the month of June of 2006 I flew down to that highly ethnic town to research backgrounds for the fifth book in the Murder in México mystery series I was working on. I found the city in the grimmest of moods. It was my first visit and I was aware of some turbulence there before I arrived, but I could not have predicted what I was walking into. This was a bit more than a year before I moved to México.

Oaxaca is a town known to have strong political feelings—the word *militant* would not overstate its intermittent condition—and labor disputes can get ugly. The teacher's union was on strike over a budget dispute with the Governor of the State of Oaxaca, Ulises Ortiz, and the national presidential election was about to be held on July 2, a Sunday, only days away. The air was electric with extreme tension on both sides.

I had chosen that time to visit because I thought the confluence of these events might give some added pizzazz to a murder mystery, since it provided at least two ways to get killed. Crossfire can have a uniquely ambiguous dynamic when plotting a story, and uncertainty gives any plot momentum. Because I'd never flown that route before, I did not think it was odd that my incoming plane was nearly empty, nor did

I guess it would be full when it left again an hour later. Many one-way tickets going north must have been sold.

Back in Minnesota, my principal news source for Oaxaca had been the Internet, and it was never better than spotty. The U.S. foreign news on television gave the problems there little notice. It didn't even merit a sidebar, so I was in no way prepared for the hornet's nest I walked into when I arrived. My bed and breakfast was on the far edge of the central district, a place lovingly built by an ancient man named Chencho, and at first I saw nothing unusual after I unpacked and walked toward the *zócalo*. About six blocks from my goal I encountered a heavy police presence. No one looked at me as I walked through it. Had I been going the other way, some might have. Then for a while I saw nothing more, but the streets were strangely empty. The storefronts were nearly all shuttered, although it was only early evening on a Wednesday. Political graffiti was everywhere, mostly framed with the words, *Ulises asesino!* (Branding the governor a murderer.) The images usually showed him eviscerating babies, or submerging them in washtubs headfirst. The small hairs on the back of my neck began to stand up as if I had entered a kind of no man's land that the skimpy reports I'd seen online did not sufficiently explain. It was somewhat like a scene from the *The Twilight Zone*.

Two blocks before the edge of the *zócalo*, I was halted by the barricades. Pavers, timbers, and corrugated sheet metal all formed a six-foot-high continuous blockade that allowed access to one person at a time on one end only. I hesitated briefly, playing the smiling, ingratiating, and not too bright intruder, one who was possibly quite lost, watching the striking teachers on the other side looking me over; then I walked in. I didn't raise my arms in the air, but I thought about it. By that point I knew that my trump card was that I didn't look like a cop and I never had. Overhead, strung between the buildings on nylon cords, orange and blue tarps blocked out the sky. People, even whole families, lined the sidewalks cooking over small charcoal braziers. Children are always part of the action here, even when it's a militant standoff. Some pointed at me in surprise. Waving, I returned an uneasy smile as I walked the two remaining blocks to the plaza, where I started talking to people gathered under the trees. The news I discovered was a bit too tense for my research needs.

Three days earlier, the police had killed six people as they cleared the first round of the *zócalo* occupation. Three of these were teachers and the other three were children. All were unarmed. On the following day the teachers returned in multiples of the previous numbers and pushed out the police, who had suddenly become reluctant to kill any more, at least for a while. This was the current impasse I had blundered into. The return of the police was expected at any moment. I did not consider myself a journalist then, but I quickly learn to walk the walk. If being a journalist meant you were uncomfortable on unfamiliar ground in a combat zone, and with a deadline, I had it down.

Until that evening I had found no title for the book, but during that walk I decided to call it *Strike Zone*, after the dominant emotional theme. It was not about baseball.

I spent a week in that crucible of unrest. The police did not return during this period as I gathered my background material and engaged in a number of conversations with the striking teachers. As always, I saw myself as an observer, a term not well-respected by the public, but indispensible when the need to write the truth is the main consideration. The atmosphere continued to crackle with tension, since the return of the authorities was expected at any moment. Over the weeks that followed my departure the death total ballooned to twenty-seven strikers and journalists. (I only learned this several weeks after my return to Minnesota.) The radio station at the university was shut down and the broadcasting equipment demolished. I found myself getting into the rhythm of these tense front lines, I saw myself there again, but I also knew that unstable rhythm could change at any time. The word *incoming* kept returning to my nervous mind, but in this context it could mean only tear gas. Ultimately, the reporter I had been following on the Internet for day-by-day reports of action in the streets was himself killed by the police. My book became once again a mystery, not a chronicle of war.

On Sunday afternoon, the presidential election day, I was the only customer among the outdoor tables of a deserted café overlooking the *zócalo*—now crowded with teachers having a lunch away from home—as I sipped a beer in a coffee cup, since alcohol is not permitted to be served during an election. The waiter appeared now and then to refill it inside, out of view. Although I didn't realize it yet at that time, México is a lawless land, mostly in a good way, but not always when you're lost on a dirt road edging toward the Pacific coast with old maps, and at night. Ten meters away from me a man strolled past carrying a white female store manikin over his shoulder. The enticing buttocks displayed an optimistic attitude as they glistened in the sun. Here, they reflect a different sensibility. It is the rear view of Jennifer Lopez that is welcomed more than that of Kate Moss. Ample more than lean, and abundance over diet and health club. Beyond those observations, I couldn't have begun to guess what this display was about, or how it fit the sour collective mood, other than business as usual no matter what.

As I sat there no other tourists walked by. I felt I must be the sole outsider to witness these events so closely. The locals may not have seen this lethal spasm as unique, but only one in a long series of political ruptures in the daily fabric of

Oaxaca the town, one perhaps more severe than many others. At that time, of course, I had no idea of doing this book.

Now I was back in the city of Oaxaca, after a more than seven-year intermission. Courage, as I had come to know it then, both for myself and those who talked to me for this book, was now simply nothing more than telling the truth as they saw it. This visit to Oaxaca was uncomplicated by politics or demonstrations, and I was able to enjoy the drive into town from the airport, where hundreds of flowering trees were in bloom. It had been an uncomplicated landing—there was not a single other commercial airliner in view at the Oaxaca Airport. The city has an official population of about 250,000, although I've heard estimates of 100,000 more. The reality is often somewhat different, but in any case, it's a comfortable size—large enough to have some sophistication and quality infrastructure, yet small enough to get around in easily, traffic permitting.

It was mid November, and the temperature was in the 70s and 80s Fahrenheit, more welcoming that the chill I'd left behind in San Miguel. I was staying at a bed and breakfast named Casa Ollin, a place we'll revisit in this chapter. Eight blocks away on the northern edge of *centro* I was expecting to meet Jon Swanson. The home he lives in is part of an informal enclave of seven houses on the northern edge of the central district. I found the compound easily enough, but since the houses within all had the same address I was grateful that he had alerted the ground staff to expect me.

All the houses appear to be relatively recent and designed in a more contemporary style that you would find closer in to town. While he rents long term in Oaxaca, he also owns a house in Ann Arbor, Michigan. He divides his time about equally between the two, and his wife was still in the States where she was wrapping up some singing engagements.

At seventy, Jon is trim and affable. He has kept most of his white hair and looks very much like the descendent of Swedish immigrants that he is. He would easily find himself at home on the streets of Minneapolis. His white-painted house is simply furnished. As he made coffee for us in the kitchen he began to speak about his background.

Jon Swanson was bitten by the travel bug early in life, starting with a trip by Icelandic air to Luxembourg when he was twenty-one. After visiting relatives in Sweden, he hitch-hiked through Europe and the Middle East.

"I got as far as Iran before returning through Iraq, Jordan, Palestine, Syria, and Lebanon. My travels inspired an interest in anthropology and later I received my doctorate in that field based on research in Yemen. When I was unable to find work in the 1980s, I turned to social work and was employed in community mental health in a heavily Hispanic neighborhood in Detroit until I retired ten years ago. Along the way I was involved in community organizing and union politics."

"And that road also led you to Oaxaca."

"I first came to Oaxaca after I retired in order to learn Spanish and just kept coming back. I now spend half my year here and that may well increase. The other 50% is passed in Ann Arbor where I live in a cohousing community. I rent my Oaxacan home year round. I love the climate here, which is very similar to highland Yemen, though with more abundant and reliable rainfall. Also like Yemen, Oaxaca enjoys warm days and cool nights. It's close to coffee growing country and that's where the weather is always best.

"I love living in this vibrant city that is at once histori-cal and quite alive. It is a quintessentially Méxican city with a strong indigenous tradition. Proud of its customs and tradi-tions, its people are warm without being obsequious. I love walking around the city visiting the markets and engaging the local people who are unfailingly forgiving of my poor Spanish.

"The city boasts a very good English language library and one can always find English speakers to talk with about a wide range of topics. I enjoy reading, walking, and occasionally writing when I am not overcome with sloth."

We settled in his living room with the coffee.

"Did you look at other places in México before you chose Oaxaca?"

He shook his head. "Not really. I came down here after I left a job where I was a social worker in a neighborhood agency with a largely Hispanic clientele. My first boss was a Méxicana, and then I started working in another unit where the boss was a Peruvian. I felt a need to learn the language, which I wished I had done when I was working. A friend had studied Spanish in Oaxaca, and she said this is a good place to do it. So I came down to study Spanish, and then the first day I was here I met a fellow from Chicago, Don Watanabe. As a social worker, he had a similar background to mine, and he was married to an African American woman, as was I. He had come down to study Spanish and he had the same leftist point of view that I had. We became fast friends. That made life here more interesting to me. I came back here the next year, and the next year after that, for a little longer each time. I've been here now ten or eleven years. I could stay longer than six months a year, but my wife wants to be up north because she likes to sing, being part of several choruses. She's not here now because she's doing some Christmas concerts."

"When I think of Oaxaca I see a strong, well-defined and diverse indigenous presence, and left-leaning politics. Does that agree with your view?"

"I think there is a strong indigenous presence here, although it seems to me that the elites here, as in México as a whole, tend to be more creole, in the sense of being Europeans who were born here. Or people who immigrated. I read an article a few years ago about people who came over after the Spanish Civil War (1936-9), and they were Anarchists and Communists, but now they've become the elites in México."

"Do you see this town as at all magical?"

"It's hard for me to speak to that, because although I've driven through Oaxaca several times, I don't have much familiarity with México as a whole. I spend most of my time right here. This is my point of reference."

"You must find it interesting from the perspective of your anthropological background."

"Yes, the cultural differences. There is a woman I'm doing an *intercambio* with (these are conversations at the library either in Spanish or in English, where one is a native speaker and the other is not). She's preparing to do her English proficiency test. She's very bright—her background is in physics and mathematics. She's a Mixe speaker from the village of Totontepec. It's up on the border with Veracruz. She said to me that I have to come up for the San Sebastian fiesta in January. It's cold then, but I want to go so I can see that area. She's very proud of her language, which is not always the case here. My wife was taking a Spanish class, and her teacher was speaking derisively about indigenous people, and then it turned out that her own grandmother was a native speaker. My wife was upset by the attitude that somehow to be a speaker of an indigenous language might be a handicap. But I think that's pretty common. México was always a country where the constitution was written by a Zapotec Indian, and still the racism is not the same here as it is in the States."

"You're talking about Benito Juárez."

Juárez became president in the late 1850s and broke the Catholic Church's massive control over property by confiscating everything but the church buildings themselves. He was a local Oaxaca boy, an orphan at the age of three, whose rise to national leadership became a standard and an example for indigenous people all over México. To me, it's typical of Oaxaca that he had his roots here.

"But still," Jon said, "the racism is still present. You know how people say, 'oh, this person's too dark.' It's just crazy stuff, but my wife doesn't experience much of that here because most people think she's Cuban."

"I think that indigenous people in México are more integrated because of interbreeding, and therefore their combined offspring became the great majority and stayed in plain sight, but in the U.S. they were mostly pushed off onto reservations and made invisible."

Jon was nodding to this.

"I read an article some years ago that suggested areas in México that had a strong indigenous centralized state system, like the Aztecs and the Maya, were areas where the language and culture persisted longer than areas where the government had been less highly centralized. I think that's true here as well. Native languages all over the world are disappearing. I don't know how long they'll persist here. There are lots of Nahuatl speakers up in México City and Puebla. Lots of Maya speakers in Guatemala. I think in some places in Sonora there are many native speakers, too, like the Yaquis.

"When I studied anthropology I thought, well, I don't want to go and study in México. That's not an exotic enough place. I have to go somewhere far away, so I went to Yemen, which was pretty interesting and really off the beaten track when I went there in 1974. But México is just amazing!"

"I always say that it's as foreign as Tanzania," I said. "What would you change about Oaxaca if you could?"

"Nothing, although I wish the sidewalks were a little

smoother and didn't have any dog shit. Aside from that, I can't think of anything."

I couldn't help reminding myself here that Jon was trained as an anthropologist, which has a point of view the complete opposite of a missionary. You go in and observe, but you change nothing and leave no footprints.

"Does your anthropology background give you a different connection to this culture, including the role of expats here?"

"I'm not sure whether being an anthropologist is a factor, but experience in other cultures gives me a different perspective. I recall that when I went to Yemen for the first time I lived in a town that had less than a dozen Europeans there, and only one American. There were four or five Swedes, I think. There were a couple of Scottish Presbyterians who were Gaelic speakers, and then there was a Frenchman who was a Breton speaker. What a skewed sample of European languages! Of all these twelve Europeans about half of them spoke a Gaelic language. When I came home I was in culture shock."

I had a hard time imagining Jon Swanson being shocked by any culture. "What did you speak for a language in Yemen?"

"Arabic."

Of course. "What's your day-to-day life like here?"

"Well, I get up and fix my coffee, just like when you arrived. I'm diabetic so I test my blood sugar. Then I read some poetry and a bit of philosophy, or some Thomas Merton, or I write a little bit."

"What kind of things do you write?"

"I work on my journal, and I'm also going to write something I've been doing research on. My major focus in research was migration. I want to write about my own family's migration to the United States and contextualize that in terms of the social and economic circumstances that prevailed in the Midwest at that time, and over time, because my grandparents came to Iowa about the time they were transitioning from prairie to corn belt. I grew up at a time when agriculture was beginning to be industrialized and moving from a family farm model to a corporate environment. The little towns were drying up. It's a totally different world now. That took place between 1945 and 1975."

I suddenly saw him in a different light, and myself as well, along with everyone I had talked to for this book. "Are we now part of an emigration of expats, dispersing southward from the U.S.? Will you and I find ourselves featured in some future study?"

I had already been interviewed by a student from a U.S. college for a thesis on expatriates. He had used my first book as a resource.

"I think there is some of that, and I guess you could look at it in those terms. I think more people will leave the U.S. and become expats because it's gotten too expensive to live there now."

"You said earlier that you were involved with union organizing in Michigan."

"Yes, and there was a group of people who were representing indigenous people here. I'd love to get involved with that, but I haven't yet. That's an area where I have a lot of sympathy—anything dealing with labor. I feel remiss in not doing that. For a while I was working a lot on Palestinian issues and I built a website. I want to do this writing on my family, and I'd also like to look at emigrant return, because there are a lot of Méxicans coming back here from the U.S. now. I don't know if you have looked at remittances, but they were down more than six percent recently."

"Is that more than just the economy in the U.S.?"

"The Obama administration has deported thousands of people. They've dumped a lot of them back across the border. Sometimes it's pretty cruel. I met a guy who had spent his teens in the States and been there almost twenty years. He was thoroughly Americanized. There's always a problem when you spend a lot of time outside the U.S., and you come back—you've always got one of your feet outside. It's the same with immigrants. For instance, my grandfather was Swedish American, but he was neither one. I think that's pretty common. For these guys, who came back here, their kids are coming back with them and they don't speak any Spanish. They have a hell of a time. They get bullied in school."

"How does that work for you personally, having one foot here and one there?"

"As an anthropologist I've always felt a little estranged from the U.S. I think that's part of it. When you learn another culture your own starts to appear a little odd to you."

"Odd how?" I could've answered this myself, but I didn't want to prompt him.

"You question the values. You know, in Yemen and in México, too, people spend a lot of time with one another, and that's a real value. In the U.S., human relationships are secondary. They're on their cell phones all the time. The pressure is that you have to be successful—your job is everything. You have to be productive. Human relations have to have a purpose. Well, they have a purpose in México and Yemen as well. Those relationships are called upon in times of need. They're like a social insurance policy, but it's a little different than in the States. Social relations are not as primary as they are here."

I don't know anthropology, but I felt like *primary* was a term with real significance. "Do you think it's still 1950 here?"

"Well, I don't think I'd put it that way. We tend to

idealize the 1950s a lot."

"I don't, but I see its influence as a long thread."

"I think there was a lot of bad stuff about that period, including McCarthy and the treatment of women and blacks, which still isn't very good in the U.S. The United States thinks it's not racist anymore, but Christ, racism in the U.S. is like the air we breathe."

"So, your Swedish relatives in the States, do they come down here to visit?"

"My sister came down here."

"She didn't listen to the press."

"My daughters come down. I wish my son would come down, but he's unemployed. He was a project manager at IBM for seventeen years. They cut way back."

"How do you react to the American media's views about México?"

"I think of the research they did on the American soldier back in the forties. The people who were most virulently anti-Japanese or anti-German were the ones furthest from the lines. When you live in a place close to it, it's never as bad as the press thinks."

"When you're face to face with anyone you can't help but see their humanity," I said.

"Yes, and they're scared of the same things you are. It's amazing how we can adapt. I remember talking to people during the Lebanese civil war who lived in Beirut. I would say, 'My God, aren't you worried about that?'

"'Oh no, the fighting is two blocks away from us.' So you adjust to it. What goes on up on the border states is a long way from here."

"You don't have any sense of that in Oaxaca?"

"I think it's here, but this is not a contested place like some areas in Michoacán. I don't see that presence. We don't have the kind of violence that they have elsewhere. In San Miguel do you ever worry about this kind of thing?"

"San Miguel is about as dangerous as the same size city in Iowa," I said. "You can find trouble if that's your goal, but that's true of any place."

"There are places here where I don't go at night, but that's true of the U.S. even more."

"You feel safe. What does it cost to live here?"

"It probably costs more than some people reckon."

"I think in some ways it's more expensive than San Miguel," I said. "The restaurants are certainly higher here."

"I think you need about $25,000 a year. I rent my place here. I own a house in the States, but I don't have a house payment anymore."

"Do you have a sense of city government, how effective they are or not?"

"We have kleptocrats here."

"What has living in México taught you?"

"I guess I have a real appreciation for the struggle of the migrant going into the U.S. When they passed NAFTA, it opened the borders for trade, which served the interest of the elites on both sides very well, but it didn't do much for American and Méxican workers, especially Méxican peasant farmers, who were not in a position to export much. It undermined parts of the rural economy."

I said goodbye to Jon Swanson and walked back down the hill toward the center of town. Soon I picked up a broad street called Calle Macedonio Alcalá that was limited to pedestrian traffic. Alcalá was a local composer who died at the age of thirty-seven in the 1860s. He would be proud to see the splendid promenade that now bears his name. I passed the great Santo Domingo Church with its attached cloister that houses a museum of the area's past, including the contents of the intact Tomb 7 from Monte Alban. Many of the colonial buildings are constructed of the local pale green *cantera*, a variety of limestone you can see in the highway cuts as you drive through the hills into town. After weathering for several hundred years, they have acquired a graceful mellowness that I've not seen in other towns, where many of the period buildings are covered in stucco. The fine old buildings in Morelia are the reddish variety of *cantera*.

This broad street is like a promenade through Oaxaca's colonial history. The gracious scale of the architecture reminds the visitor that this was one of the first great cities in México, after México City. The king of Spain gave this area to Cortés as his personal domain after the Aztecs told him this was where their gold came from.

At the end of Alcalá the *zócalo* now has a different air than when I last saw it seven years ago. The atmosphere is upbeat and lively. The vendors of balloons and street food are back. The shoeshine stands are busy; with the slap and beat of the polishing cloth, they have their own special panache. One clear difference between the *zócalo* here and the *jardin* in San Miguel is the presence of huge trees. Rainfall is more plentiful, and the altitude is 5,100 feet, 1,300 lower than San Miguel, which also has more of a high desert aspect during the dry season.

The *zócalo* is the living room of Oaxaca. It is often crowded and chaotic, reflecting the emotional and politically charged life of this town. Under the shady tree canopy, drama is part of the air here. Political speeches are not unusual. I saw one small demonstration of women against domestic violence. In another corner a band was playing.

When I was here during the strike most of the government buildings were spattered with graffiti; only the venerable cathedral at the corner, which had taken from 1535 to 1633 to construct, had been spared.

The following day I met Jim Breedlove at the bed and breakfast. He had sent me some notes on his background that would help me frame some questions for our conversation.

"I was born in 1937 and raised in Fort Worth, Texas, where I went to Catholic schools and was with Méxican Americans on a daily basis. Early on I liked their family closeness, their good humor, and their food. I thought being a Méxican was a great thing.

"I graduated with a BA in history and went on to the University of Texas at Austin to study Latin American history, I got an MA and intended to go on to a doctorate but I began to run out of money to support my family—a wife and four kids, so I took a job in the Latin American Collection of the UT libraries. I became more and more hooked on books, especially the Latin America rare book collections and the Latin America manuscript collections. I moved up the ladder a bit, and even though I didn't have a library degree I was given a professional position in the Latin America Collection where I worked for six years. In 1968 I was offered the job of Latin American Curator of the Stanford University Libraries, charged with developing and building the collections in history, literature, and social sciences. Included in the job was a position as Lecturer in the Stanford Institute of Latin American Studies. My job took me on frequent book buying-trips to Latin America. I worked at Stanford for twenty-five years, until 1993 when I retired. Within a year I was living in San Cristóbal de las Casas in Chiapas—I had always planned to live in México."

With his background, it was no surprise that Jim had not chosen the beaches for his retirement. We were sitting out by the pool at Casa Ollin. Jim was wearing khakis and a shirt with a subtle graph paper print. His hair is white and he has a small goatee.

"So your Méxican residence started out in Chiapas as planned," I began. "Were you driven out then by the troubles?"

"I wasn't driven out. I moved there in January of 1994, right as the Zapatista rebellion had broken out. I found it fascinating that I was in a place where we didn't know where the rebellion was going to go next."

"Were you in San Cristóbal de las Casas?"

"Yes. I moved there because before I retired, the Anthropology Department at Stanford gave me a trip to Chiapas as a gift. I had never been there, and I went with an anthropologist whose specialty was that region. It was a wonderful experience for me because I had really been thinking more about Xalapa in Veracruz, and not about Oaxaca at all. I had visited Oaxaca in 1960, and hadn't been back since then.

"Eventually I got tired of the climate in San Cristóbal; it's cold and wet most of the year. I was doing photography at the time, but I did find the town an enriching experience, since I was there four and a half years at an exciting time. I'm not a Méxican citizen, so I didn't participate in anything at all political. I was going to make my own dark room and I needed a space, so I rented it from a group of indigenous photographers. They were from various language groups there. I got to know these people quite well, since I was going there every day to use the darkroom. That was an enriching experience. My interest in photography helped me make the decision about San Cristóbal because at that time Antonio Turok, one of México's most important photographers was living there. I met him, and there were others who I also admired. I was new to photography, and I was doing black and white. It was an exciting time, but it was also a tense time."

"Did you feel at risk because of that?"

"No. I never did, except once. I went with that anthropologist to San Pedro Chenalho. We just went out to see it. He spoke the language fluently. People there immediately thought he was a missionary, because the missionaries in that area do speak the native languages well. They became very angry and started chasing us, and picked up some two-by-fours and we ran out of town. We had a car, so we were able to get out safely. But that was the only time whether in the country or the city itself that I felt unsafe. The way I looked at it was that, since I was a foreigner; they weren't interested in me."

"Was there any unrest in San Cristóbal itself?"

"What I began to realize was that the non-indigenous Méxicans in San Cristóbal, they call them *coletos* (this could also mean a mop, a jacket, or a person's insides), are the source of a lot of racism in the town, and there was considerable discomfort about that. Some neighbors asked me why so many indigenous people came to my house. I said, ' Well, they're friends or acquaintances, and I work with them in photography.' They didn't say I shouldn't do that, but they just asked me why. When I answered, it was left at that."

I could see the pattern forming here, a matter of growing discomfort for a variety of reasons.

"Also, in San Cristóbal there was no movie theater, and only one or two bookstores. I found the expat community very different from the Oaxaca community, in that they were not terribly open or welcoming to new people or expats. I don't want to exaggerate that, because I did make some good friends there."

"By then you must have started to look around at other places." He nodded slowly. Jim has a restrained, unhurried style, and a thoughtful look, as if little got past him even in the troubled times in Chiapas.

"I knew people in Oaxaca from my work, including a book dealer here that I'd done a lot of business with when I was still working. I came up to see her and I started meeting expats in Oaxaca, and I liked this town. As I said, I had been here before in 1960, which was before the restoration of the colonial center was done, and I found it really lovely. The plaza around the Santo Domingo Church is one of the most beautiful spaces in the world, where you can stand there and see the mountains. I really liked the people I met here. At first there were more expats than Oaxaqueños. They were friendly and interesting, so I decided to move here. I was really tired of the climate in Chiapas. This was in 1998. I found the house I still live in. I didn't buy it, I rent. I love the house. It has a big place to garden. I still had a car at that time and I was very happy here. We had far less traffic then, although there was an explosion of cars in Oaxaca in the early 2000s when credit was eased. More and more people could afford cars. Before that you could park anywhere you wanted in town, whatever the hour.

"I have been very happy to live here. I have no idea of the size of the expat community, but there are some people I'm very close to."

"You're mainly within the small subgroup of your friends. Are you connected to the Oaxaca Lending Library?"

"I'm a member. At one time, ten years or so ago, I was temporarily on the board to finish out someone else's term. It was a time of some rancor and unhappiness in the library but that has since been smoothed out. It's a very important place to most expats who are new and don't know anyone here yet. Have you been there?"

"I spent some time there this morning. I found it very vibrant, full of people. I thought it had great vitality."

"They have a lot of programs and activities. Over the years it has also become a place for Oaxacan people to use because part of the collection is in Spanish. Students get a discount on membership—it's a subscription library. There are English classes there, and you probably saw people doing *intercambios*. It has a good collection in English. This has been a very good place to live. Because I'm only a permanent resident, I don't participate in any political activity here. I'm interested in politics anyway, and you'll probably have a question or two about that."

"My sense of it is that it's very active in that way, and not only because I was here for part of the strike in 2006. I know that the village cultures contribute enormously to the atmosphere here."

"Well, Oaxaca certainly has a strong indigenous presence. There are seventeen different language groups here, in the city and in the valley. There are towns that are truly indigenous. The people in the central part of the state can usually speak Spanish. There are certainly more remote areas where people don't speak any Spanish. In the primary schools in some places the children are taught both the local language and Spanish. There is a strong desire on the part of adults to work on the preservation of their languages. Younger people are often not that interested."

"I suppose some areas are more militant about this than others."

Jim nodded slowly. "All of these traditional communities have their own *usos y costumbres* (uses and customs), and they are ratified by the state. They are allowed to use these means in electing town officials, and in other ways too. They are concerned with how to settle disputes, legal issues, investigations and trials. They are finally subject to Oaxacan state law and federal law, but in much of their proceedings they can use their own customs."

"Ones they have used for centuries, even before the Conquest."

"Yes, and Oaxaca is also quite a left-leaning place today. It has a long history of vocal and militant protests. For a while the most active area in that way in the state was the isthmus, down around Tehuantepec. It still is. The teacher's union is a very powerful force in Oaxaca and it is definitely leftist."

"Have they made peace with the state government?"

"No. The government and the feds don't want to get involved. So the short answer is that the teachers have neither made peace with the state, the federal government, or among themselves."

"What is your day to day life like here?"

"My daily life is that of a retired bum in some ways. I read a lot, I garden some, I have a dog and we walk."

"And you're doing some writing?"

"I write every day, mainly poetry, and I write in a journal, in prose. I belong to a group of writers here. We meet every two weeks, and it's a particular system that we use. It's called the Amherst method. One person is the leader for each session and keeps time."

"Is it one of those meetings with a dictated topic?"

"That leader has chosen three topics, and there are three sessions of twenty minutes each where you write about each one."

"What do you get from that kind of structure?"

"It disciplines me and makes me write. It's all treated as fiction when we're discussing what people have written."

I could sympathize with this; I have frequently asked myself whether nonfiction really exists.

"I've done some things that have surprised me," Jim

went on, "being prompted that way and having to come up with something in just twenty minutes."

"I think I've run into this system before. Is it a situation where there are only positive comments allowed?"

"Right. And you speak like you and I are friends and in my commenting about what you have written I would call you the narrator. I would say what I liked, what stood out to me, and what I would remember about it. I had never written in that kind of situation before and it has sparked my creativity. Some of the pieces I've written I'm going to definitely develop, either as poetry or as prose. It's a good group—regularly there are about ten people. You are not required to read, only if you want to. Sometimes I don't want to. But usually I read, and the comments can be quite helpful. It's always good to get positive reinforcement on what you've done. People aren't bullshitting you, and you don't have to comment either. We've gotten very comfortable with each other."

"So that's an important part of your social life."

"Right, and there are five or six other guys that have breakfast together on Thursdays. I no longer have a car. It finally died and I haven't replaced it."

"I find the driving here is too aggressive."

"It is, and the traffic has gotten horrendous in the past ten years or so. There are times when I wish I had a car, but overall, I haven't really regretted not having one. The bus system and the *collectivos* are good."

"Do you find this place at all magical?"

"Yes, but I'm resistant to that term."

"I'm not fond of it either. It can be a means of sentimentalizing a place. I think that people who have lived in México, and this includes me, are not sentimental about it. I don't go around with blinders on, but I still would rather live here than any other place."

"I would too, and I feel the same way. But you know, it is magical. Talking about this one place in the center of town, that open space around the Santo Domingo Church must be one of the most beautiful spaces in the world. Yet, there are so many other beautiful places here. The towns are often very interesting, as are the markets. South of the *zócalo* you'll find a lot of the less expensive stores that sell materials and hardware. I love to go down there about six or seven o'clock at night just to see the commercial life. There's so much going on. The Sierra Norte mountains are beautiful. It *is* magical. There is, as you say, a tremendous variety of geography and cultures, and Oaxaca is unique in México. There are certainly other beautiful places in this country, too; Chiapas is one of them."

"I've had to travel a great deal for this book, and as it draws to a close, I still feel that Oaxaca is unique. There's no other place I've seen that has quite the flavor and character of this town. Even with its rough and occasionally radical edges."

"You're right about that."

"Would you change anything about it?"

"The traffic, but I don't know what can be done about that in a town with narrow colonial streets. There's a terrible habit people have of double parking. It's nightmarish. I wish that the political protesters here would back off. There are many besides the teachers; there are protests because of political prisoners, or ill treatment of a particular village or group. They block the streets and major intersections. I wish there could be some way to regulate that, but then you'll loose the point of the protest. I have talked politely to people in those situations, and said, 'You know you're not bringing anyone over to your side. Everybody is angry because we can't get to where we're going. People can't go to work.'

"The response is often, 'We have to show our power.'

"There's not much I would change. I wish there was less poverty. The city looks quite prosperous, and it is. It's even becoming kind of ritzy. A lot of people from northern México and México City have moved to Oaxaca for the same reasons we did."

"Do you feel that the expat group here is close and cohesive?"

"No, despite what you saw at the library this morning, the expat community is not an integrated community." The tone of his voice suggested that this was an issue he had considered more than once in the past.

"Would you describe it as a community at all, or only as a looser, less cohesive group?"

"It's much looser than a community. There are expats here who prefer to not have much to do with other Americans. They're usually people who speak the language well and they can connect with the local community, even though that too is a more traditional group. I speak Spanish reasonably well and I do have Oaxacan friends. They socialize, as you're aware, mainly with their families."

"It is a different style, as I've often seen in San Miguel. Do you go back to the States much?"

"I do. I have children in Texas and one in California. I lived in California for twenty-five years and I still have strong friendships there."

"Do your kids come down here?"

"When they can, although they're all working so hard. Friends come down too. But with my friends, that's dropped off since 2006. People I know who have really loved their experience in México and who always felt favorable about this place, it surprises me now that they're afraid to come."

"You're referring to the teacher's strike."

"Right, and after that, the increase in drug violence.

That has really frightened people off."

"Or, at least, the drug violence publicity in the press. Do you sense much of a presence of that here?"

"Well, if there is, I haven't heard much about it. The Zeta group I have heard, and this is rumor, that they have a presence here, but they do extortion, protection rackets. The accuracy of that I'm not sure of. I certainly know that Oaxaca is nothing like Michoacán or the border states. It's not a place where I feel afraid, although there are parts of town where I don't go at night, with all the bars and hookers."

"Let's talk about your role in the kids' library project." He had mentioned this in our preliminary conversations.

"Libros para Pueblos (Books for the Villages). It's a project that started in the late 90s. A neighbor and old friend of mine is married to a Méxican woman. He had the idea through just talking to people in the villages, and he became interested in how many books are available to children outside the city. There aren't many, as he discovered. In one town he talked to the school principal and found out that while they had some textbooks, they had no books for the kids to read for enjoyment. So he started hitting people up, like, give me twenty-five bucks and I'll buy some books for these kids and take them out to this place. He asked me to help him, and we started a library in one village. We worked with the Padres de Familia (PTA). We told them if they would find a space and build the shelving, we would provide the books. Then we both began to hit people up. It began as a purely volunteer project that has grown to seventy-two libraries. We have a website titled *Libros para Pueblos*. Now for the first time we have a halftime paid person to do a lot the staff work for us, but the rest of the board, now ten of us, are completely volunteer. As I've gotten older (Jim Breedlove is 76) I do less and less. I don't do much traveling now that requires an overnight stay or a twelve-hour drive. Our purpose from the beginning is not to change the culture of Oaxaca, but only to provide books for children that they can read for pleasure. We want to emphasize that."

It's not to change the culture of Oaxaca. Or anywhere.

This has emerged as an underlying theme of this book. I was not sad to see it come up again, unprompted, in these final conversations, because more than anything, it defines the difference between these exiles off the beaten path and those who settle into places that are more like colonies where expats have a choice of both cultures. I offer no judgments about this choice, because I live in San Miguel too.

"For them to read these books is not a task," I said. At that moment, however, I realized that none of these books was likely to be written in any of the native languages. Yet, even so, the point was about reading and the engagement that brings. You couldn't have it every way possible, because who among those publishers was bringing out native language texts, where there were fifteen to seventeen possibilities for the choice of languages in a single state?

"Right, it's not a task, and it's never homework, either. They don't have to do it. Over the years we've developed programs for their parents too, who sometimes can't read, although most of them do. The only point is how important it is to read to your children. The government now is promoting this."

"Have they helped your project at all?"

"No. We made an application to a government agency, but we didn't meet their requirements. The money that drives this has all been private money. We now have an angel, a wealthy man in México City who found out about us and came down to take a look at our efforts. He now makes it possible to start about twelve new libraries each year, which costs around $2,400. Then we find sponsors for each library who will commit to giving $800 a year for five years to add to the collections. We've been quite successful with this. You mention kids and books to people and they come aboard. Tom, who started this effort years ago, early on negotiated a discount with the big publishers of kids' books, so we get 45% off retail prices on what we buy. We've become one of the major purchasers of kids' books in Oaxaca. It's a great program that's personally been wonderful for me. I've gotten to meet people all over the state."

Considering Jim's history, this had to be a terrific way to carry on his mission.

"The teachers are a big issue here, and they don't always do things right, but nonetheless I have great admiration for many of them who are in rural areas. When we first started they didn't even have chalk or blackboards."

"So we don't need to search very far to find reasons for their militant behavior."

"That has now changed for the better, paradoxically for someone of my political views, under Vicente Fox, who did a lot for education in México." (President from 2000 to 2006, from the PAN, a center-right party.)

"Your political views, let's talk about that. Living in México as you have for some time, how do you look at the U.S.?"

"Unfortunately, with an increasingly negative view. Like how insular we are. The kind of things we do in the world, like the drone bombings. I find it horrifying. I think the immigration policies are outrageous. In Oaxaca we get a lot of Central Americans coming through. There's a train from the south called the Beast. That's what these people come up on. I'm not sure it goes all the way to the border."

"But it doesn't have that purpose."

"No, it's only a freight train. But people fall off and get run over."

"Yes, and we have these trains going through San Miguel too on that route north."

"It's horrifying. I have two friends here doing work on this, one a photographer and one a writer. They're documenting a lot of it and the stories are chilling, what these people go through. So my political views on the U.S. are that it's a mess, and it's becoming more and more reactionary in its politics."

"Even though the Democrats are in power."

"Yes, and I think personally that Obama is a great, great disappointment. You and I could go on about this all afternoon. Méxicans are very polite, mostly, and they don't want to say bad things to you or criticize your country, but there's a lot of resentment here. Oaxaca is one of the major exporter states of people. They usually go to Los Angeles where there's an enormous Oaxacan community. There is a lot of resentment, and more about those of us who come down here and don't have to work and we can spend our money pretty much any way we want to. When I go to the States I get tense."

"Is that partly the pace?"

"Yes. It's the pace. There are more and more unemployed people. It's a mess that has nothing to do with who we used to be. I think the country has become much more racist, partly because we have an African American president and people can't bear that. The immigration reform isn't likely to pass. I don't like speaking against my own country. I don't care for that. I'm from Texas, and it's one state you could be most critical of, and yet there are things I love about it."

"When you reach a certain age, you tend to look back on your life and track some of the threads that have gone through it. Is this part of your life on that main thread?"

"As an adult, yes. I've always been something of a

lefty. I grew up in the segregated state of Texas. Because I was sent to Catholic schools, I knew a lot of Méxican kids. Had I gone to public schools, I wouldn't have known them. I loved their family life, the warmth of it and the craziness of it—all the noise they made. My family were nice people but they were very proper. We were quiet and we didn't yell at each other. And we didn't hug the way they did. The mothers of the kids I went to school with would just take me and hug me, and the fathers would too, and kiss me on the cheek. And then I thought too, and I don't know where this came from, that segregation was simply wrong. I was seventeen before the Brown versus Board of Education case."

"What has living in México taught you?"

"I suppose the most important lesson is that we're all the same, aren't we? We're human beings. We all have the same troubles. Being a white American, my troubles are not so severe, but we are all the same, and we should care about one another. That's one thing I really feel about the U.S.; even though we did have legal segregation, and although we treated the Indians badly, we did have some sense when I was a child of community responsibility. Now we seem to have become greedy, selfish people who don't want to pay taxes so that the kids can have decent schools. We can send our children to private schools. But we're responsible too for all the kids who are going to grow up."

The following morning a driver picked me up and took me out to the small Zapotec town of Tlacolula, about forty kilometers east of the capital. We drove down through a long valley flanked by rounded-over green foothills with more rugged mountains behind on both sides. The day was brilliant sunshine. Much of the farmland was given over to agave, the main ingredient for mescal, which is insanely popular here.

Although we passed some bigger distilleries, like Benevá, most of the production came from small artisanal makers. They have a wide variety of recipes and processes that provide a topic of endless discussion among mescal aficionados.

With a population of about 15,000, Tlacolula is famous for its traditional Sunday market. We parked next to an eight-foot-high pile of paving stones in the walled yard of a private home behind iron gates. It had space for about eight cars under the trees and was a nice moneymaker for the owner during market days. He stood beside us leaning on a cane and collected his fee in advance as we got out of the car.

The market is erected for the day only on eight blocks of the city streets, with offshoots to the sides. Food is the biggest item, with vast tables of dried chiles, fruits, vegetables, and baked goods. There was one whole block of meat and poultry vendors, and in the street between, a line of charcoal grills waited ready to prepare your purchase to order. Half a dozen dogs lounged hopefully underfoot. Further down, stalls offered masks, wooden kitchen implements, leather goods and flowers, weaving in the native styles. A woman walked past with a turkey on his way to dinner. Feet tied together, he calmly watched the action.

The main church is a relic of the sixteenth century. I wandered through the interior, which houses the statues of many saints along the walls. In the case of martyrs, each one demonstrates the means of his death. Many are standing there carrying their heads in their arms.

On the rest of the week these crowded streets revert to their normal life and pace, and the people change back to their workday clothes. This is a glimpse of pre-Conquest México, a market it shared with Spain even before they met, because the format of market day goes back to prehistory.

With his wife Judith, Jon McKinley is the owner of the bed and breakfast where I was staying. I decided to talk to him because, like Julie and David Winslow in Pozos, and like Rose Calderone in Morelia, innkeepers often like to keep their finger on the pulse of the town. Jon had spent the first fifty-three years of his life in San Diego, where he practiced law in his own one-man firm, specializing in litigation, a head-to-head game that can be full of nasty surprises. It's usually better to settle out of court.

We took a seat at the poolside table. Inside I could see Judith in the kitchen talking to one of the staff people. She wore a hat that looked like a modified fedora, and it suited her. Jon was ready to tell his story.

"I first visited Oaxaca in September of 1999 when I arrived here in search of the 'essence' of Mexico. I not only found the culture to be what I was looking for, for but I also started on a path that led to my marriage to my then tourist guide—a Mixteca woman from Oaxaca.

"When I came back here for the Day of the Dead in the year 2000, I once again used Judith as a tourist guide. There was still nothing romantic about the relationship. I returned again in the spring of 2001 for the Semana Santa (Easter Week) and to spend time with my favorite guide. I came back again for a week of every month in 2001, renting an apartment in the fall of that year. I continued that for the next two years and Judith and I built a house in the Xochimilco barrio. In 2004 we got married.

"In 2005 we bought an older house in the central historic district and converted it to this bed and breakfast, and we've been running it ever since. Now I see myself as a recovering attorney. I've escaped from an atmosphere of aggression and discontent to arrive at a place where our closest associates (our guests) are positive and happy to be here."

I took *older* in this context to mean old in the sense of houses you'd find in San Diego, because this house where we sat was in no way colonial.

"Sure, Oaxaca has its problems," Jon continued, "I don't deny that. But the weather is good, the people here are warm and generous, and the food is wonderful. I feel that I made the right decision in moving here."

Jon is in his mid sixties. His ginger-colored hair is intact and he wears a gray goatee and two gold earrings, a style I suspect he acquired after he settled here. As we talked, his delivery was unhurried and relaxed. It was not a cross-examination.

"Did you look at any other places in México?

"I've always been a México fan, interested in all things about this country. I took Spanish in high school and enjoyed it. My teacher was from México. I loved the culture and at an early age I began forming an image of my ideal México, my Camelot version of it. I had met people from different parts of this country but I couldn't get a grasp of what a real Méxican was, and what the real México was like. I visited a number of different cities over a period of years: Guadalajara, México City, Mérida, and some of the northern cities closer to the border of Arizona. I never did find my Camelot version of México."

"Were you thinking at that time that you might cut short your work life in the States and move down here?"

"No, never. I was mainly curious about the culture and the people that I met in the States; some were born here and some there. They all had such different personas that I couldn't figure out what a real Méxican was, outside of someone who was simply born in México or was of Méxican heritage. In 1999 I took a trip to México City and spent four days, and then it was a choice between Oaxaca and Puebla.

As luck would have it, I chose Oaxaca. So I spent those four days here at the end of September. By the end of the first day I answered my own question about what the real México was—it was Oaxaca. Of course, there are a lot of other places I might have visited, but when I got here I thought this was the real thing."

"What was it about this place that brought you to that conclusion?"

"I think the bottom line is the indigenous culture. In figuring out what a Méxican was, and I'm still having trouble with that question, I think the color of México comes from the indigenous people, not from the European or American imports. When I came down here for the first time I looked on the Internet for an indigenous guide because I wanted someone local from one of those cultures to show me that aspect of the area. Actually, the only choice of an indigenous guide was Judith, who is now my wife. That's how we met. I tell people we met over the Internet, which is partially true, because that's how I found her as a guide. Through her eyes I began to see and form my own idea about what the real México is, as Oaxaca has either fifteen or sixteen different indigenous groups all in the same state. They're the ones that provide the color and texture of Oaxaca."

"At that time were you in the process of burning out on your law practice?"

"I was by myself, a sole practitioner for twenty-five years doing mostly civil litigation, and I had some health issues because of the tensions of being a litigation lawyer, but I didn't imagine that I would stop doing that in the near future. I wasn't looking for a different place to live. I knew that I couldn't stay in litigation forever, and I had started doing estate planning, which is a lot less pressure-driven."

"Trusts and wills."

"Right. I wasn't totally burned out, but I was trying to get out of litigation. I'll be sixty-five in a couple of weeks."

"So, there was a transition when you decided to move. At some time as you were coming down here every month, you must have thought, 'I'm just going to pack it in.'"

"Yes, and looking back now it's kind of difficult to pick out any certain event that made me decide to move on. Part of it was that I have three children and they had all moved out of San Diego. Before that I had felt attached to San Diego because of their presence. But once they found spouses and moved on to other cities, it was like springing open the door to the cage. That was one of the reasons that had kept me there, but there was no other place in the States I wanted to live. It was mainly because I fell in love with Judith after about the third visit here that I decided to rent an apartment in September of 2001. With that I started living down here, but without any intention of making it a 100% move."

"Because of my earlier visits, when I think of Oaxaca, I think of a strong indigenous presence, and a left-leaning political life that can be vocal or even militant."

"It's hard to define it in terms of leaning one way or the other, because the PRI party has run Oaxaca, as it has most of México, for seventy years, until they were voted out of the presidency (in 2000). But they never have been eliminated from the local and state scene. They have such a strong mechanism for obtaining votes, both legally and not, that they're always a part of the culture. Although they may have started out as being left-leaning they have turned into a staunchly conservative party over time. In most of the small villages people are more inclined toward the PRI than they are toward any other. The party gives them bags of groceries, sacks of cement, and they make a lot of generous gifts to people to keep their vote. The political scene down here is very difficult, because even when we had the mega marches of the teachers, you really couldn't tell who all the players were. In 2006 when everything was falling apart here, and it looked like a revolution, I suggested to my wife that maybe a revolution would be a good thing for Oaxaca. She just laughed and said they would only change the names and everything would just return to the way it had always been. I don't define the culture here in terms of politics."

"Same horse, new rider, as they say here."

"Exactly."

"How does Oaxaca express that essence of México you were looking for?"

"To me it's expressed more than anything else when I go to the *zócalo* and watch people for a while. I noticed the first few times I came here that there were concerts there. The interesting thing was that they weren't just older people coming to listen to the concerts, there were young mothers wearing their village *huipiles* with three or four children. They would come and stand for an hour listening to classical music. They'd be standing next to someone who appeared to be a bricklayer with dusty clothes and callused hands reverently listening to the music too. I noticed that it was a real mixture of cultures coming together and enjoying the classics, or watching a theatrical performance. Beyond that, it's hard for me to answer that question because so much of my pleasure in Oaxaca is provided by my wife and her family. It's also seeing Oaxaca from the inside from a family viewpoint, one that I'm part of, instantly from the first time I came here."

"Did they accept you right away?"

"At first there was a little hesitation, not really a test period, but almost all of her family accepted me, including her mother, very quickly. Her mother was a strong independent person. She thought any friend of Judith's was a friend of hers also."

"Is her father still alive?"

"No, her father died eight years ago."

"But he was still around in the early phase of that relationship, and for your marriage."

"No, he wasn't here for that. The first time I saw him I asked Judith to introduce me to him, and she said, 'No, I think it's better if we don't.' He was very unpredictable. But her mother and I got along very well."

"Do your kids come down here, and how do they connect with this other family?"

"Very well."

"You are divorced or widowed?"

"Divorced. My children have been down, the last one being my youngest son. He's very outgoing and enjoys the culture here, the mescal, enjoys Judith's family, and is accepted very well by her family. They're very warm and generous, I have to say."

"Is having a business easier here because she's part of it?"

"Absolutely. She takes care of running all the difficult aspects of the business, like when we do construction changes. If it weren't for her I probably wouldn't be in business here. It was a fluke that we ended up doing a bed and breakfast. When my family came down for the wedding I checked out other places because we didn't have this place. We put them up in a hotel close to the entrance to the Botanical Gardens. We had checked it out and it was beautiful. Nice rooms, a very traditional Méxican-looking place. We thought my family would be very happy there. Next morning over breakfast I asked them how it went, and they said, 'Terrible, we want to move.'

"I asked what could be terrible about it and they started describing their service there. It's a beautiful setting but the service was terrible. The night clerk was flirting with the maid."

"Playing slap and tickle."

"Yes. They didn't bring any towels or toilet paper when they asked for it. For some reason it passed through my mind that Judith and I could do a much better job than they did. It might even be fun to run a business like that. I mentioned it to my wife and she said, 'No, absolutely not. I have no interest in that, no way.' She was a licensed tour guide and she had once run a little hostel with three rooms or something like that."

"What brought her around?"

"I sold her on the idea of what I thought we could do, and finally she agreed. She had been thinking hotel, and I was thinking bed and breakfast. She didn't have much concept of a B&B, as most Méxicans don't. It's getting more popular now. We've been operating for eight years, and during that time it's gotten better known."

"As I look around here I see a tremendous attention to detail. Is that your influence or hers? Everything is thought of—I couldn't help but notice a sheet of paper on the side of the refrigerator that gives the staff doing breakfast in the morning the phrases to say in case they can't recall them quickly enough. Because I write mostly fiction, I know it's always the details like that which make the story come alive."

"It's a combination. Judith has a lot of ideas, and she does most of the decorating. I've also had some ideas that were successful, but a lot of them come from the guests. When they leave I always send them an email asking what we could do to make their next stay better. The guests have suggested the computer we've set up for them, then the Wi-Fi, the water refill station, the book exchange, the mescal bar, and a lot of others. I think the only one we haven't put into effect was having a buffet breakfast. But we're looking for feedback all the time. Neither one of us had any experience running an operation like this one."

"Do you foresee any further changes?"

"We're planning at the end of this month to merge two upper rooms across the pool into one suite. Next spring we'll do the same thing to the small rooms beneath."

"In terms of the business climate, how do you get along with the city government and the bureaucracy?"

"To give you an example, when we bought this house it was just a private home and it needed a lot of modifications. It had three bathrooms then and now we have thirteen. So being in the center we're part of the historic district, which has a committee that watches over any changes to the buildings. We have two levels of bureaucracy where we are, since we have them and the municipal offices. So, wanting to comply with the law, Judith went to the office of the historic district and told them we were thinking about buying a building, but not placing it in any location. She said it was going to need some changes and we wanted to know what to do to get permission to do that. The answer was that we had to get an architect to approve the design. She asked them for a list of acceptable architects. Well, they didn't really have one right now but maybe in three or four months they thought they might be able to recommend one or two who would be acceptable. She thanked them and came back and told me we were doing it without permission. This meant that a lot of the noisy work was done on the weekends, because they go around looking for places under construction."

The house they bought has the look of the mid-twentieth century, as does the block where it stands, on both sides of the street. It's unselfconsciously modern, more like gently contemporary. I guessed it was built in the 1950-60 era.

Walking through the public areas, I saw no colonial elements. Behind us inside was the great room that on this end held a leather sofa and chairs. In the wall behind, a wide niche displayed about forty mescal bottles in a variety of presentations.

The center of the room held two long dining tables with colorful tablecloths of local weave that were changed daily. On the left was the kitchen behind an arch painted with floral motifs.

"And did ignoring the bureaucracy work out?"

"It did. So to answer your question, when we can do it easily, we work with the city. For most projects, like on altering these two back rooms, Judith runs the job. She's done a lot of construction. She was in charge of building our house up on the hill."

I was now progressively discarding any preconceptions I had about what a woman from a small Mixtec village might be able to do in a twenty-first century Méxican world.

"I don't know her educational background, but she seems awfully savvy."

"Judith started off with a degree in teaching, and then decided she didn't want to be a teacher. She finally ended up with a degree in chemical engineering too. For an engineering job she went to Veracruz for a while (the center of the oil industry) and said it smelled bad so she came back to work for the power company inspecting poles out in the boondocks."

"She been around the block then in business in a variety of ways before you started this."

"When I first met her as a tour guide, she was renting a place over on García Vigil, a big colonial house with two courtyards. She was subletting the front to other people to pay the rent. She lived on the back patio with her three boys."

"Has the town settled down now after the terrible summer of 2006?"

"Yes, on the surface."

"But some of those issues are still unaddressed?"

"It's hard to tell because although the teachers are the highest paid group in Oaxaca, they always say they need more. It's not clear to me whether it might be the leaders who are trying to increase their power base. Only two or three days ago they shut down the major chain stores here. They just circle the buildings and squat down in the doorways and don't let anybody through. Sam's Club, Sears, Soriana, Wal-Mart, and all the other big chain stores were shut down for most of the day."

"Is that an effective way of getting things done for them?"

"The fact that they do it frequently indicates to me that it's not very effective. They always seem to be complaining that they want something else. It's not clear whether they hope to get anything out of it or they're just showing how powerful they are. The teachers don't have much to say about it. It's the leaders who make the decisions about what they're going to do."

"México has tremendous variety in culture and ethnicity, but to me it seems like Oaxaca has a special kind of uniqueness. Maybe I'm romanticizing it. Perhaps as an antidote I should go up to Costco and watch the protesters in action."

"Let me give you a couple of examples. Judith and I went to Santa Fe and Albuquerque four or five years ago for the World Folk Art Festival. In the portion from México, which has thirty-one states, two-thirds of it was from one state: Oaxaca."

"Was the other third from Michoacán? Because that aspect of their cultural life is extremely rich."

"A lot of it was from there, and then some from the

state of México too, but most of it was from Oaxaca. We've gone to other art events and usually the ratio is the same. Most of that art originates in the indigenous part of the culture, not from the European side. It's that side that also produces the painting, music and theatrical works. It's all about the indigenous culture and the color that it brings."

"When you use the word color here, as you did just now, you're talking about the entire fabric and texture of it. What would you change about this town if you could?"

"I would have the people be more respectful of their city and state, to not throw garbage out the window of their cars, not to put the garbage out on the street for the dogs to tear apart first thing in the morning, to not graffiti the walls and break off new trees that have been planted. You drive along the highway and you see a lot of trash. They don't show much respect. It's not too different from when I was a young boy in the States in the fifties. People didn't think anything of throwing a sack of trash or a burning cigarette out of the window of their cars. Here it's still that way."

I have mentioned this in an earlier chapter, but San Miguel has the same problem, but with less graffiti. Years ago, traveling in Croatia, one of the most beautiful countries in the world, I had observed the same thing.

"That and the other thing I would change are the politicians who could be more respectful of their constituents. Maybe it's not just here, but worldwide, where people will say, 'This guy wasn't too bad, he didn't steal as much as the last one.' It's kind of a joke and it shouldn't be. México has a tremendous amount of natural resources and a strong labor force. My opinion is that the only thing keeping México from leaping ahead in the worldwide marketplace is the lack of interest on the part of the politicians, who seem to be more concerned with padding their own pockets than in advancing their own country."

"Does your marriage to a local woman give you a special connection to this culture?" I couldn't help but feel Jon McKinley's position in that regard was a perfect counterpoise for Lenya Bloom and Rebecca Hurd in Puebla.

"Absolutely. Not only the larger Méxican culture, but the Oaxacan culture and the Mixtec culture, too. Judith's background is Mixteca, so I get to do things other expatriates here don't get to do. Saturday we went to a barbecue at her brother's house, a pit barbecue in this case, and that's the way they do the lamb for his birthday. I sat with other Mixtecos, drinking mescal and eating lamb, and just enjoying their company. These are things I couldn't do if I wasn't married to a Méxican."

"Correspondingly, that must affect your relationship with other expats here. Perhaps it mutes your dependence or your need for association with others more like yourself?"

"Maybe it does. Frankly, I don't really see the point of spending time with other expats. I'm sure there are a lot of nice people here. I know there are, because I've met a few. But I don't see any reason to spend time with them. I have friends who are Méxican and I spend time with them, although I'm not prejudiced toward the expats. The lending library here is a good place if you want to meet other expats, and you can play bridge or chess with other Americans and Canadians. I don't know whether I don't have time, or I don't make time, or I just don't have the interest. In any case, I don't see the need to do that."

This was my final conversation for this exploration of expats off the beaten path. I could see now a long thread in these chapters that does not wind through expat communities. Where there are affiliations, they are more incidental than fundamental. Oaxaca has the largest expat community of any town in this book, yet none of the three people I spoke with there were deeply engaged with it.

"What is your day like here? I sense that you're in the bed and breakfast every day, and for long hours."

"It's pretty idyllic, really. Sometimes I feel like I'm a college student on spring break. After all, I have to spend my time someplace. I don't really work very hard when I'm here. I have a few responsibilities I need to do, mostly involving reservations and the Internet. I could do that in an hour or so each day, but when I'm here I take courses online, I download them, like from The Teaching Company. It's a great opportunity for me to do things I could never do when I was an active lawyer. I didn't have time to study the historical aspects of the Bible, or the science of neurology, and all kinds of other things."

"But your very presence in this building must have a guiding influence on the staff, and you're certainly here as a point of reference when issues come up, as they must at times."

"Yes, but I'm not called upon to do that very often. When I arrive in the morning at seven or a bit before, the staff arrives soon after and they offer me coffee. They treat me with respect, just as I treat them with respect. It sounds a little irreverent, but sometimes I feel like Mel Brooks in *The History of the World*, where he says, 'It feels so good to be king.' I'm very privileged that somehow I've conducted my life in such a way that I can afford to live here in a nice style and be coming to a place every day that I'm happy to be part of."

"Have you developed any special insight running a business where the employees are all Méxican? Because in the United States, working in your own practice, you would probably have had only a secretary."

Jon made a broad gesture. "The staff is all hired by

my wife. She knows how to do that. It can be difficult hiring for a business like a bed and breakfast because you have to find someone who *is* honest without question, and not only is honest, but has all the appearances of being honest. They're entering into people's rooms that have left cash or cameras, cell phones, lying around. It has to be someone who is unquestionably honest. Somebody reliable. They come in every day on time more or less and spend the day working, not dinging around or talking on the phone. Judith has been very good at hiring."

"You probably don't have a lot of time to get involved with community organizations (NGOs)."

"I have all the time in the world, but there are so many other things I want to do. I could leave here and do something else. Sometimes I'll go down to the *zócalo* and have my shoes shined and watch the people. Have a beer and some peanuts. I have a lot of time on my hands but I choose to spend it in different ways, mostly learning things I don't know."

"Has living here affected your view of the U.S.?"

"No. It's kind of compartmentalized in my mind when I'm there. I have my criticisms of it as I always have, and I also have my criticisms of México. I don't try to compare them. The lifestyle and the culture are completely dissimilar. It's just two different places with different cultures and standards of living, and I accept that. When I'm here I realize that my staff lives in what would be considered illegal housing up there. But they're happy. They may live in a house with a corrugated tin roof, and they may have an indoor toilet but they don't have showers. They bathe themselves using a fifty-gallon drum of water and a little cup they use to pour cold water on themselves."

"And you pay competitive wages."

"Right. One of the benefits of not having to rely on

the income from this place is that we can afford to pay our people more than they could earn anyplace else. Then when they receive tips from the guests over and above that, it keeps them happy and loyal."

"You're saying you don't live on the income from this business."

"We do in the sense that it pays the bills here and we eat most of our meals here. We're not doing this for the money. If we were, we would've shut down in 2006 when the uprising came. We kept going at the same pace and paid the staff 100% through the whole thing even though we were empty for months. We wanted to keep our staff because they're good."

"What's your reaction to the U.S. media treatment of México?"

"It's funny about that. People in the U.S. are generally afraid of México, and that's because of what they read in the media. It's not usually based on any personal experience down here. Last year three different groups came in with the same leader, some book clubs out of Minneapolis. Each time the group arrived they wanted us to say a few words. These were mostly parties of women in their fifties, sixties, and seventies. I asked whether any of them had been warned or told not to come to México. In all three groups every single person, about sixty in all, raised their hands to say that they had been told not to come down here. I think that comes from the fact that people don't distinguish between the border city violence and what might be happening in other parts of the country."

"And it's because the press makes no attempt to distinguish that either. They delight in generalizing. I started out many years ago in journalism and I know that it's possible to lie by using the facts."

"My analogy is the Méxican who wants to go to LA, and reads about the killings in Detroit and decides not to go. Most Americans don't know México. People here know more about U.S. history than Americans do about México's history."

"Would it be safe to say you have experienced no problems yourself here?"

"Zero. We did install a camera out front just as a preventive measure, only because the police force here is not very reliable. We would rather put up a camera in a cautionary manner than rely on the police if something did happen."

"Do you have water supply problems?" I was thinking again of the Winslows running their splendid small hotel in Pozos.

"We do, and I was surprised to hear earlier that where you live in Guanajuato there was plenty of water."

"Plenty overstates it, and we do have less rainfall than you do. Maybe it's managed differently. In the dry season the water is often turned off for a while in the afternoon, but we keep our cisterns full so we don't have any supply problems."

"Here a good part of every day is spent dealing with water issues."

"There are times when you have to purchase water?"

"We have a cistern with 15,000 liters of storage capacity. When we're full and the city water doesn't come on, we have to purchase a tank truck of water, which comes with 12,000 liters at a time. That will be good for only a few days if we don't get the city water turned on. People come down here and take showers like they would in the States."

"Prom showers."

"Exactly. You take a twenty or twenty-five minute shower, and there goes a good chunk of our cistern. Sometimes they shower twice a day. In fact at one point I had the idea of heating the water in the pool with solar panels." He pointed at the edge about eight feet away from our table. "We investigated the project and it sounded great, but then Judith said, 'You know if we heat the water, more people will use it and there will be more towels to wash and they'll take two showers a day.' End of subject. We decided to leave the water cold so only a few will go in."

"What do the locals do for a living? Is there any big industry here?"

"There's a fine industrial park on the edge of town, but now it's mostly abandoned. One of the last industries out there was a jeans factory and that shut down five or six years ago. Now there's a glass artist out there and not much else. For whatever reasons, industry is not encouraged by the government here. The income of Oaxaca consists of money coming in from the federal government, the income of the teachers, the government workers, and tourism. So when the teachers step on the tail of tourism they're cutting off a large portion of the economy here. Probably a third of everybody in town is dependent on tourism in some way."

"What has living in México taught you?"

"It's taught me to try to live with less stress." Jon was nodding now as if this was at the crux of all these issues, as it has been for others in these conversations. "It's given me a different way to prioritize my life; what is important to me and what's not. Things that I used to think were important in the States no longer matter that much. When I first came down here having a nice car was important to me, and I realized that in my wife's family, she was the only one with a car. Well, her brother had a car, but it was a beat-up old Plymouth. None of them seemed to think much of it. A car wasn't that important."

"And México is hard on cars."

"Very hard. So the other thing that strikes me is that holidays like Christmas here are all about family, not about presents or Santa Claus. Now all of a sudden that's changing somewhat. Things like Christmas that were important to me in the States now have a different importance."

"What would you say to someone who is sixty years old and looking at Oaxaca as a place to retire?"

"The first thing is that you have to expect that this is not just the same as the United States, but only cheaper. You have to expect that the level of medical care is not as modern as at home."

"But is it still sound?"

"Not very. I'm just about to start Medicare in the States, and I plan to hang on to that, because unlike some who are willing to risk the medical care here for something serious, I'm not."

"You know that you can't use it here, you have to go to the States to use it."

"Yes, although my supplemental policy is good in other countries. And the care is cheap here. When Judith fell down and shattered her elbow, it cost us less than $1,000 to have the surgery on her elbow and remove the pieces."

"And in spite of your overall view of medical care here, you were happy with that experience."

"Yes, but we don't have health insurance down here because it's not very effective. They reject most preexisting conditions."

"And other than that?"

"You should learn to speak Spanish and learn to get around without a car. The climate is ideal here, probably better than anything in the United States or most of México. We have a very tolerable range of temperatures. While it's a beautiful place to live, it's going to lack some of the comforts you might have up north. You're living in a third world country. Police protection is an issue, if you have any problems. Bribery is a problem with the police. Yet, there are truckloads of police wandering the streets with machine guns."

"It's a great show of force," I said, "but does it work?"

"I'm not sure there are any bullets in their guns. Thinking about the medical again, a lot of the people here believe in the *curanderos*, they're sort of like witch doctors. One day my wife took me to one because she wanted to buy some herbs that she could only get there, and as I was waiting for her I saw a sign on the wall. If you are suffering from *susto* (fright, or being badly startled), they have a remedy for that. If you have lost your shadow, they will help you find it and can reattach it for a fee. There was also a list of services related to the evil eye."

"I haven't looked into Obamacare in great detail, but I think your supplemental coverage under Medicare probably wouldn't go that far."

"I'll have to check on that."

Indeed, and that was good advice. After a serious search for his Camelot south of the border, Jon McKinley had entered the México experience in depth. This thrust had its early roots in his high school interaction with the Spanish language. He had done his homework, even then, when he could not have imagined how and where it would finish.

Check it all out, rent before you move. Look before you jump. México can be a trap for the unwary, even as it is a place of blooming for those moving on with their lives. It is an experience for people still capable of taking risks and trying to understand what they are looking at. But for those who would like to stay young, who can experience the challenge of change, come on down.

The next morning I stood in the kitchen staring at the refrigerator. On it was the hand-lettered sheet with prompts for the kitchen help that Jon and I had talked about:

> Hello good morning how are you?
> Would you like to sit down?
> Would you like *fruts* with yogurt and granola or plain?
> Can I take your plate how was your breakfast?
> Me, I take it.

Although I was eager to return to San Miguel and start work on writing this last chapter, I was also reluctant to end my week in Oaxaca. My journeys through Mexico's colonial heartland have taken me to many compelling places, but I had found an atmosphere, a way of life, and an uncompromising flavor of indigenous culture in Oaxaca that went a few degrees further into the heart of México.

For myself, I usually resist using the term *magical*, since it often has sentimental overtones, and my task is always to be the unsentimental observer. Still, Oaxaca possesses a degree of color, to use Jon McKinley's term, a textured fabric that delights not only the eye, but all of the senses. This has to be the legacy of the vivid and diverse cultures of the Oaxaca Valley, where the indigenous people work at maintaining their lifestyle on an active and daily basis. The only close parallel would be the craft villages of Lake Pátzcuaro, which is less diverse in its cultural heritage, but in no way less vivid.

CONCLUSION

You're not supposed to ask about such things. There are stories no one is willing to tell you.

-Sandra Cisneros, *Caramelo*

Perhaps that's the case here, since I know I haven't arrived at the entire truth. Indeed, a number of people refused to talk to me about their experiences and declined to explain why.

Maybe I didn't want to hear all of it, since this is not a how-to book. It looks at examples, but like life itself, it provides no instructions. Since each of us in México and elsewhere approaches the expat experience differently, there is no single *key* to this puzzle. With the same pieces to start with, it can still fit together in different ways. Yet I was fortunate to find people who *would* speak with me, who didn't mind telling of their personal journeys and ultimate connection south of the border, mostly because I had the raw nerve to ask. Yet, what a long, diverse journey this has been. If I could sum it up in a phrase, it would be that I think life has a different *measure* here. If that simple view lacks drama, it still possesses a strong element of truth.

This book illustrates a few of the many ways people can choose to live. Indeed, one of my early assumptions was that even later in life we still possess the ability to reset our own self-imposed limits and to push out the boundaries beyond what we might have guessed possible in the past. Perhaps doing that can almost be easier later rather than earlier in life, since the expectations of the people around us are diminished. The effect is magnified when the soil on which we choose to play out our lives is foreign—and to northerners, whether Canadian or American, no soil is more foreign than that of our southern neighbor.

Most of us have a natural instinct to stick within the territory of our own tribe or clan, to maintain a little distance from those who are not members, people we define as *others* for reasons of race or culture. To pull up our roots and settle uninvited in the midst of those *others* on their own turf requires an uncommon kind of nerve, a special self-confidence that not everyone possesses. From the conversations in this book, it appears that the smaller the nearby expat support community is, the larger the quantity of that confidence is required.

One question I asked of many people was what they had learned from living in México. These answers were among the most revealing, and in many cases gave them a way of distilling their experience. Patience was a component in nearly every response.

These conversations also furnished me with a question for myself. Why was it that the process of visiting widely separated regions and examining divergent expat lifestyles made me feel circumscribed and somewhat isolated in my own way of living in San Miguel de Allende? For the reader who does not live in México, those questions may loom even larger. Surely one of the lessons of these stories is that México is immensely diverse, and if your desire is to reinvent yourself, whether in total or in minute detail, or simply to move on to the next phase of your life, then some haven exists here in which it can happen for you, with or without the support of large numbers of other expats. After all, the energy to bring about changes of this kind comes from within. One aspect these places have in common is that they are supportive in spirit, provided that you supply the decision to launch the process.

Another effect I see in these pages is what I call the *flicker of recognition*, that instant or that hour when, with no special preparation or warning, you realize that you are standing in a place like no other in your entire life. It calls up the image of Rick Davis, as one example, going out one morning to find a good cup of coffee in Pátzcuaro—no more than that—and in the process recognizing that he would live out his life in that small city, no matter what or how long it took to arrange it. Experiences like this are not uncommon among expats. It is impossible to speculate on how often they are not acted upon, because we only observe them when they are. The rest is all a muted fumbling in the background, the noise of making do offstage, without drama, challenge, or often, fulfillment. The sound of silence can be what we hear when life misfires and we surrender to a lesser goal we never thought of settling for.

While I am no believer in fate, I do recognize tipping points, those unexpected moments of decision that are forced upon us by mindless circumstance. One door closes and another opens without reason or apparent need. A new horizon is revealed, and suddenly we are on a different path. Or not. Maybe the next book should be about looking back on those paths not taken, although, like a fizzled rocket, that trajectory seems less compelling as it evaporates in a smudge of vapor on the wind. Choices become visible in moments like that in order for us to make them, not so that we can avert our eyes.

Writing is like teaching: in the process of making a book for others, we reveal to ourselves its hidden lessons, its subtle subtexts. We absorb its curious nuances and probe its tangled implications. In that spirit I have approached this book as if it were a work of fiction, in the sense that I've avoided generalization, and instead embraced the detail of the lives I've been privileged to glimpse. Its truths are not universal, but particular, in the way they must be for each of us. We are neither saved nor enlightened by the experience of crowds or the rant of political parties, but by our dedication to our own individual path. The rest is only boilerplate and handouts. My aim throughout has been to be a true observer, burdened neither by judgment nor advocacy. I am a cheerleader for no single place or for any particular lifestyle, but I do find the expat condition endlessly fascinating in all its variety.

This is what I have tried to portray on these pages.

INTO THE HEART OF MEXICO